Clashing Views in

Human Resource Management

TAKING SIDES

Clashing Views in

Human Resource Management

Selected, Edited, and with Introductions by

Pramila Rao
Marymount University

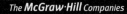

TAKING SIDES: CLASHING VIEWS IN HUMAN RESOURCE MANAGEMENT

Published by McGraw-Hill, a business unit of The McGraw-Hill Companies, Inc., 1221 Avenue of the Americas, New York, NY 10020. Copyright © 2011 by The McGraw-Hill Companies, Inc. All rights reserved. No part of this publication may be reproduced or distributed in any form or by any means, or stored in a database or retrieval system, without the prior written consent of The McGraw-Hill Companies, Inc., including, but not limited to, in any network or other electronic storage or transmission, or broadcast for distance learning.

Some ancillaries, including electronic and print components, may not be available to customers outside the United States.

Taking Sides® is a registered trademark of the McGraw-Hill Companies, Inc.
Taking Sides is published by the **Contemporary Learning Series** group within the McGraw-Hill Higher Education division.

1 2 3 4 5 6 7 8 9 0 DOC/DOC 1 0 9 8 7 6 5 4 3 2 1 0

MHID: 0-07-352733-5
ISBN: 978-0-07-352733-8
ISSN: 2152-9795 (print)
ISSN: 2152-9809 (online)

Managing Editor: *Larry Loeppke*
Director, Specialized Production: *Faye Schilling*
Senior Developmental Editor: *Jill Meloy*
Editorial Coordinator: *Mary Foust*
Production Service Assistant: *Rita Hingtgen*
Permissions Coordinator: *Shirley Lanners*
Editorial Assistant: *Cindy Hedley*
Senior Marketing Manager: *Julie Keck*
Senior Marketing Communications Specialist: *Mary Klein*
Marketing Coordinator: *Alice Link*
Senior Project Manager: *Jane Mohr*
Design Coordinator: *Brenda Rolwes*
Cover Designer: *Rick D. Noel*

Compositor: MPS Limited, A Macmillan Company
Cover Image: Steve Cole/Getty Images

www.mhhe.com

Editors/Academic Advisory Board

Members of the Academic Advisory Board are instrumental in the final selection of articles for each edition of TAKING SIDES. Their review of articles for content, level, and appropriateness provides critical direction to the editors and staff. We think that you will find their careful consideration well reflected in this volume.

TAKING SIDES: Clashing Views in HUMAN RESOURCE MANAGEMENT

EDITOR

Pramila Rao
Marymount University

ACADEMIC ADVISORY BOARD MEMBERS

Editors/Academic Advisory Board continued

Preface

I have never in my life learned anything from any man who agreed with me.

—Dudley Field Malone

It is better to debate a question without settling it than to settle a question without debating it.

—Joseph Houbert

Taking Sides: Clashing Views in Human Resource Management contains 40 selections, presented in a pro and con format, which provides you with 20 interesting and controversial topics in human resource management (HRM). We encourage you to consider each of the HRM selections for lively classroom debates to predict what management outcomes might prevail at the workplace.

Debates have been used as a teaching method since the early times of Greek philosophers. The Greek philosopher, Protagoras, considered the pioneer of debates, encouraged the Greeks to always see the positives and the negatives to any topic. He had profound discussions with Greek philosophers on various questions relating to human nature. The word "debate" originated in the thirteenth century from the French word *debattre,* which means to beat down.

In the United States, debates had their origins in the well-known presidential debates. While such political discussions began in the nineteenth century during Abraham Lincoln's era, it was the first televised debates between the charismatic John F. Kennedy and Richard Nixon that set the stage for the widely publicized televised shows that we see today.

In the academic world, debates are considered a very engaging learning method as it follows a learner-centered approach. In such an approach, students are self-directed, construct their own knowledge, develop conceptual positions, and collaboratively augment their subject knowledge. A debate-style learning format also allows students to develop several additional skills, such as engaging in critical thinking skills, becoming active learners, building their own knowledge, participating collaboratively, thinking quickly (for rebuttals), and developing oratory and listening skills. While this method of learning might seem to place the burden squarely on students, the outcome of such independent learning is immense. Finally, debates provide students an opportunity to take a stand and support their viewpoint, which is an important competency in business and policy-making environments. Generally, business and policy leaders make decisions after understanding both sides to an issue, which allows for better judgments.

Each selection issue has an Issue Summary or brief synopsis of the YES and NO readings that helps set the stage for the debates. This is followed by an Introduction that usually involves a historical introduction, definition of important terms, relevant statistics, high-profile court cases (wherever relevant), rhetorical questions, and a summary of both the YES and NO readings. This edition also provides an international perspective to each selection as students are encouraged to acquire a global view on management perspectives. This is followed by a Postscript section that provides a brief summary of the two readings, identifies any pertinent information that would allow readers to expand their subject knowledge, and poses additional questions (wherever relevant). This section also has a list of Suggested Readings that will help readers glean a better understanding of the debate topic. At the end of the book, there is a brief bio section of all the contributors of the issue articles, providing their professional background and credibility on the subject matter.

It is very important students do not to limit their scholarly readings mainly to the YES and NO articles and Suggested Readings sections. Students should conduct their own research and identify new articles related to the topic matter to develop new and additional perspectives. Such an increased understanding on the topic will provide participants enhanced subject knowledge and also make debates more lively and engaging.

A Word to the Instructor   This is the first edition of *Taking Sides: Clashing Views in Human Resource Management.* It includes 20 issues that were carefully selected after conducting a market research survey on the importance of these topics to HRM. Scholars identified these issues as relevant topics in HRM. An *Instructor's Resource Guide* with issue synopses, suggestions for classroom discussions, and test questions (multiple choice and essay) is available from McGraw-Hill/CLS. This resource is a very useful accompaniment for this text. A general guidebook, *Using Taking Sides in the Classroom,* which discusses methods and techniques for integrating the pro/con approach into any classroom setting, is also available. Online versions of both resources, as well as a correspondence service for *Taking Sides* adopters can be found at http://www.mhhe .com/cls.

Acknowledgements   I would like to acknowledge the support of my husband and love of my children that made this writing project possible. My immense thanks also goes to Marymount University—both my Dean (James Ryerson) and Chair (Dr. Virginia-Bianco-Mathis)—who were very supportive in providing a course release that allowed me to meet this writing deadline. Finally, I would like to recognize the diligent work of my graduate assistant, Gisella Zelaya, who helped me in more ways than one on this book project.

Pramila Rao
Marymount University

Contents In Brief

Contents

UNIT 1   LEGAL ENVIRONMENT   1

Issue 1.   Is Affirmative Action Still Necessary?   2

Award-winning educational journalists reported that race can be used as a criterion for admissions as the University of Michigan won a milestone court case. Supreme Court judges are of the opinion that racial diversity should begin at the university level to help students transition better into a multicultural workforce. Joe Messerli, author of the BalancedPolitics Web site, provides his thoughts on both pros and cons of several management issues. He suggests that one of the main pitfalls of affirmative action is that our business world will continue to live in a colored society.

Issue 2.   Will the Americans with Disabilities Act Amendments Act (ADAAA) Be Abused in the U.S. Workplace?   15

Award-winning writer, Dina Berta, suggests that the ADA (Americans with Disabilities Act) has always been controversial because it was difficult to define and understand. Now that the act has been redefined to ADAAA (Americans with Disabilities Act Amendments Act), it will allow more employees to fall under the disability category, which could increase the number of lawsuits. Legal attorney Victoria Zellers argues that sufficient training of HR professionals could substantially reduce litigation expenses for organizations. The HR department should be proactive to understand and provide for the special needs of their employees.

Ira Blank, litigation attorney, suggests that personality tests are excellent predictors of job performance because they identify several critical work-related skills needed in today's team and multicultural environment. Erin White, reporter for the *Wall Street Journal,* cites the studies of Dr. Griffith, which state that student always fake their personality when they realize the outcomes are different. Questions on these tests are so transparent that it is easy to manipulate the answers.

Lessing Gold, attorney and writer, contends that organizations have a liability in checking the background references of both their permanent or temporary applicants. He indicates how applicants with criminal records emerge back into the work environment with false records, potentially putting customers and co-workers in jeopardy. Chad Terhune, senior writer for *BusinessWeek,* asserts that information from background checking companies is so inaccurate that it is very unfair to several whose employment records have become blemished. He feels that the unregulated nature of this industry could be one of the main reasons for such employment errors.

Martha Frase, freelance writer, suggests that cognitive ability tests are excellent predictors of work performance because they are objective, valid, and reliable. Further, these tests can be administered to a variety of job categories from entry to executive levels. Raj Parthasarathy, process improvement manager, states that emotional intelligence is the best predictor of job performance because it involves critical components of self and relationship management. Researchers are paying increasing attention to emotional intelligence (EI) as its components have positive consequences on job performance.

Jessica Marquez, journalist at *Workforce Management*, suggests that women face a glass ceiling, possibly because their careers generally begin much later and they have more career interruptions due to family commitments. *Black Enterprise* journalists state that women do occupy top-notch positions. The effort is in finding the right universities and organizations that will actively support such diversity initiatives.

Ann Pomeroy, senior writer for *HR Magazine*, illustrates how organizations have identified that women are better business leaders with an example from Safeway. She states that women have some innate characteristics that serve them well as leaders. According to the research studies of INSEAD Professor Herminia Ibarra and her doctoral student, Otilia Obodaru, women demonstrate low visionary skills. These business skills are very important for strategizing and understanding the dynamic environment.

Steve Allison, technical consultant for Adobe Connect, believes that e-learning provides excellent opportunities for employees to learn at their own pace. Businesses also profit because e-learning is very cost-effective compared to traditional methods. Penny Reynolds, trainer and consultant, implies that e-learning training methods are not for everyone because the lack of interaction might impede learning. Also, most e-learning initiatives pack in too much content, which hinders mastery of the subject matter.

Paul Hemp, a Harvard Law School graduate and editor of the *Harvard Business Review*, argues that our current society is facing loss of productivity due to excessive dependence on technology (such as BlackBerrys, cell phones, etc.), blurring boundaries between home and work. Michelle Labrosse, one of the 25 Most Influential Women in Project Management, contends that modern technological devices allow employees to be connected to form virtual teams.

The American Federation of Labor and Congress of Industrial Organizations (AFL-CIO) Web site identifies the work of Professor Harley Shaiken, from the University of California-Berkeley, who states the positive impact of unions on HRM outcomes. Dennis Berman, *Wall Street Journal* journalist and 2003 Pulitzer Prize winner, argues that the current state of the auto industry is mainly due to excessive demands of the unions. The high cost of maintaining labor is passed on to the consumers and reduces organizational profit margins.

Fay Hansen, contributing editor for *Workforce Management*, provides studies of leading professors from Stanford and MIT who suggest that merit pay has lost its meaning because employees are not being actually rewarded for performance. They assert that this compensation system is not distinguishing between success and failure and hence has lost its meaning in the workplace. Laura Meckler of the *Wall Street Journal* contends that workforces that are traditionally underpaid will benefit from such a pay system. Such workforces will feel motivated to perform better because they have been constantly paid poorly.

Michael Armstrong, who writes extensively on rewards and pay, identifies the benefits of intrinsic rewards and indicates that financial rewards or external motivators are often short-lived and do not contribute to employee retention. However, intrinsic rewards contribute immensely to job satisfaction and employee retention. Frank Hayes contends that pay or external factors contribute to employee satisfaction and job retention. High compensation has a unique way of attracting and retaining talent.

Alex Blyth reiterates the thoughts of Microsoft leaders on forced ranking. This performance approach is very good at identifying the underperformers and rewarding the stars. Gail Johnson, former editor of *Training* magazine, suggests this method is flawed because it encourages a very competitive and dysfunctional work environment.

Compensation expert and IPS Fellow Sarah Anderson and her colleagues argue that U.S. CEOs are substantially overpaid in a 2008 study conducted for the Institute for Policy Studies. Professor Reich from Berkeley states that the capitalistic system promotes a principle of supply and demand. There are very few qualified executives, so they are in high demand. Executives have distinguished educational and work records that result in their elaborate pay levels.

Dr. Charles Woodruffe, author and CEO of a company that focuses on managing winning talent, states that, based on experience, expectations, and personality needs, Gen-Yers might need a new set of management practices. Dana Kyles, freelance writer for *Business Week* and *Strategic Finance* magazines, believes that multiple generations can work together harmoniously. Several HRM practices appeal to all the generations unanimously, and it is these common practices that organizations should try to identify.

This article helps to identify how HRM practices have provided phenomenal success and growth to the Google, Inc. organization. HRM leader of Google Lazlo Bock, insists that it is employees that make his organization outstanding. Tony Pettengell suggests that HRM leaders are never in the forefront in most organizations. Hence, they do not provide any substantial profits or growth in organizations.

Professors from the University of Memphis insist that outsourcing is a good business strategy because it creates higher profits, delivers cheaper products, and enhances customer response time. Professor Weidenbaum from Washington University suggests that there are several barriers to a smooth outsourcing process such as language barriers, technology glitches, and intellectual rights.

Correlation Guide

The *Taking Sides* series presents current issues in a debate-style format designed to stimulate student interest and develop critical thinking skills. Each issue is thoughtfully framed with an issue summary, an issue introduction, and a postscript. The pro and con essays—selected for their liveliness and substance—represent the arguments of leading scholars and commentators in their fields.

Taking Sides: Clashing Views in Human Resource Management is an easy-to-use reader that presents issues on important topics such as *talent acquisition, women in corporate levels, employee performance and organizational productivity,* and *compensation and performance appraisal.* For more information on *Taking Sides* and other *McGraw-Hill Contemporary Learning Series* titles, visit www.mhhe.com/cls.

This convenient guide matches the issues in **Taking Sides: Human Resource Management** with the corresponding chapters in three of our best-selling McGraw-Hill Human Resource textbooks by Noe et al., Cascio, and Bernardin.

Taking Sides: Human Resource Management	Human Resource Management, 7/e by Noe et al.	Managing Human Resources, 8/e by Cascio	Human Resource Management, 5/e by Bernardin
Issue 1: Is Affirmative Action Still Necessary?	**Chapter 3:** The Legal Environment: Equal Employment Opportunity and Safety **Chapter 5:** Human Resource Planning and Recruitment	**Chapter 3:** The Legal Context of Employment Decisions	**Chapter 3:** The Legal Environment of HRM: Equal Employment Opportunity **Chapter 5:** Human Resource Planning and Recruitment
Issue 2: Will the Americans with Disabilities Act Amendments Act (ADAAA) Be Abused in the U.S. Workplace?	**Chapter 3:** The Legal Environment: Equal Employment Opportunity and Safety **Chapter 6:** Selection and Placement **Chapter 13:** Employee Benefits	**Chapter 3:** The Legal Context of Employment Decisions **Chapter 5:** Planning for People **Chapter 7:** Staffing **Chapter 15:** Safety, Health, and Employee Assistance Programs	**Chapter 3:** The Legal Environment of HRM: Equal Employment Opportunity **Chapter 10:** Compensation: Base Pay and Fringe Benefits **Chapter 14:** Employee Health and Safety **Chapter 12:** Managing the Employment Relationship **Chapter 4:** Work Analysis and Design
Issue 3: Is the "Living Wages" Concept the Best Answer for High Employee Turnover Among Lower-Skilled Employees?	**Chapter 10:** Employee Separation and Retention	**Chapter 2:** The Financial Impact of Human Resource Management Activities **Chapter 11:** Pay and Incentive Systems	**Chapter 1:** Human Resource Management in a Changing Environment

(Continued)

Taking Sides: Human Resource Management	Human Resource Management, 7/e by Noe et al.	Managing Human Resources, 8/e by Cascio	Human Resource Management, 5/e by Bernardin
Issue 4: Should Employees be Allowed to Wear Symbols of Faith to the Workplace?	**Chapter 3:** The Legal Environment: Equal Employment Opportunity and Safety	**Chapter 16:** International Dimensions of Human Resource Management	**Chapter 3:** The Legal Environment of HRM: Equal Employment Opportunity
Issue 5: Are Social Networking Sites Good Recruitment Sources?	**Chapter 5:** Human Resource Planning and Recruitment	**Chapter 6:** Recruiting	**Chapter 5:** Human Resource Planning and Recruitment
Issue 6: Are Personality Tests a Good Predictor of Employee Performance?	**Chapter 9:** Employee Development	**Chapter 7:** Staffing	**Chapter 6:** Personnel Selection
Issue 7: Would Mandatory Background Checks for all Employees Reduce Negligent Hiring Lawsuits?	**Chapter 6:** Selection and Placement	**Chapter 7:** Staffing	**Chapter 6:** Personnel Selection
Issue 8: Is Cognitive Ability Testing a Good Predictor of Work Performance?	**Chapter 8:** Performance Management	**Chapter 9:** Performance Management	**Chapter 7:** Performance Management and Appraisal
Issue 9: Does the Glass Ceiling Still Exist in U.S. Organizations?	**Chapter 1:** Human Resource Management: Gaining a Competitive Advantage **Chapter 9:** Employee Development	**Chapter 3:** The Legal Context of Employment Decisions	**Chapter 3:** The Legal Environment of HRM: Equal Employment Opportunity **Chapter 4:** Work Analysis and Design **Chapter 9:** Career Development
Issue 10: Do Women Make Better Business Leaders?	**Chapter 5:** Human Resource Planning and Recruitment **Chapter 6:** Selection and Placement **Chapter 9:** Employee Development	**Chapter 1:** Human Resources in a Globally Competitive Business Environment **Chapter 4:** Diversity at Work **Chapter 5:** Planning for People **Chapter 10:** Managing Careers	**Chapter 3:** The Legal Environment of HRM: Equal Employment Opportunity
Issue 11: Does E-Learning Actually Promote Employee Learning and Development?	**Chapter 7:** Training **Chapter 9:** Employee Development	**Chapter 2:** The Financial Impact of Human Resource Management Activities **Chapter 8:** Workplace Training	**Chapter 8:** Training and Development
Issue 12: Does Increased Dependence on Laptops, Cell Phones, and PDA's Hurt Employee Productivity?	**Chapter 1:** Human Resource Management: Gaining a Competitive Advantage	**Chapter 1:** Human Resources in a Globally Competitive Business Environment	**Chapter 12:** Managing the Employment Relationship
Issue 13: Do Unions Help Organizational Productivity?	**Chapter 14:** Collective Bargaining and Labor Relations	**Chapter 11:** Pay and Incentive Systems **Chapter 13:** Union Representation and Collective Bargaining	**Chapter 13:** Labor Relations and Collective Bargaining

Taking Sides: Human Resource Management	Human Resource Management, 7/e by Noe et al.	Managing Human Resources, 8/e by Cascio	Human Resource Management, 5/e by Bernardin
Issue 14: Has Merit Pay Lost its Meaning in the Workplace?	**Chapter 12**: Recognizing Employee Contributions with Pay	**Chapter 11**: Pay and Incentive Systems	**Chapter 11**: Rewarding Performance
Issue 15: Do Intrinsic Rewards Provide for Better Employee Retention?	**Chapter 5**: Human Resource Planning and Recruitment **Chapter 8**: Performance Management	**Chapter 9**: Performance Management **Chapter 11**: Pay and Incentive Systems	**Chapter 11**: Rewarding Performance
Issue 16: Is Forced Ranking an Effective Performance Management Approach?	**Chapter 8**: Performance Management	**Chapter 9**: Performance Management	**Chapter 7**: Performance Management and Appraisal **Chapter 11**: Rewarding Performance
Issue 17: Given the Current State of the National Economy, Is Executive Pay Unreasonable?	**Chapter 1**: Human Resource Management: Gaining a Competitive Advantage **Chapter 11**: Pay Structure Decisions	**Chapter 6**: Recruiting **Chapter 11**: Pay and Incentive Systems	**Chapter 1**: Strategic Human Resource Management in a Changing Environment **Chapter 5**: Human Resource Planning and Recruitment **Chapter 10**: Compensation: Base Pay and Fringe Benefits
Issue 18: Does Attracting, Developing, and Retaining the Millennial Generation Require Significant Changes to the Current HRM Practices?	**Chapter 1**: Human Resource Management: Gaining a Competitive Advantage		**Chapter 1**: Strategic Human Resource Management in a Changing Environment **Chapter 5**: Human Resource Planning and Recruitment
Issue 19: Do Human Resource Management Practices Contribute to Increased Firm Performance?	**Chapter 1**: Human Resource Management: Gaining a Competitive Advantage **Chapter 2**: Strategic Human Resource Management **Chapter 8**: Performance Management	**Chapter 2**: The Financial Impact of Human Resource Management Activities **Chapter 9**: Performance Management	**Chapter 1**: Strategic Human Resource Management in a Changing Environment **Chapter 7**: Performance Management and Appraisal
Issue 20: Is Outsourcing a Good U.S. Business Strategy?	**Chapter 1**: Human Resource Management: Gaining a Competitive Advantage **Chapter 2**: Strategic Human Resource Management **Chapter 15**: Managing Human Resources Globally	**Chapter 1**: Human Resources in a Globally Competitive Business Environment **Chapter 2**: The Financial Impact of Human Resource Management **Chapter 16**: International Dimensions of Human Resource Management	**Chapter 1**: Strategic Human Resource Management in a Changing Environment **Chapter 2**: The Role of Globalization in HR Policy and Practice

Introduction

Today, organizations regard human resource leaders as strategic partners and seek their expertise and input for their organizations' profit and growth. Organizations compete with one another to provide the best for their employees, which suggests that employees are the most important assets. Google Inc., the Internet giant, refers to its HRM department as People Operations, emphasizing that employees make the difference. Container Store, a storage retailer, offers 50–100 percent above the industry wages and family-friendly hours. SAS Institute, a technology company, mandates 35-hour workweeks. How did this human resource management (HRM) journey begin?

Scholars suggest that employee–employer relationships could have had their beginnings in the craft associations of carpenters, masons, and leather workers during medieval times. Early apprentices were encouraged to live with and learn from their masters about their trade and work. In the course of being apprenticed, masters took care of their apprentices by providing them with shelter, food, and profits. This set the stage for identifying an employment relationship between a worker and his master or an employee and employer.

These paternalistic work relationships slowly faded with the advent of steam engines and the Industrial Revolution. The Industrial Revolution began in the mid-eighteenth century and introduced the concept of mass-production and employment of thousands in factories. Machines slowly began to replace time-consuming hand craftsmen's labor, and employees were hired to mainly perform routine and repetitive labor tasks. Henry Ford, founder of the Ford Motor Company and father of mass production, is said to have commented that employees do not need to bring their brains to work but only need to use their hands and legs.

The concept of division of labor also began as employees started to specialize in their jobs because this created an increase in production of goods. Organizations became very successful as profits increased tremendously, but slowly the rift between employers and employees began to emerge. Employees complained of lack of motivation, very low wages, and poor working conditions. Employees began to realize that they do not have a voice to protect their interests and work-related needs. Therefore, employees began to form labor groups so that they could have some balance of power at the workplace. However, there were no federal acts established that supported employees or recognized them as a source of bargaining power.

In the late 1870s, Frederick Taylor pioneered the scientific management movement with the revolutionary suggestion that management should be viewed as a science to enhance workplace productivity. Science is based on core facts and factual experiments; similarly, his study suggested that job performance should be based on records and data. His scientific research, referred to as time and motion studies, was conducted in steel factories and identified that employees were not functioning at their best performance levels. Therefore, he started timing employees' work using a stopwatch to monitor how employees worked and coordinated to produce their final products. This study provided three major results. First, he suggested that employees should be selected based on their physical or mental capacities to perform the job. He observed several steel workers struggling to move the heavy tons of steel; hence, some employees were physically not suited for their jobs. Second, he added that jobs should be procedurally defined that will allow for work perfection. Finally, he insisted that there should be work incentives or rewards for employees for performing the job correctly. Factories across the county embraced Taylor's management concept. Organizations that adopted his school of thought observed increased profits and employee satisfaction, suggesting that there could be truth in considering job performance as a science. His research also introduced the piecework (quantity produced versus time spent) incentive scheme to motivate employees to increase productivity. Scientific management was the dominant management approach until the early 1930s.

Around 1883, the federal Pendleton Act was mandated, which established that applicants take competitive exams to be hired into federal jobs. This step established the process of test-taking in hiring and also recognized that merit is an important selection criterion. Prior to the establishment of this act, selecting applicants for the federal services was largely based on personal favors and nepotism, resulting in staffing unqualified applicants. Different HRM practices were slowly beginning to take some shape and form.

Toward the end of the nineteenth century, the employment conditions in factories were becoming so bleak that employees wanted to institute some kind of communication with management. Employees perceived that better communication with management would help in better wages, improved working conditions, and fair rewards. This saw the emergence of welfare secretaries to help organizations and their employees communicate cordially. Research also suggests that welfare secretaries were predominantly women who started out mainly to look after the well-being of their employees (sick, pregnant women) and slowly incorporated other labor functions into this role. Welfare secretaries acted as liaisons between management and employees and played a neutral role in hearing employees' concerns and communicating those concerns to the management.

Around the early 1900s, industrial psychologists began to study the effect of applicants' mental characteristics on job performance. Hugo Munsterberg, chair of the psychology department at Harvard, pioneered this school of thought with the launching of his book *Psychology and the Industrial Efficiency*. The book was divided into three main sections: (1) how to hire the most qualified, (2) how to get maximum productivity, and (3) how to improve work techniques. He developed mental and job simulations tests and conducted these tests in several job professions to demonstrate that mental characteristics are important predictors of job performance. World War I provided a great opportunity to conduct these tests on thousands of applicants and identify the results of the test scores on job performance.

It was around the early 1900s that the term "personnel" first appeared in print. The civil service commissions primarily initiated the use of this term in their annual reports to indicate specific labor needs. Organizations hired personnel specialists and began to identify these departments by several names such as "Welfare," "Sociological," "Employment and Service," and "Personnel and Training." The primary purpose of these personnel departments was to provide for the well-being of employees in terms of safety, training, and benefits.

However, while the goal of these departments was to help employees, some organizations' departments were quite invasive. For example, the Sociological Department of Ford Motor Company had a policy from 1914 to 1917 of enforcing company visits on their employees to ensure that employees' personal living styles were not a social aberration. Employees who did not meet the organizational standards of living styles were either dismissed or denied company profits. Subsequently, this practice was abolished due to the injustice and unfairness caused to several employees.

Around the 1920s, behavioral psychologists contributed another breakthrough research, the Hawthorne studies, in understanding the function of human resource management better. This investigation, conducted from 1924 to 1933 at the Western Electric Company in Chicago, studied the effects of working conditions (such as lighting and temperature) on job performance and productivity. The study provided mixed results with some experiments suggesting that working conditions did impact job performance while others indicated that they did not. As a result of such irrational results, the organization conducted a deeper research investigation with the help of researchers from the Harvard Business School. Industrial researcher Elton Mayo and his associate Fritz Roethlisberger identified that human factors contributed more than environmental factors in enhancing productivity. Their study, referred to as the Relay Assembly Test Room, singled out six women to understand the effect of working conditions on productivity. After a year, the research concluded that these employees did not place much importance on their working conditions. However, they deeply valued the human factors such as how their supervisors treated them, how their co-workers interacted with them on a daily basis, and how they were recognized for their hard work. Organizations realized the importance of having a workplace that emphasized human relations and not just robotics.

In 1935, the National Labor Relations Act (Wagner Act) was established, which was another major step for employees to champion for equality at the workplace. This act allowed employees to work together as an entity (a labor union) to collectively bargain for their interests. The mutual agreement between management and employees known as collective bargaining included work-related concerns and interests of any labor union. Though employees could form labor unions even prior to the formation of this act, employers were against it and were very anti-unions. Employees were fired for taking part in any unionized activities and became very fearful and hesitant to join labor unions. However, this federal act mandated that employers cannot interfere in the formation of labor unions and also have to bargain in good faith with labor unions. This also saw the formation of labor relations departments in organizations to manage the employment relationship between employees and employers.

In 1964, federal law Title VII or the Civil Rights Act brought increased attention to the importance of HRM. The act prohibits workplace discrimination based on race, sex, color, or national origin. The law recognized that employees should get fair treatment in the workplace and introduced several other federal acts over the decades (Equal Pay Act of 1963, Age Discrimination in Employment Act of 1967, Rehabilitation Act of 1973, Americans with Disabilities Act of 1990, and Civil Rights Act of 1991). Though the presence of HRM was strongly acknowledged, this department was still regarded as predominantly administrative.

In the 1970s and 1980s, the business world witnessed several important trends such as increased globalization, stiff domestic competition, changes in workforce demographics, and reduced firm productivity. These trends held HRM departments accountable for employees and their job performances. Traditionally, strategic models dictated that organizations compete mainly on the basis of external market factors. However, the new model was suggesting that organizations consider their internal factors and resources—HRM practices and employees—as important organizational assets.

Around the early 1980s, academic scholars also began to show an interest in organizations' internal resources and their importance to strategic goals. In 1984, Birger Wernerfelt introduced the term "resource-based view" to the academic literature to emphasize how effective HRM practices can contribute to organizations' strategic goals. However, it was in the 1990s that Jay Barney laid the foundation to this concept with his revolutionary resource-based view theory or RBV. This theory identified that HRM practices that are valuable, unique, inimitable, and nonsubstitutable can contribute to increased firm performance. Therefore, an increased awareness that employees and their HRM practices can provide organizations with sustainable competitive advantage became entrenched. During the 1990s, several academicians published scholarly work indicating that HRM practices do contribute to enhanced firm performance.

U.S. corporations provide several examples of strategic HRM practices that are valuable, unique, inimitable, and nonsubstitutable. Internet king Google Inc. has a work policy of allowing employees to decide their own work time with a 70-20-10 policy (work project, personal development, and creativity). The ROWE (results only work environment) flexible work policy of U.S. electronic retailer Best Buy has revolutionized the traditional concept of not having to be physically present at work by providing employees absolute work flexibility. The ROWE program has demonstrated a 35 percent work productivity increase and more than 50 percent decreased employee turnover. In the hospitality industry, Ritz-Carlton's daily employee line-ups, elaborate talent-hiring process, and $2,000 frontline empowerment culture is applauded in the hospitality industry, albeit very difficult to duplicate. Booz Allen, a U.S. management consulting firm, recognized as the best in training and development, offers $5,000 in tuition reimbursement (graduate education and professional development) annually to its employees and considers employee development as a shared task between the employer and employee.

In 1997, Dave Ulrich also contributed to the strategic orientation of HRM by providing a four-role model of HRM, which is recognized both by practitioners and scholars. He suggested that HRM professionals have four specific organizational roles: administrative expert, change agent, employee advocate, and strategic partner. Each role allows HRM professionals to deliver valuable organizational outcomes. As an administrative expert, the HR leader is the authority on identifying effective HRM practices to employees. As a change agent, the HR leader must be proactive to adapt HRM practices according to the dynamic business environment. As an employee advocate, the HRM leaders sponsor employees concerns and also champion their causes. Finally, as a strategic partner, the HR leader contributes strongly at the board level and to the strategic orientation of the organization.

In the past decade, HRM has witnessed yet another transformation—the emergence of e-HRM (electronic human resource management). e-HRM is the process of using technology for human resource management practices, such as recruitment, training, performance appraisal, and benefits. e-HRM has provided HRM leaders with two important options for self-service and outsourcing. Organizations are predominantly using e-recruitment, e-learning, virtual teams, and online benefit planning, which allow employees personal access to HRM functions. Technology has also redefined the meaning of the workplace as employees work increasingly with laptops, PDAs, and cell phones, converting their personal spaces into offices. In addition, organizations can outsource certain HRM functions to external vendors that are not core or prove more cost-effective. Practitioners and scholars suggest that reliance on e-HRM could possibly enhance the strategic orientation of human resource professionals because they will have more time to focus on core and strategic activities.

Yet several studies suggest that becoming strategic partners is an elusive dream for HRM leaders. Research in 2002 by the Society of Human Research Management (SHRM) indicated that only 34 percent of the organizations' HRM leaders performed any strategic role. Even after such a long journey, HRM does not seem to receive the same importance as their peer departments such as finance, marketing, and sales. And the norm continues to be that HRM leaders struggle to find that prominent place at the board level. What could be the reasons for this?

A 2002 study done by Accenture on HRM practices suggests the reasons that HR leaders do not have strategic importance is because the measurement of the effectiveness of HRM practices is still obscure. While it is easy to identify the output of sales or production departments, it is more difficult to get such tangible results from HRM departments. Organizations are not able to clearly articulate how their staffing practices impact firm performance or how their training practices enhance bottom-line profits. Further, practitioners and scholars also suggest it is important to adopt a holistic approach for HRM so that the various practices are interrelated and distinguished as one large system. A systematic method allows corporations to see clearly the inputs and outputs and identify the benefits to the organization in terms of critical indicators such as return on investment and organizational growth.

What does the future hold for HRM professionals? As the business world is becoming a global marketplace and information is getting more digitized, HRM departments have to constantly consider the external environment to develop their strategic HRM agenda. Further, these leaders will be held more accountable for their tactical input as organizations are trying to outsource routine administrative work to allow HRM leaders to have quality time for business planning. Consequently, there is a very strong emphasis on adopting measurement metrics that predict a linear relationship between HRM practices and organizational effectiveness. Human resource management has come a long way from the early days of a paternalistic employer–employee relationship to a digitized work environment.

References

R. Bradley, "Lessons in Productivity and People," *Training & Development* (vol. 49, no. 10, p. 56, October 1995).

John F. Burnum, "Secrets About Patients," *The New England Journal of Medicine* (April 18, 1991).

M. Esdaille, S. Alleyne, "HR Growth," *Black Enterprise* (vol. 34, no. 11, pp. 85–92, 2004).

B. Friedman, B, "Globalization Implications for Human Resource Management Roles," *Employee Responsibilities and Rights Journal* (vol. 19, no. 3, p. 157, 2007).

F. Glaspie-Ellis, "From Paper-Pusher to Strategic Partner: The Changing Role of the Human Resource Professional," (Dissertation, Capella University).

R. Greenwood, "Employee Privacy Issues of the Early 20th Century: 1900 through Hawthorne Studies," *Journal of Applied Management and Entrepreneurship* (vol. 9, no. 1, pp. 94–99, 2004).

E. Gubman, "HR Strategy and Planning from Birth to Business Results," *Human Resource Planning* (vol. 27, no. 1, pp. 13–23, 2004).

J. Jamrog, M. OverHolt, "Building a Strategic HR Function: Continuing the Evolution," *Human Resource Planning* (vol. 27, no. 1, pp. 51–63, (2004).

F. Landy, "Early Influences on the Development of Industrial and Organizational Psychology," *Journal of Applied Psychology* (vol. 82, no. 4, pp. 467–477, 1997).

R. Levering, M. Moskowitz, "In Good Company," *Fortune* (vol. 155, no. 1, pp. 94–114, 2007).

R. Vosburgh, "The Evolution of HR as an Internal Consulting Organization," *Human Resource Planning* (vol. 30, no. 3, pp. 11–23, 2007).

Web Sites

SAS institute: Best Places to Work: http://www.chartcourse.com/article_SAS.html

Frederick Taylor and Scientific Management: http://www.netmba.com/mgmt/scientific/

Pendleton Act (1883): http://www.ourdocuments.gov/doc.php?flash=old&doc=48

Internet Source for Biographies on Psychologists: Hugo Munsterberg: http://faculty.frostburg.edu/mbradley/psyography/hugomunsterberg.html

Personnel Management: A Short History: http://www.cipd.co.uk/subjects/hrpract/hrtrends/pmhist.htm http://www.u-s-history.com/pages/h1612.html: National Labor Relations Act.

RBV Barney: http://www.valuebasedmanagement.net/methods_barney_resource_based_view_firm.html

Internet References . . .

The History of Affirmative Action Policies

This Web site frequently produces articles on various current issues and outlines key points in the history of affirmative action policies.

http://www.inmotionmagazine.com/aahist.html

A History and Timeline of Affirmative Action

This Web site provides information on several current domestic and international events and provides a history and timeline of affirmative action.

http://www.infoplease.com/spot/affirmative1.html

Facts About the Americans with Disabilities Act

This Web site defines who is considered an individual with disabilities, and outlines the facts about the Americans with Disabilities Act in detail.

http://www.eeoc.gov/facts/fs-ada.html

Americans with Disabilities Act

This Web site brings reference information and Q&A content together specific to the Americans with Disabilities Act. It is built to deliver the best answers on the Internet.

http://www.answers.com/topic/americans-with-disabilities-act

Center for Labor Research and Education (Labor Center)

The Center for Labor Research and Education (Labor Center) is a public service and outreach program of the UC Berkeley Institute for Research on Labor and Employment. The Labor Center carries out research on topics such as job quality and workforce development issues, work with unions, government, and employers to develop innovative policy perspectives and programs.

http://laborcenter.berkeley.edu/livingwage

Living Wage Calculator

This site, developed by Dr. Amy K. Glasmeier estimates the cost of living in your community or region. The calculator lists typical expenses, the living wage, and typical wages for the selected location.

http://www.livingwage.geog.psu.edu

FindLaw

FindLaw is a legal resource for up-to-date online legal information on relevant employment topics.

http://employment.findlaw.com/employment/employment-employee-discrimination-harassment/employment-employee-religion-discrimination-top/employment-employee-religion-workplace.html

Religion and the Workplace

The Entrepreneur Web site provides answers for several work-related concerns or issues, like religion.

http://www.entrepreneur.com/management/legalcenter/legalissuescolumnistjeffreysteinberger/article184334.html

Legal Environment

*W*hat rights should employees have? Should federal laws support employees? Human Resource Management (HRM) practices in the U.S. corporate world enjoy very strong federal support. This section addresses some laws that have been introduced to attain an equal opportunity work environment. Affirmative action was introduced in the 1960s to reduce racial discrimination, while the American Disability Act appeared in the early 1990s to mitigate disability discrimination. The living wage ordinance was started in 1994 to enhance the quality of living for lower-skilled employees. Should employees be allowed to freely express their religion at the workplace? Do we need federal interventions?

- Is Affirmative Action Still Necessary?
- Will the Americans with Disabilities Act Amendments Act (ADAAA) Be Abused in the U.S. Workplace?
- Is the "Living Wages" Concept the Best Answer for High Employee Turnover among Lower-Skilled Employees?
- Should Employees Be Allowed to Wear Symbols of Faith to the Workplace?

ISSUE 1

Is Affirmative Action Still Necessary?

YES: June Kronholz, Robert Tomsho, Daniel Golden, and Robert S. Greenberger, from "Race Matters: Court Preserves Affirmative Action—Preferences in Admissions Survive, but Justices Condemn Point System—Win for Business and Military," *Wall Street Journal* (June 24, 2003)

NO: Joe Messerli, from "Should Affirmative Action Policies, Which Give Preferential Treatment Based on Minority Status, Be Eliminated?" *BalancedPolitics,* www.balancedpolitics.org/affirmative_action.htm (2009)

ISSUE SUMMARY

YES: Award-winning educational journalists reported that race can be used as a criterion for admissions as the University of Michigan won a milestone court case. Supreme Court judges are of the opinion that racial diversity should begin at the university level to help students transition better into a multicultural workforce.

NO: Joe Messerli, author of the BalancedPolitics Web site, provides his thoughts on both pros and cons of several management issues. He suggests that one of the main pitfalls of affirmative action is that our business world will continue to live in a colored society.

President Kennedy introduced the term "affirmative action" in 1961 to address the issue of racial discrimination that existed at that time. It was federally mandated in 1965 by the issuing of Executive Order 11246. The main goal was to remedy past acts of discrimination against protected groups (such as African Americans and women) who did not have similar labor representation in the workforce. The Affirmative Action policy is legally mandated for all federal contractors ($50,000 and 50 or more employees) and can also be a legal settlement in discrimination lawsuits.

Affirmative Action is implemented through utilization analysis and affirmative action plans. The utilization analysis is a statistical method of comparing the percentage of an organization's internal labor force with that of the external labor force. The affirmative action plans provide a statement to remedy any underutilization of protected groups.

The result of the Affirmative Action policy when it was implemented in the 1960s was that educational institutions saw a reduction of achievement gaps between white and minority students during the 1970s and 1980s. In the 1990s, as businesses became increasingly global, they benefited from a diverse qualified workforce that was able to provide better heterogeneous work solutions.

However, preferential treatment and reverse discrimination have become contentious outbursts of affirmative action plans. *Preferential treatment* refers to the process of proactively hiring underutilized groups into the organization's workforce. *Reverse discrimination* is when dominant groups (e.g., white males) begin to feel discriminated against during the employment process as preferential treatment begins to take prominence. A high-profile reverse discrimination court case is that of Alan Bakke, a qualified white male student who was refused medical school admission in 1978 due to a quota system (a predetermined number). The quota system kept 16 seats out of 100 seats for minority applicants. The outcome of this case was that courts prohibited the use of quota systems in any admission process.

The Supreme Court ruling in 2003 supported the view that affirmative action plans can be applied to students at the university level. The judges affirmed that a diverse university student population will help students understand the dynamics and nuances of today's global workforce. Organizations are becoming increasingly global in their interactions today, with almost 700 out of 1,000 large U.S. firms stating that their international operations exceed that of their domestic. Further, such proactive efforts will also gradually mitigate racial disparity experienced at U.S. universities. Affirmative action also will attract diverse individuals to careers and universities they might have not considered if there was no such federal support. Do we not want to see a diverse society?

However, proponents of anti-affirmative action plans feel that providing preferential treatment sets a stigma suggesting their performance (academic or job) requires federal intervention and support. Employees and students have expressed negative peer behavior because of preferential treatment. Further, it attributes any individual's hard work for academic or job admission to be a result of external factors. Further proponents argue that if we continue with the Affirmative Action policy mandated three decades ago, U.S. society continues to live in shades of black and white. Do we still need such a color-biased society?

A concluding twist to this debate is whether such programs are quintessentially American. Have other countries initiated federal programs for disadvantaged groups? In fact, yes they do. Some countries that offer such programs are India, which provides affirmative action programs to people from different castes (distinct labor groups), and Malaysia, which offers support to different ethnic groups (Muslims and Chinese).

YES ← June Kronholz, Robert Tomsho, Daniel Golden, and Robert S. Greenberger

Race Matters: Court Preserves Affirmative Action—Preferences in Admissions Survive, but Justices Condemn Point System—Win for Business and Military

Abstract (Summary)

The decision striking down the undergraduate formula will force Michigan and other public universities with huge applicant pools to hire more admissions officers to read applications individually. University of Michigan President Mary Sue Coleman said she didn't "anticipate problems" in redesigning the school's undergraduate-admissions system, which automatically gave minority students a 20-point bonus on a 150-point scale. The court upheld the more-flexible admissions process used by the university's law school, which sought only to assemble a "critical mass" of minority students.

In a separate dissenting opinion, Justice Clarence Thomas called the majority's goal of ending affirmative action in a quarter-century "a 25-year license to violate the Constitution." Justice Thomas also suggested that one reason the higher-education establishment fought so hard for affirmative action was its fear that, if racial preferences were eliminated, schools would be forced to drop another admissions advantage: that enjoyed by children of alumni. Most elite colleges regard policies favoring so-called legacy admissions, which tend to help white students, as key to their fund raising.

Chief Justice [William Rehnquist] and Justice Anthony Kennedy also dissented from the law-school ruling. The dissenters, joined by Justices [Sandra Day O'Connor] and Stephen Breyer, formed the six-member majority in the undergraduate-admissions ruling. Joining Justice O'Connor's majority in the law-school ruling were Justices Breyer, Ruth Bader Ginsburg, David Souter and John Paul Stevens.

In a landmark decision with wide-ranging implications for affirmative action across American society, the court ruled that it is legal to give some preferential treatment to disadvantaged minorities, calling the diversity that they bring to education, business and the military necessary to the cultivation of "a set of leaders with legitimacy in the eyes of the citizenry."

But the victory for the status quo was conditional, as the court emphasized that racial preference should be a temporary rather than permanent fixture of American society, and called for "periodic reviews" and "sunset provisions" for race-conscious admissions.

The court, by a 5-4 vote, upheld a program at the University of Michigan's law school that allowed race to be considered in admissions. Going beyond the 1978 Bakke ruling that allowed colleges to use affirmative action, the court yesterday appeared to encourage businesses and others to do the same.

Viewed broadly, the decision endorsed a hotly disputed policy that has launched millions of blacks and Hispanics into the middle class but has alienated some whites and Asians. But more than that, the court has helped set the tone for race relations for years to come by putting its moral and legal imprimatur on programs that try to increase the number of minority-group members in civic and business leadership roles. "Effective participation by members of all racial and ethnic groups in the civic life of our nation is essential if the dream of one nation, indivisible, is to be realized," Justice Sandra Day O'Connor wrote in the majority opinion.

But in a second decision, this one on a 6-3 vote, the court struck down a separate University of Michigan undergraduate-admissions process based on a point system because it made race a "decisive" factor, rather than just one of many in determining who was admitted. This ruling will force state schools that use similar numerical methods to revise them, and it could cause companies to rethink their reliance on quantitative evaluations of job applicants and employees.

Even while endorsing affirmative action, Justice O'Connor, the swing vote on the law-school decision, urged that time limits be placed on affirmative action in admission because reliance on racial preference is "potentially so dangerous." She wrote, "We expect that 25 years from now, the use of racial preferences will no longer be necessary."

Although Michigan is a public university, the decision is considered likely to apply to selective private universities as well because they receive government funding. It also will affect admission practices at selective public high schools where affirmative action has also been eliminated or besieged.

Politically, the decision won't go down well with the Bush administration's conservative base. The White House has advocated ostensibly race-neutral substitutes for affirmative action, such as automatic college admission for high-school seniors in the top slice of their class. And the ruling overturns lower-court bans on affirmative action in Texas and Georgia, giving public universities in those states the option of resurrecting racial preferences. The University of Texas said it is likely to do so, at least on the graduate-school level.

Justice O'Connor's opinion makes a strong argument for racial diversity. Her thinking seems to have been heavily influenced by briefs filed in the case by a group of military officers and by businesses, including General Motors Corp. Diversity prepares students for the workplace and society, the justice wrote. Businesses "have made clear that the skills needed in today's increasingly global marketplace can only be developed through exposure to widely diverse people, cultures, ideas and viewpoints," she wrote.

A number of companies yesterday applauded the high court's endorsement of their efforts to diversify the workplace, although few businesses were eager to discuss the details publicly. Almost all large companies employ affirmative action, especially if they deal with the federal government. But employers rarely offer more than broad, long-term goals. Companies could now face increased pressure from civil-rights advocates to diversify their higher ranks.

Coming after a series of conflicting lower-court decisions, the Supreme Court ruling also left military leaders relieved that the affirmative-action pipeline had been preserved. Joseph Reeder, a former Army under-secretary who enlisted the support of nearly 30 retired officers of both political parties for the military brief, said the decision "allows the military to preserve the top quality we've been getting in the officer corps." The brief, which contended that an integrated officer corps is necessary to preserving armed-forces morale, invoked national security as a justification for affirmative action, seemingly taking conservative opponents and the Bush administration by surprise.

The high court's divisions yesterday reflect the continuing conflict in American society over public policies based on race. But the court strengthened a critical aspect of its 1978 precedent in the Bakke case, which banned quotas while allowing race as one factor among many. The controlling opinion in Bakke that endorsed racial diversity as a "compelling" state interest had the support of only one justice, Lewis Powell Jr. Now, that view has been embraced by a five-justice majority. . . .

President Bush, whose administration filed briefs with the court opposing Michigan's admissions process, nevertheless said he "applaud[s] the Supreme Court for recognizing the value of diversity on our nation's campuses. Diversity is one of our nation's greatest strengths." The administration, pushed by conservative supporters, had told the high court that schools instead should exhaust race-neutral methods to expand minority enrollment before resorting to preferences. The president mentioned so-called percent plans, now in use in Texas, Florida and California, that commit state universities to accept a certain percentage of top performers from each high school. This approach is designed to ensure admission to state universities of the best students at predominantly minority high schools, even if they might not otherwise qualify based on criteria such as standardized tests.

It is unclear what will happen to the percentage programs now, although the Center for Individual Rights, the conservative Washington-based advocacy group that backed the challenge of Michigan's admissions policies, said it would use further lawsuits to try to stop any state that attempts to drop the race-neutral approach.

The Supreme Court decisions dealt a blow to groups opposed to affirmative action that had hoped that a strong majority decision in their favor would add fuel to their efforts to rein in racial preferences used by employers. Curt Levey, director of legal and public affairs at the Center for Individual Rights, said his group is now more likely to concentrate on ensuring that universities comply with yesterday's rulings, rather than immediately pursuing additional related litigation against companies.

The decision striking down the undergraduate formula will force Michigan and other public universities with huge applicant pools to hire more admissions officers to read applications individually. University of Michigan President Mary Sue Coleman said she didn't "anticipate problems" in redesigning the school's undergraduate-admissions system, which automatically gave minority students a 20-point bonus on a 150-point scale. The court upheld the more-flexible admissions process used by the university's law school, which sought only to assemble a "critical mass" of minority students.

In a dissent to the O'Connor majority in the law-school case, Justice Antonin Scalia called the education lessons of diversity "a lesson of life rather than law—essentially the same lesson taught to . . . people three feet shorter and twenty years younger," in places such as Boy Scout troops. Justice Scalia decried the "tribalism and racial segregation" on campuses where minority-only clubs, student centers and housing are allowed or even promoted. He wrote that these arrangements could become "tempting targets" for future litigation challenging race-based campus organizations.

In a separate dissenting opinion, Justice Clarence Thomas called the majority's goal of ending affirmative action in a quarter-century "a 25-year license to violate the Constitution." Justice Thomas also suggested that one reason the higher-education establishment fought so hard for affirmative action was its fear that, if racial preferences were eliminated, schools would be forced to drop another admissions advantage: that enjoyed by children of alumni. Most elite colleges regard policies favoring so-called legacy admissions, which tend to help white students, as key to their fund raising.

Chief Justice Rehnquist and Justice Anthony Kennedy also dissented from the law-school ruling. The dissenters, joined by Justices O'Connor and Stephen Breyer, formed the six-member majority in the undergraduate-admissions ruling. Joining Justice O'Connor's majority in the law-school ruling were Justices Breyer, Ruth Bader Ginsburg, David Souter and John Paul Stevens.

While President Bush probably would nominate an ideological twin if the chief justice were to step down, Justice O'Connor's replacement would more likely alter the court's ideological makeup. That prospect could spark a brutal fight in the Senate and protests in the streets of Washington. The recent series of nasty fights over Mr. Bush's nominees for federal appeals-court vacancies are considered a dress rehearsal for the battle that will ensue when there is a Supreme Court opening.

The Michigan rulings affect only those colleges and universities that attract so many applicants that they need to pick and choose those they accept—perhaps no more than 200 of the country's 4,000 schools. But the decision also potentially affects scholarships and career-enhancing internships and research-assistant positions that are awarded at least partly based on race. Many colleges had begun to broaden their definition of who is eligible for those benefits as the Michigan cases edged closer to a resolution.

While it allows colleges to consider race in making those awards, the court makes clear that diversity shouldn't be defined solely in terms of race and ethnicity. That will mean universities will have to look more broadly at special talents and life circumstances, such as family income and education levels, in seeking a diverse student body.

At the University of Michigan, which annually receives 25,000 applications, the decision will mean hiring dozens of additional admissions officers who can give applications the personal, "holistic" look that Justice O'Connor required. Michigan's lawyer, Marvin Krislov, said there "may be some resource issues" as a result, but the school "is not concerned at all" about the rulings. He added that the university already conducts an annual review of its affirmative-action policies but plans a more comprehensive analysis in the future, in line with Justice O'Connor's opinion.

Justice O'Connor's goal of rendering affirmative action obsolete in 25 years puts pressure on lower public schools to eliminate the persistent test-score gap between whites and minorities. Harvard president Lawrence Summers said that American society's ability to meet her goal will depend on whether "we insist on schools that set the highest standards" and have the money to meet them.

Public schools made big strides in closing achievement gaps between white and minority youngsters in the 1970s and 1980s, but those gaps began to widen again in the 1990s. Now, national tests show black 12th graders reading and doing math at levels below that of white eighth graders. No consensus exists on why the racial discrepancy has worsened in the past decade. School systems and many liberals blame inadequate funding, while conservatives say educators aren't held accountable for their failures.

In 25 years, "if we go on the current trajectory, that gap in achievement will be greater than it is now," said Harvard Prof. Gary Orfield. . . .

Should Affirmative Action Policies, Which Give Preferential Treatment Based on Minority Status, Be Eliminated?

In a Nutshell

Yes	No
1. Affirmative action leads to reverse discrimination.	1. Diversity is desirable and won't always occur if left to chance.
2. Affirmative action lowers standards of accountability needed to push students or employees to perform better.	2. Students starting at a disadvantage need a boost.
3. Students admitted on this basis are often ill-equipped to handle the schools to which they've been admitted.	3. Affirmative action draws people to areas of study and work they may never consider otherwise.
4. It would help lead a truly color-blind society.	4. Some stereotypes may never be broken without affirmative action.
5. It is condescending to minorities to say they need affirmative action to succeed.	5. Affirmative action is needed to compensate minorities for centuries of slavery or oppression.
6. It demeans true minority achievement; i.e. success is labeled as result of affirmative action rather than hard work and ability.	

Overview/Background

Affirmative action generally means giving preferential treatment to minorities in admission to universities or employment in government and businesses. The policies were originally developed to correct decades of discrimination and to give disadvantaged minorities a boost. The diversity of our current society as opposed to that of 50 years ago seems to indicate the programs have been a success. But now, many think the policies are no longer needed and that they lead to more problems than they solve.

One notable example is a case argued a few years back in the Supreme Court concerning admissions to the University of Michigan. The school had a policy of rating potential applicants on a point system. Being a minority student earned you more than twice as many points as achieving a perfect SAT score. Three white students sued citing this as raced-based discrimination.

School officials said that diversity is desirable and affirmative action is the only way to achieve true diversity. Several other cases involving affirmative action have followed similar arguments.

The following sections explore the issue and show how things are much more complicated.

Yes

1. **Affirmative action leads to reverse discrimination.** Affirmative action is designed to end discrimination and unfair treatment of employees/students based on color, but it in effect does the opposite. Whites who work harder and/or are more qualified can be passed over strictly because they are white. Contrary to many stereotypes, many minorities fall into the middle or upper class, and many whites live in poverty. Unfortunately, the way things are set up now, a poverty-stricken white student who uses discipline and hard work to become the best he can be can be passed over by a rich minority student who doesn't put in much effort at all.

2. **Affirmative action lowers standards of accountability needed to push students or employees to perform better.** If a minority student can get into Harvard with a 3.2 grade-point average, why should she push herself to get a 4.0? Although some students or employees are self-motivated, most people need an extra push or incentive to do their very best. By setting lower standards for admission or hiring, we are lowering the level of accountability. We should reward hard work, discipline, and achievement; we shouldn't reward a student simply because he or she is a certain race, nor punish another student simply because he or she isn't.

3. **Students admitted on this basis are often ill-equipped to handle the schools to which they've been admitted.** Imagine a AA minor league baseball player suddenly asked to bat cleanup in the majors, or a high school science fair contestant suddenly asked to take a rocket scientist job at NASA. There's a possibility of success in these situations, but it's more likely they will be in over their heads. Schools like Harvard and Yale have high GPA and SAT requirements because it is extremely difficult to graduate from them. Thus, when they're forced to lower standards to achieve a minority quota, some students can't keep up. This isn't to say these students are less capable, but chances are that if they can't meet minimum requirements, they probably aren't ready to go there. The far-lower graduation rate of minorities is testament to the fact that they are too often going to schools that don't match their ability. The original application criteria of schools were put in for a reason. We should adhere to them.

4. **It would help lead a truly color-blind society.** When you apply for a job or fill out a college application, how often are asked about things like your hair color, eye color, or height? Unless it's for a modeling or athletic position, probably never. Why? It's because hair & eye color or height don't have any effect on your ability to do a job or succeed at a school. There's no association between hair/eye color and intelligence, discipline, ambition, character, or other essentials. Thus, it's useless to even ask about the information. Conversely,

there's no association between skin color and intelligence/discipline/ etc. So why do we keep drawing attention to it? Wouldn't it be great if we one day lived in a society when skin color was ignored as much as hair & eye color?

5. **It is condescending to minorities to say they need affirmative action to succeed.** When you give preferential treatment to minorities in admission or hiring practices, you're in effect saying "You're too stupid or incapable of achieving on your own, so let me help you." It is condescending and insulting to imply that minorities cannot achieve their goals through hard work and ability.

6. **It demeans true minority achievement; i.e. success is labeled as result of affirmative action rather than hard work and ability.** Ask Condi Rice or Colin Powell how they got to where they are—hard work or affirmative action? Both were hired because they are bright, articulate, and well-suited for their positions. My guess is that both would be offended if you said they got to where they were strictly because of affirmative action. The same can be said of minority doctors, lawyers, business leaders, etc. Too often, their achievements are demeaned by people who believe preferential treatment got them to their current positions. Minorities must then work twice as hard to earn respect.

No

1. **Diversity is desirable and won't always occur if left to chance.** Part of the education process is learning to interact with other races and nationalities. Many students live very segregated lives up until the time they start college. Thus, opinions of other races and nationalities are based on stereotypes. Interaction allows students to learn that persons of the opposite race are people too, more or less just like themselves. The movie *Remember the Titans*, based on a true story, is an excellent illustration of this. In the beginning, the football players portrayed in the movie are heavily segregated and antagonistic to the other race. The coach forces them to room with a player of the opposite color as well as learn some essential facts about each other. To make a long story short, they become lifelong friends and accomplish an undefeated season. Since this diversity is desirable, we want to make sure colleges represent a wide range of backgrounds. Unfortunately, without affirmative action, this diversity is much less likely to occur. It's possible schools will become segregated like in past decades. Elite schools may become increasingly dominated by majority students. Diversity is so important; we can't leave it to chance.

2. **Students starting at a disadvantage need a boost.** Minority students, generally speaking, start out at a disadvantage in their college or job application process. They usually come from lower income families and have less opportunity to go to private schools as white students. Some inner city youths must also live their childhoods in high crime, drug-infested areas. Sincere, hard-working minority students are every bit as capable as white students, but because of these disadvantages, they may not have the same paper qualifications. Affirmative action evens the playing field a bit.

3. **Affirmative action draws people to areas of study and work they may never consider otherwise.** Whether it's men being brought into nursing, women brought into technology fields, or minorities brought into Ivy League schools, it is always desirable to bring people to areas of study or work that they may not have considered otherwise. The more we change stereotypes, the less we'll need affirmative action in the future.

4. **Some stereotypes may never be broken without affirmative action.** For decades blacks were considered less capable than whites. It took affirmative action to give blacks the opportunity to show they are every bit as capable. These and other stereotypes have started to change and will continue to change with the help of affirmative action.

5. **Affirmative action is needed to compensate minorities for centuries of slavery or oppression.** The first several centuries of the U.S.'s existence saw whites enslave and oppress blacks, Native Americans, and other minorities. Minorities gave decades of unpaid labor, had land taken from them, were subject to brutal punishments, and were denied most of the fundamental rights provided by our Constitution. Affirmative action simply provides a way to compensate the descendants for the wrongs done to their ancestors.

In response to white assistant coach Yoast's favorable, easier treatment of black players on the football team: *"Now I may be a mean cuss. But I'm the same mean cuss with everybody out there on that football field. The world don't give a damn about how sensitive these kids are, especially the black kids. You ain't doin' these kids a favor by patronizing them. You're crippling them; you're crippling them for life."*—Coach Boone in *Remember the Titans* (played by Denzel Washington)

POSTSCRIPT

Is Affirmative Action Still Necessary?

Affirmative Action, which was established almost five decades ago, is a highly debated and controversial issue at universities and in organizations. Proponents advocate that a diverse society is extremely beneficial to businesses and therefore should be initiated at the university level. Further, pro-affirmative action groups suggest that some disadvantaged groups may need external support to create a flat playing ground where everybody has access to the similar opportunities. In addition, the Affirmative Action policy helps alleviate stereotypes commonly associated with certain protected groups.

The Supreme Court provided a landmark decision in 2003 when it delivered that the Affirmative Action policy may be used in the admission process to increase diversity. Diversity is a compelling national interest that should begin in university classrooms. Corporate America applauded this decision because as its workforce is becoming more and more multicultural, employees demonstrating sensitivity to different cultures will be a definite business advantage. The courts still prohibited the use of quotas or predetermined numbers in an admission application process.

Opponents of the Affirmative Action policy are convinced that it results in reverse discrimination. Reverse discrimination suits continue to haunt legal courtrooms even today. Recently, white firefighters in New Haven, Connecticut, won a reverse discrimination suit as the city of New Haven decided not to promote white firefighters. The city threw out test scores of white employees because African American firefighters did not receive high test scores.

Further, opponents argue that nonprotected groups have to work harder to get similar academic or employment opportunities. Is this fair? Also, protected groups who get preferential treatment may not be competent and may be merely satisfying numbers for admissions in universities or organizations. In addition, antagonists believe that the color of a person's skin and the person's gender should not be hiring predictors in any process. Do protected groups need federal programs today when we have minorities serving as the highest leader in the political and U.S. Supreme Court offices?

The introduction and postscript are based on the following readings also.

Suggested Readings

Bakke v. University of California Appeal: 1978—Reverse Discrimination Claimed: http://law.jrank.org/pages/3291/Bakke-V-University-California-Appeal-1978.html.

High court backs firefighters in reverse discrimination suit
http://www.cnn.com/2009/POLITICS/06/29/supreme.court.discrimination/
index.html.

Reverse-discrimination case splits Supreme Court
http://www.csmonitor.com/2009/0423/p02s01-usju.html%20.

Michigan ruling reaffirms drive for student diversity
http://www.timeshighereducation.co.uk/story.asp?storyCode=177865&
sectioncode=26.

Alison B. Marshall, "U.S. Supreme Court Tackles Affirmative Action in University Admissions: Will the Outcome Affect Corporate Diversity Efforts?" *Employee Relations Law Journal* (vol. 29, no. 1, p. 96, 2003).

June Kronholz, Robert Tomsho, and Charles Forelle, "High Court's Ruling on Race Could Affect Business Hiring," *Wall Street Journal* (Eastern Edition, p. A.1, June 2003).

Madison J. Gray, "Nationwide Attack on Affirmative Action," *Black Enterprise* (vol. 37, no. 7, p. 29, February 2007).

ISSUE 2

Will the Americans with Disabilities Act Amendments Act (ADAAA) Be Abused in the U.S. Workplace?

YES: Dina Berta, from "Labor Lawyers: Changes to Americans with Disabilities Act May Lead to More Workplace Discrimination Suits," *Nation's Restaurant News* (October 2008)

NO: Victoria Zellers, from "Make a Resolution: ADA Training," *HR Magazine* (January 2009)

ISSUE SUMMARY

YES: Award-winning writer, Dina Berta, suggests that the ADA (Americans with Disabilities Act) has always been controversial because it was difficult to define and understand. Now that the act has been redefined to ADAAA (Americans with Disabilities Act Amendments Act), it will allow more employees to fall under the disability category, which could increase the number of lawsuits.

NO: Legal attorney Victoria Zellers argues that sufficient training of HR professionals could substantially reduce litigation expenses for organizations. The HR department should be proactive to understand and provide for the special needs of their employees.

The Americans with Disabilities Act (ADA) was introduced in 1990 to reduce the discrimination against disabled people. Traditionally, society tends to segregate people who are disabled, and this federal act was instituted to mitigate this negative social trend. A proactive federal intervention would help disabled people integrate better with the main society and also help them achieve economic independence. Approximately 43,000,000 Americans have one or more physical or mental disabilities, with this rate increasing constantly.

The ADA defined disabled individuals as those who have a physical or mental impairment that drastically limits their major life activities. The definition of "major life activities" included walking, speaking, sitting, and reading, among several others specified. Specifically, an individual must demonstrate that he or she a) has a physical or mental impairment that substantially limits one or more of his or her major life activities; b) has a record of such an impairment; or c) is regarded as having an impairment. The disabled category also includes "controlled impairment", that is, individuals who have conditions that are controlled with medication (e.g., epilepsy) and also individuals who are perceived as disabled (e.g., morbidly obese).

The main controversy with the ADA is the very strict interpretation of the word "disabled." This has led to several lawsuits. The number of disability legal suits that the EEOC received is ranked third after sexual harassment and race legal suits. The other contributing factor for increased lawsuits under ADA was the inability of employers to provide reasonable accommodations.

An important court case illustrates how the interpretation of the word "disabled" can be misconstrued. In *Sutton v. United Airlines,* twin sisters sued the airlines when they were not hired as airline pilots due to severe myopia. The sisters claimed they were not hired because they were perceived disabled due to their poor vision. However, the court concluded that severe myopic problems do not classify as a disability because it did not impede the sisters from getting other industry jobs and also they functioned perfectly well with corrective measures (eyeglasses).

The ADA has been amended to the ADAAA from January 2009 in view of broadening the definition of disability. The term "major life activities" was redefined with an exhaustive list of activities such as walking, standing, lifting, eating, bending, reading, writing, and sleeping, among several others, including critical functions of the body. Further, employers have to disregard mitigating factors when determining if individuals have a disability. *Mitigating factors* are defined as external factors that help disabled individuals reduce the impact of any disability (such as hearing aids or medications). However, corrective measures such as eyeglasses and contacts were excluded. In addition, chronic illnesses that could reoccur (such as cancer) qualify as disabilities because such illnesses in their active stage would substantially limit an individual's life activity. Given such a broad expansion to disability, many more individuals will qualify as being disabled, and employers may face increased lawsuits.

On the other hand, HRM professionals are confident that sufficient training is the key to reducing costly lawsuits. While organizations invest sufficiently in sexual harassment and diversity training, organizations do not spend enough for disability training. Disability training can make employers feel well prepared and identify any loopholes in managing the process. During the hiring process, disabled individuals should not be asked specifically about their disabilities but only whether they can perform essential job functions. Further, HRM managers suggest using a very collaborative approach in managing information with line managers about employees in the context of the broadened definition of the term "disabled." HR managers should be informed of employees who may be having problems with major life activities so that they can be prepared when such employee-related problems arise. The main goal for HRM departments and line managers is to develop a well-coordinated approach before such employee concerns become litigation.

YES ↵

Dina Berta

Labor Lawyers: Changes to Americans with Disabilities Act May Lead to More Workplace Discrimination Suits

Employers should expect to see more workplace lawsuits under the newly amended Americans with Disabilities Act, according to labor lawyers who advise restaurant operators.

Unhappy with strict interpretations the U.S. Supreme Court has made since the ADA statute was passed in 1990, Congress acted to expand the law and make it easier for individuals with mental or physical impairments to file discrimination lawsuits. . . .

The law applies to workplaces with 15 or more employees for at least 20 weeks during a year, including part-time and temporary employees.

"The bottom line is that when it comes to ADA litigation, restaurants should now have the same expectation for ADA claims as they do for other discrimination claims, such as gender, race, religion, age and etc.," said Michael Mitchell, a partner in the New Orleans office of Fisher & Phillips and executive editor of the Hospitality Workforce Trends newsletter.

The amended law redefines and expands the definition of a disabled person as someone who is unable to perform a major life activity or is significantly restricted in the duration of a major activity.

Included in the list of major activities are such tasks as walking, standing, lifting, eating and sleeping, and mental tasks such as communicating, reading and thinking. Any major body functions, such as cell growth, digestive and reproductive functions, are also considered major life activities.

"It will no longer be difficult to prove that you have a right to bring such a claim," Mitchell said. "Although employers still have the same ability to argue to a jury that they had a legitimate and non-discriminatory reason to justify an employment action, they can no longer count on being able to defeat such a claim before it gets to that point."

Employers currently are able to avoid litigation by asserting that some employees do not qualify for protection under the law, given the strict interpretations the courts were making, explained attorney David Jordan of the Fulbright & Jaworski employment law firm in Houston.

"But Congress said [the courts] have gone too far," he said. "There were too many people being locked out of protection of the ADA. They wanted more people protected."

After a series of pro-employer decisions by the Supreme Court in 1999, lower courts began applying a "demanding standard" when determining whether a plaintiff was considered sufficiently disabled to advance an ADA lawsuit, Mitchell said.

"Disability advocates reacted angrily to what they considered be an undermining of the act's original intent," he added.

To further broaden the definition of a disability, "mitigating measures" can no longer be considered in determining whether a person is disabled enough for ADA protection, the lawyers said. A mitigation measure, for example, might be a prosthetic leg or hearing aids or medications. Corrective eye glasses or contact lenses were excluded.

"If you have a prosthetic device that enables you to walk just fine, then an employer could argue you were not disabled under the [ADA] act," Jordan said. "The courts said you had to take into account that with such a mitigating measure, you no longer fall under the protection of the ADA. The new legislation removed that."

Mitchell warned that operators, owners and human resources executives will need to update their policies and offer wider accommodations to their workforce. He and Jordan both are encouraging employers to err on the side of caution in considering employee requests for accommodations.

However, "the most prudent and cautious employers are probably already doing enough to protect themselves under the changes of the ADA," Jordan said. His firm is advising clients to be "thorough and seek counsel for close calls. Those who are always making close calls in favor of the employees should be fine."

Make a Resolution: ADA Training

Abstract (Summary)

As the New Year rang in, the Americans with Disabilities Act (ADA) Amendments Act took effect, bringing millions more people within the ADA's protection. The ADA Amendments Act's (ADAAA) vast expansion of disability means that many more applicants and employees are eligible for reasonable accommodations and that employers need a fresh ADA compliance strategy. The ADAAA defines and vastly expands the term major life activities as including caring for oneself, performing manual tasks, seeing, hearing, eating, sleeping, walking, standing, lifting, bending, speaking, breathing, learning, reading, concentrating, thinking, communicating and working. The ADAAA does not require ADA training, but provides a strong business case for it. Sexual harassment training isn't specifically required by Title VII of the Civil Rights Act of 1964 either, but employers recognized the importance of regular sexual harassment training after the US Supreme Court decided Burlington Industries Inc v Ellerth and Faragher v City of Boca Raton.

Now is the time for stand-alone, dedicated coursework.

As the New Year rang in, the Americans with Disabilities Act (ADA) Amendments Act took effect, bringing millions more people within the ADA'S protection. The ADA Amendments Act's (ADAAA) vast expansion of "disability" means that many more applicants and employees are eligible for reasonable accommodations and that employers need a fresh ADA compliance strategy.

In the past, employers often won ADA cases by filing motions for summary judgment and establishing that the plaintiffs were not disabled, avoiding expensive jury trials.

Employers will need to alter their approaches and take a page from what worked in the sexual harassment context. Employers can curb litigation risks through ADA training separate from general equal employment opportunity or nondiscrimination training.

Although training budgets are being squeezed in these tough economic times, training could save employers time and expense in the long run.

The ADAAA broadened the ADA's definition of disability by expanding the term "major life activities," doing away with the "substantially limited" requirement for those regarded as having a disability, and overturning two U.S. Supreme Court decisions that interpreted the ADA'S definition of disability narrowly.

From *HR Magazine*, 54:1, January 2009, pp. 81–83. Copyright © 2009 by Society for Human Resource Management, Alexandria, VA. Reprinted by permission via the Copyright Clearance Center.

The ADA still covers only qualified individuals with disabilities and provides that to be disabled, an individual must have "a physical or mental impairment that substantially limits one or more major life activities," or must have a record of such an impairment, or must be regarded as having such an impairment.

However, with the ADAAA, the only requirement for the "regarded as" prong is that the impairment must not be minor—a criterion the law does not define—or transitory, defined in the law as lasting less than six months.

The ADAAA also defines and vastly expands the term "major life activities" as including "caring for oneself, performing manual tasks, seeing, hearing, eating, sleeping, walking, standing, lifting, bending, speaking, breathing, learning, reading, concentrating, thinking, communicating and working." The amendment states that major life activities include the operation of a major bodily function, such as "functions of the immune system, normal cell growth, digestive, bowel, bladder, neurological, brain, respiratory, circulatory, endocrine and reproductive functions."

Decisions Overturned

In addition, the ADAAA overturns two U.S. Supreme Court decisions that had limited the ADA'S coverage. One decision let employers consider the ameliorative effects of mitigating measures, such as hearing aids and medication, when determining whether someone has a disability (Sutton v. United Airlines Inc., 527 U.S. 471 (1999)). The ADAAA instead requires that employers evaluate impairments without regard to mitigating measures. Thus, a mental disorder such as depression controlled by medication must be considered in its unmedicated state to determine if it is a disability. The ADAAA does have an exception that permits employers to take into account the effects of eyeglasses and contact lenses.

The ADAAA also overturned a Supreme Court decision that concluded that the term "disability" should be viewed narrowly and that said the ADA requires a demanding standard to prove one is disabled (Toyota Motor Manufacturing, Kentucky Inc. v. Williams, 534 U.S. 184 (2002)). The ADAAA instead provides that disability should be viewed broadly and asks the U.S. Equal Employment Opportunity Commission (EEOC) to issue regulations to further address this issue.

Another important change requires that impairments that are episodic or in remission qualify as disabilities if in their active stage they would substantially limit a major life activity. This revision, along with the one regarding mitigating measures, moves numerous conditions such as cancer, diabetes and epilepsy from a case-by-case determination to almost certain status as ADA disabilities.

The Argument for Training

The ADAAA does not require ADA training, but provides a strong business case for it. . . .

Employers . . . should recognize the value of training HR personnel, managers and supervisors on the ADA and its amendments. While the ADAAA did not alter the ADA'S reasonable accommodation and nondiscrimination requirements, many more individuals will qualify for these protections. So it's essential that key professionals understand what the ADA, as amended, involves.

Training should include review of:

Who is covered. Given the expansion of "major life activities" and the removal of mitigating measures from consideration in disability determinations, almost anyone who has, or is regarded as having, a serious impairment or disease that is not temporary will qualify as disabled. Ensure that training covers any applicable state laws prohibiting disability discrimination.

How hiring policies and practices are affected. Since applicants are covered, re-evaluate hiring processes. Case in point, reading is now a major life activity. Thus, you will need to look at how reading may affect your hiring process. If reading isn't an essential function of the job, such as for a maintenance staff position, and if a candidate can't read, an employer probably will have to provide a reasonable accommodation to help the candidate complete the application process.

However, if reading and/or writing are essential job functions, the employer doesn't need to provide such assistance. The amended ADA does not require employers to change essential job duties. And you are not expected to be a mind reader—you will need to offer assistance only if the applicant requests help.

Employers also should remind those who screen applicants that employers are not allowed to ask whether individuals have disabilities. Interviewers can ask whether someone is able to perform essential job functions with or without accommodation.

The interactive process and its requirements. When someone requests an accommodation, the ADA requires an employer to engage in the interactive process with the person to determine if a reasonable accommodation can be provided to enable that person to perform the requirements of the position. However, many courts have held that an individual does not need to use the magic words, "I'm requesting an accommodation for my disability." Rather, if someone simply states, "I need help or assistance because of my impairment," that triggers the process.

Here are some additional examples of triggers for the interactive process:

- An employee tells his supervisor he is having trouble reading an internal memo because of his poor vision.
- An employee asks her supervisor if she can come to work two hours late because of an appointment with her physical therapist.
- An employee informs his supervisor he cannot work overtime because of his sleep apnea.

Supervisors need to be trained to report statements like these to the HR department.

What accommodations are reasonable. Determining reasonable accommodations varies greatly according to employer and position. It may be unreasonable to require a small construction company to provide a bucket truck to an employee who cannot climb a ladder, but this accommodation may be reasonable for a large utility. Train supervisors to work with HR and corporate counsel to determine reasonable accommodations.

What is prohibited. In addition to providing training on nondiscrimination and reasonable accommodations, teach managers that harassment actions can be brought under the ADA. Of the 27,262 total harassment charges made to the EEOC and state fair employment practices agencies in fiscal 2007, 4,934 were for disability harassment—third after race and sexual harassment and more than the amount for age, national origin or religious harassment. Train all employees to prohibit harassment and to report complaints of impairment-related harassment to HR.

Similarly, retaliation is prohibited. If an individual requests an accommodation, regardless of whether the employer provides the accommodation, that individual is protected from retaliation for making the request.

It's also important for training to cover the interplay between the ADA, as amended, and other laws, including the Family and Medical Leave Act, state nondiscrimination and state family-leave statutes, workers' compensations laws, and Social Security disability.

The amendments will make ADA compliance more complicated and expansive. Now is the time to train the entire HR team and management on the ADA—to minimize mistakes and, should you have to go to trial, aid your defense.

This is one New Year's resolution you need to keep. . . .

POSTSCRIPT

Will the Americans with Disabilities Act Amendments Act (ADAAA) Be Abused in the U.S. Workplace?

The ADA introduced several important employment terms to the American corporate world. *Essential functions* are defined as the tasks and duties that employees must perform to be effective in their job. *Marginal functions* are considered peripheral duties that are not critical to the job. The ADA allows employers to make decisions based on the ability of individuals to perform the essential job functions. *Reasonable accommodations* are accommodations that employers must provide for disabled employees (such as wheelchair access). *Undue hardship* is when an organization perceives that it might incur a lot of cost or difficulty in providing accommodations to the disabled.

The new expanded definition of the ADAAA has created both concerns and answers to disability activists. The current broad definition has an exhaustive list of activities not included in the earlier version of the act and also has added additional conditions to the disability clause. Therefore, more individuals would qualify as disabled, which is a big change from its former elucidation. ADA legal complaints are ranked third by EEOC, suggesting that there could be a lot of gray areas still unanswered by the law. The current ADAAA requires disabilities be considered without mitigating factors; that is, employers must evaluate disabilities without the support of medication or external aids. Would the Sutton twin sisters win their case against United Airlines now?

On the other hand, HRM professionals contend that organizations have not given enough attention to providing employees with disability training. Because hiring managers perform several HRM functions (such as staffing and training), line staff also needs to be thoroughly trained on current laws and possible outcomes. Adopting a collaborative environment between HRM and line employees will definitely ensure that the disability law is not abused. HR professionals insist that disability training must be given the same rigor as other training opportunities if organizations want to reduce potential lawsuits.

Two other court cases illustrate the interpretation of the word "disabled" as being controversial. Consider *Toyota Motor Manufacturing* v. *William* to glean information on how the courts upheld and reversed decisions to reach a correct definition of the word "disabled." The plaintiff, William, sued Toyota after she developed carpal tunnel syndrome and requested reasonable accommodation. However, when the organization terminated her subsequently, she sued under ADA, claiming that she was fired because of her disability. It is interesting to read how long-drawn court cases can get and also how the word "disabled" is interpreted in the court of law. Does the current ADAAA support the outcome of this court case?

Similarly, in *Murphy* v. *United Parcel Service* (UPS), Murphy, a UPS driver, sued when he was terminated from his job when employers realized his hypertension figures exceeded the norm for UPS drivers. Murphy sued under ADA as he felt he was fired because he was perceived disabled. However, the court supported UPS, as they concluded that Murphy performed his daily activities normally with blood pressure medication and hence does not qualify for ADA.

Suggested Readings

Anonymous, "Revised ADA Regs Already Present Challenges," *HR Focus* (vol. 86, no. 9, p. 2, September 2009).

Andrew Slobodien and Katie O'Brien, "The ADA Amendments Act of 2008 and How It Will Change the Workplace," *Employee Relations Law Journal* (vol. 34, no. 3, pp. 32–39, December 2008).

J. Shoskin, "The ABCs of the NEW ADAAA," *American Agent & Broker* (vol. 81, no. 6, pp. 28–30, June 2009).

Americans with Disabilities Act: http://www.u-s-history.com/pages/h2050.html#.

ADA Accessibility Lawsuits Causing Headaches for Small Business Owners: http://www.sfgate.com/cgi-bin/article.cgi?f=/g/a/2008/06/13/carollloyd.DTL.

Toyota Motor Manufacturing, *Kentucky* v. *Williams*: http://www.arentfox.com/publications/index.cfm?fa=legalUpdateDisp&content_id=1143.

ISSUE 3

Is the "Living Wages" Concept the Best Answer for High Employee Turnover among Lower-Skilled Employees?

YES: Annie Gentile, from "Wage Laws See Varied Results over 14 Years," *The American City & County* (October 2008)

NO: Diane Cadrain, from "States and Cities Square Off over Living Wage Laws," *HR Magazine* (March 2004)

ISSUE SUMMARY

YES: Annie Gentile, freelance writer and expert on employment issues, contends that increasing wages of low-skilled labor definitely will contribute to positive organizational outcomes.

NO: Diane Cadrain, legal attorney, suggests that higher low-skill wages would squeeze the profit margins for organizations and make the final product or service more expensive.

Living wages is a wage concept that has been introduced to provide reasonable wages so that low-skilled employees can have a comfortable standard of living (housing, nutrition, and clothing). These wages are higher and different from the minimum wage, which is mandated by the federal or state government and usually does not provide sufficiently for employees to enjoy reasonable living standards.

The living wage has also been spurred by the fact that the minimum wage is comparatively stagnant or rising very slowly in contrast to the cost of living, which is increasing by leaps and bounds. Minimum wage cannot support a family of four (husband, wife, and children) and is geared more toward single individuals such as teenagers, college students, and part-time workers. The living wage ordinance (LWO) requires businesses to pay employees average wages between $6.25 and $12.00. It has been estimated that $8.20 is the average wage for a family of four to survive above the federal poverty line.

The LWO began in Baltimore in 1994 when labor unions and community activists demanded that businesses receiving state assistance or government contracts (of \$10,000 or more) should provide higher or "living wages" for their employees. Subsequently several localities such as Boston, Washington, D.C., San Francisco, and Santa Fe, among several others, have passed the LWO. Currently, there are almost 140 LWO cities adopting this ordinance, and proponents are advocating more cities to be included.

Proponents advocate several positive outcomes with providing living wages to employees. First, businesses will experience reduced employee turnover, which is so chronic among low-skilled workers who are frequently job-hopping for better wages. Second, providing better wages will also reduce absenteeism and increase employee morale as employees feel a sense of accomplishment with higher wages. Third, this would promote a sense of corporate social responsibility on businesses as they share their profits with their lower-skilled employees.

Further, employees who are on living wages will have more disposable income to buy consumer products, creating a cyclical effect on the local economy. How can we have a universal wage system when we know the cost of living varies significantly across the states? Finally, and an important point for policymakers, if businesses do not support living wages, the burden of maintaining individuals who fall under such poverty levels will fall squarely on the American taxpayers. Does our society want this?

In contrast, opponents of living wages argue that businesses will face increased labor costs that will be passed on ultimately to consumers. This could dampen business profits that rely predominantly on low and cheap prices. Further, some advocates are pushing LWO to cover entire jurisdictions of big cities regardless of whether businesses have obtained government contracts. This has created a controversial debate between retail/hospitality establishments and policymakers as small and mid-size companies fear that they will have no profits at all.

Some argue that if American businesses are obliged to pay certain wages, this could increase the likelihood of outsourcing and offshoring, which have become contentious in today's business world. For employees who are not well educated and also those who do not have any employment skills, low-paid entry-level jobs (non-living wages) might be their only method of living and sustenance. Do we really want to hurt those that need help? One community organization that proactively supports LWO is ACORN (Association of Community Organizations for Reform Now), which strongly advocates living wages and robust self-sufficient communities among low- and moderate-income families.

Is living wages solely a domestic concern, or do other countries also promote such labor issues? Yes, other countries are actively promoting this kind of wage act. In Asia, "the labor behind the label" is trying to promote higher wages for garment workers on the basic premise that employees deserve a decent community living regardless of what work they do. Further, having a "floor" or wage system based on the local cost of living in Asian countries will ensure multinationals do not exploit cheap labor. The Baltimore wage concept has spread to the United Kingdom also and gained quite some momentum over the years with new jobs for the 2012 Olympic workers stipulating living wages.

YES

Annie Gentile

Wage Laws See Varied Results over 14 Years

Abstract (Summary)

Since 1994, when Baltimore became the first municipality in the US to pass a living wage ordinance (LWO), scores of cities and special districts have followed suit. In general, LWOs require government contractors or companies that receive publicly funded economic subsidies to pay their workers at a rate that exceeds the federal ($6.85 per hour) or state minimum wage. LWO advocates claim that employers who do not pay their workers a living wage pass a burden on to taxpayers, who are forced to subsidize low-wage earners with government-funded programs.

Some ordinances fall to politics while others thrive.

Since 1994, when Baltimore became the first municipality in the nation to pass a living wage ordinance (LWO), scores of cities and special districts have followed suit. Fourteen years later, some of the ordinances have been repealed, others have been modified, while a few are prompting neighboring jurisdictions to adopt similar labor rules.

In general, LWOs require government contractors or companies that receive publicly funded economic subsidies to pay their workers at a rate that exceeds the federal ($6.85 per hour) or state minimum wage. LWO advocates claim that employers who do not pay their workers a living wage pass a burden on to taxpayers, who are forced to subsidize low-wage earners with government-funded programs. And, they claim that LWOs ultimately benefit employers and their workers because higher wages help reduce workforce absenteeism and turnover, and improve morale.

In August, Manchester, Conn., repealed its 27-monthold LWO in a 5-4 vote. The change was prompted by the discovery that a contract with the town's health insurance administrator did not meet the city's wage standard for some of the company's employees in other states. The insurer asked for a waiver, and some board members proposed an amendment to the ordinance to require large employers to meet the wage standard only for those employees who may work directly or indirectly on Manchester contracts. Instead, the board of directors repealed the ordinance.

From *The American City & County,* 123:10, October 2008, pp. 16–17. Copyright © 2008 by Penton Media Inc. Reprinted by permission.

Flexibility has helped sustain the LWO that Ann Arbor, Mich., officials adopted in March 2001. The ordinance exempts seasonal parks and recreation workers, and applies only to city contracts of $10,000 or more. Presently, Ann Arbor's LWO calls for employers who contract with the city to pay $10.85 per hour to their employees if they provide medical benefits and $12.56 per hour if they do not. City Administrator Roger Fraser says a few exemptions have been made to the ordinance over the years, including one for a recycling operation that employs approximately 20 low-wage manual labor employees. Including the recycling employer in the LWO would have significantly increased costs to the city, Fraser says.

Additionally, in April, the Ann Arbor City Council voted to exempt the city's annual summer festival from the ordinance because many of the festival workers are high school and college students. "[Those exempted] are mostly students who are not supporting a family, and not the type of people that were in mind when the ordinance was designed," he says. In the past, the city's contribution to the festival was held to just under $10,000 to avoid triggering the law, and the exemption meant the city could increase its donation.

Meanwhile, LWOs around Ventura County, Calif., have been expanding steadily since the county passed the first ordinance in the region in 2001, says Santa Barbara Councilman Das Williams. Since that time, the city of Ventura, Oxnard and Port Wynemie have adopted LWOs, and Santa Barbara enacted one in 2006. Santa Barbara adjusts its living wage rate annually. In fiscal year 2008–2009 Santa Barbara's LWO calls for employers to pay either $11.86 or $12.94 per hour depending on the benefits provided, or $15.10 per hour if no health benefits are included.

The concentration of LWOs in the area means that no one city is at a disadvantage when competing for contracts. "We now have such a critical mass of jurisdictions that any business serious about contracting with cities needs to think strongly about paying a living wage," Williams says. . . .

Diane Cadrain   ➔ **NO**

States and Cities Square Off over Living Wage Laws

Abstract (Summary)

Many state legislators are expected to lock horns with city officials around the country this year over the increasing popularity of living wage ordinances in municipalities. Since Baltimore enacted the first such ordinance in 1994, 116 localities have followed suit, requiring employers who work on public contracts, or who receive government economic development subsidies, to pay their employees enough to lift them out of poverty. But business groups in some states, alarmed by the effect of living wage ordinances on commerce and competition, are fighting back by seeking statewide legislation barring localities from passing such requirements.

Many state legislators are expected to lock horns with city officials around the country this year over the increasing popularity of "living wage" ordinances in municipalities.

Since Baltimore enacted the first such ordinance in 1994, 116 localities have followed suit, requiring employers who work on public contracts, or who receive government economic development subsidies, to pay their employees enough to lift them out of poverty. But business groups in some states, alarmed by the effect of living wage ordinances on commerce and competition, are fighting back by seeking statewide legislation barring localities from passing such requirements.

The living wage movement is a reaction to two catalysts, said Nathan Newman, associate counsel with the Brennan Center for Justice of the New York University Law School. "One is that the federal minimum wage has remained at $5.15 per hour since 1996. The other is the trend in local governments toward taking decently paid municipal jobs and putting them in the hands of private contractors."

Typically, living wage ordinances require businesses that receive public contracts or economic development funds to pay their employees enough to keep them at or above the federal poverty level. The hourly wage equivalent to the poverty line for a family of four is currently $8.20 per hour, and the ordinances have required wages ranging from $6.25 to $12 per hour.

Without a living wage, advocates say, employees can only survive with help from charities and emergency rooms. Thus, municipalities may spend on social services what they save on contractors' labor costs.

To opponents, the irony of living wage ordinances is that they hurt those they most intend to help. "They force the least skilled workers out of the marketplace," says Craig Garthwaite, Research Director of the Washington, D.C.-based Employment Policies Institute (EPI). "It really means that lower[-paid] workers are out of the workforce and lose opportunities to learn new skills."

Even more worrisome, opponents say, is the fact that localities that have enacted living wage ordinances are tempted to expand into local minimum wage ordinances covering all employers operating within a jurisdiction, not just those with public contracts or public subsidies.

"The living wage movement is shifting its attention to local minimum wages in localities where they have already passed living wage ordinances," said Garthwaite, citing San Francisco and Santa Fe, N.M.

Business groups have lobbied for state laws barring localities from enacting either living wage ordinances or local minimum wages. Florida and Texas passed pre-emption legislation in 2003, South Carolina in 2002, Utah and Oregon in 2001, Louisiana and Arizona in 1997, and Colorado in 1996.

In Tennessee, a pre-emption proposal that died in the 2003 legislative session is expected to resurface. Connecticut also is expected to consider pre-emption legislation. The Santa Fe minimum wage ordinance will face a court challenge to its constitutionality, brought by a group of business leaders who claim that only the state, not local government, has the power to set minimum wages.

Despite resistance to mandating higher wages, at least three states are pondering setting or increasing minimum wage statutes in 2004. Florida, one of a few states with no minimum wage of its own, will have a statewide minimum wage proposal on the ballot in November. . . .

POSTSCRIPT

Is the "Living Wages" Concept the Best Answer for High Employee Turnover among Lower-Skilled Employees?

The living wage movement began in Baltimore when community activists and labor unions decided that economic enhancement of low-skilled employees should be a collaborative effort between local governments and businesses. Economists suggest that living wages contribute to a productive economy and also provide a stable low-skilled workforce to businesses. LWO is actively promoted in various metropolitan cities with some states, such as Maryland, mandating living wages for the entire state. Maryland promoted two different living wages for different parts of the state: $11.30/hour in the Baltimore and Washington, D.C., metropolitan areas and $8.50/hour for the rest of the state.

Opponents fear that retail businesses that thrive on a cost leadership strategy will be unable to pass on any benefits to consumers due to high labor costs. Community activists also do not support retail establishments that do not provide living wages. Retail giant Walmart's effort to expand into Los Angeles was thwarted because activists did not endorse such large-scale low-wage employment. Antagonists also perceive that providing living wages might impede low-skilled employees from having any jobs at all. Do we want to increase economic disparity in our society?

Finally, let's consider some important court cases for LWO. First, in the State of Missouri versus local business groups in 2001, the court upheld that cities in Missouri can provide living wages. An earlier ruling in 1998 had indicated that the state of Missouri cannot enact LWO. Second, in the court ruling for the city of Santa Fe in 2004, it upheld the decision that living wages could be applied throughout the city. In 2007, in another dramatic win for living wages, the city of Los Angeles upheld that 13 private hotels around the Los Angeles International airport would pay living wages to their 3,500 low-skilled employees.

Suggested Readings

P. Dreier, "Good Jobs, Healthy Cities," *The American Prospect* (vol. 20, no. 8, pp. A10–A13, 2009).

Joanne Deschenaux, "First Living Wage Law Passed in Maryland," *HR Magazine* (vol. 52, no. 6, pp. 28, 40, June 2007).

J. Wicks-Lim, "Should We Be Talking About Living Wages Now?" *Dollars & Sense* (vol. 281, pp. 11–13, March 2009).

Should Minimum Wage Be Abolished? http://www.balancedpolitics.org/minimum_wage.htm.

Potential Pros and Cons of a Living Wage Ordinance in Sacramento: http://www.acorn.org/index.php?id=247.

Missouri Court Declares That Cities Have Power to Enact Living Wage Laws: http://www.brennancenter.org/content/resource/missouri_court_declares_that_cities_have_power_to_enact_living_wage_laws.

"Living Wage" Identified for Asia: http://news.bbc.co.uk/2/hi/business/8294531.stm.

Researching London's Living Wage Campaign: http://www.geog.qmul.ac.uk/livingwage/.

Appeals Court Upholds Santa Fe living Wage Law: http://www.brennancenter.org/content/resource/appeals_court_upholds_santa_fe_living_wage_law/.

ISSUE 4

Should Employees Be Allowed to Wear Symbols of Faith to the Workplace?

YES: Robert Grossman, from "Religion at Work," *HR Magazine* (December 2008)

NO: Robert D. Ramsey, from "When Religion and Work Clash," *Supervision* (September 2007)

ISSUE SUMMARY

YES: Robert Grossman, editor and professor of management, suggests that organizations should adopt a faith-friendly approach and allow employees wear their symbols of faith and express themselves religiously at work.

NO: Dr. Robert Ramsey, author and freelance writer, argues that accommodating religious requests might become a never-ending list of requests that could hamper business goals and profits.

Today's workplace includes a diverse mix of employees from various religious backgrounds. Title VII, established in the 1960s, dictates that there will be no religious discrimination in the workplace. The question that concerns HRM leaders today is whether employees should be allowed to express or wear external symbols at the workplace, which is getting increasingly diverse in terms of religion.

In 2008, the Society of Human Resource Management (SHRM) reported that 64 percent of its organizations had a religiously diverse workforce in comparison to 36 percent in 2001. The results indicate a substantial increase of employees from different religious faiths as more and more immigrants from different faiths arrive.

David Miller, Director of Princeton University Faith and Work Initiative, suggests that diversity initiatives should advocate a free expression of employees' religion also. It seems very unfair to expect employees to leave their religious expressions behind at their homes to maintain a detached exterior at the workplace. How can organizations embrace employees' ethnicity without acknowledging their religion?

Several leading organizations, such as Coca-Cola Bottling Company and Ford Motor Company, have adopted a very faith-friendly approach. These organizations have allowed employees of different religious faiths to conduct religious meetings at the workplace. These organizations have also indicated that allowing employees to express their faith has increased their commitment to the organization and provides a very nurturing environment. Muslim employees at Ford are allowed to use on-site prayer rooms for their daily prayers. Such organizational initiatives strengthen their dedication to the organization and also make the workplace more meaningful to them. A survey by SHRM indicated that morale significantly improved when employees were allowed to wear symbols of faith or express their religion at the workplace.

On the other hand, Dr. Ramsey suggests that accommodating today's workforce of myriad religions has become a very cumbersome process for HRM professionals. Employees ask for several religious accommodations such as to observe religious holidays, dress accommodations, private space for prayers, and special kinds of food (kosher) and meat products. The list of expressions of religious faith becomes endless, and the main challenge is when to draw the line between reasonable and unreasonable requests. Many organizations might find it difficult to accommodate religious dress because they may have a strict dress code to reiterate their image. For instance, Sukhbir Channa, of Sikhism faith, was asked to leave Disney World in 2005 when his long hair and beard were against the company's dress code. Channa's religious faith prohibits him to cut his hair or shave off his beard. Disney World refers to its employees as "cast members" and adopts a very strict dress code that included minimum makeup for females and no facial hair for males. Should Disney change its dress code for certain religious groups? Another case is that of Dr. Zaki, who was refused a position in a health clinic in Texas in 2009. She was told that she could not wear her head scarf because the clinic policy did not allow wearing hats or scarves to work.

Dr. Ramsey suggests that organizations should place their business and corporate strategy as the main criterion for accommodating religious requests. Organizations should not accommodate employees' religious requests that would reduce an organization's business profits. For instance, Somali cab drivers refused to take customers that had liquor or even pet dogs because it was against their religion. Should customers be turned down because of an employee's faith? Dr. Ramsey suggests that it is very important to keep the customer's good interest in mind because that is the organization's top business priority. Further, organizations should not accommodate religious requests that might harm employees or other co-workers. For instance, Muslim women insisting on wearing religious dress in a manufacturing work environment could possibly cause harm to themselves or their co-workers.

An international perspective suggests that wearing or expressing symbols of faith is quite controversial in other countries also. In 2004, France passed a ban of wearing any religious symbols of faith in secondary schools, which included Jewish caps, Christian crosses, and Muslim head scarves. Are we trying to minimize stereotypical associations or increase discrimination?

YES ↵

Robert J Grossman

Religion at Work

Abstract (Summary)

The US educational system and other teachings say you should compartmental-ize faith, says Bob Pettus, HR veteran, who retired in 2005 as vice chairman of the US' second-largest Coca-Cola bottler. Religion remains integral to life in the US, and religious practices are increasingly diverse. In a 2001 survey conducted by the Society for Human Resource Management (SHRM) and the Tanenbaum Center for Interreligious Understanding in New York, 36% of HR professionals reported an increase in the religious diversity of their employees during the pre-vious five years. While no data are available, many experts say the number of companies that promote or encourage religious expression is trending up. Only half of the 540 HR professionals responding to the SHRM survey said religious issues were part of training for managers and supervisors; 37% said they were part of training for employees. In the end, it seems likely that HR professionals will spend more time with religion and spirituality in the future.

Many employers are weaving religion and spirituality into company cultures. The push may come from bosses or the rank and file—and their motivations vary. Either way, when religion and spirituality cross the threshold, they result in daunting legal and managerial challenges along with perceived benefits.

Bob Pettus spent his entire career with Charlotte, N.C.-based Coca-Cola Bottling Co. Consolidated—all with top-level human resource responsibility. Like an Israelite wandering in the Sinai seeking the Promised Land, he engaged in a quest—to find the keys to attracting and retaining high-performing workers and managers. After decades in the wilderness, he was losing heart.

"Our employees' salaries, benefits and perks were always a little bit ahead of others so we could attract the kinds of employees we needed," recalls the HR veteran, who retired in 2005 as vice chairman of the nation's second-largest Coca-Cola bottler with 5,800 employees in 11 Southeastern states. "I would get all excited about giving everyone a 3.5 percent increase, putting in a new insurance policy, adding a new holiday. But when I made the announcements, there was hardly any response except, 'Hey, that's what everyone else is doing. You guys should have been doing this a long time ago.' We spent all those mil-lions, and all we got for it was 'ho-hum.'"

Then Pettus—who now consults for the company—saw the light. He was meeting the physical and emotional needs of workers, but what about the spiritual?

From *HR Magazine,* December 2008, pp. 26–33. Copyright © 2008 by Society for Human Resource Management, Alexandria, VA. Reprinted by permission via the Copyright Clearance Center.

Did it make sense to keep religion under wraps and require people to leave their faith at the doorstep? Equally important, if leaders really believed in running the business in concert with God and religious values, shouldn't they say so?

Pettus knew company leaders who answer affirmatively buck convention: Most business leaders are faith-frosty, convinced that the less religious expression at work, the better. They comply with legal mandates and accommodate individuals who require special arrangements, but go no further.

The U.S. educational system and other teachings "say you should compartmentalize faith," Pettus says. "Folks who are willing to talk about their faith and live it out Monday through Friday often are viewed as fanatical. Someone can go to a football game and scream and holler, throw things in the air and dress like a slob. But at work, if you mention that you should love one another and live right every day—it's like, 'What's wrong with you?'"

Pettus took a stand. Working with the chief executive officer, he drafted a mission and values statement that makes it clear company leaders embrace and honor God. It opens the door to spirituality for all employees and champions stewardship. The statement leads with "Our Values Honor God."

Finally, an initiative that was met with an overwhelming positive reaction. When people learn they can live out their faith, Pettus says, "There's this loyalty, this willingness to go the extra mile."

Faith Focus

Coca-Cola Bottling Co. Consolidated represents one of many faith-focused U.S. companies. These organizations proactively conduct business in a manner that embraces the faiths of leaders or owners. Their faiths provide underlying values that motivate and guide the organizations. A few, such as Coca-Cola Bottling, are publicly traded. Many more—such as Austaco Ltd., a privately owned Taco Bell franchisee with 1,800 workers in Austin, Texas—number among the nation's small and medium-sized and frequently family-owned businesses.

"We classify ourselves as a Christian company—Christ- or God-centered," says Don Barton, Austaco's HR vice president. "We do things like say grace when we have a meal, something a typical company might not do. The employees know that our CEO, Dirk Dozier, is open about sharing his Christian faith in personal testimony. Our motto is to serve, which includes serving our employees on a spiritual basis."

Faith-Friendly

Also welcoming religion are faith-friendly companies. They value inclusion and promote diversity and religious self-expression. They do not align with one religion, but instead invite workers to bring all manners of religious and spiritual expression to the workplace.

At Ford Motor, for example, workers' religious groups have access to facilities after hours for meetings and communicate through newsletters. "Being able to bring your whole self to work is essential to us," says Allison Trawick, global manager in Ford's Office of Diversity and Inclusion in Dearborn, Mich. "That means everyone." At the centerpiece of Ford's religious diversity: the Ford Inter-faith Network (FIN), one of eight recognized and supported affiliate groups.

Led by a board of representatives of Buddhism, Catholicism, Church of Jesus Christ of Latter-day Saints, evangelical Christians, Hinduism, Islam, Judaism and Orthodox Christianity, FIN welcomes all religious and spiritual groups. One discovery: "how many values we have in common," says Daniel Dunnigan, manager of worldwide volumes and FIN chairman. "We all value family, integrity [and] personal industriousness and are committed to leading morally upright lives."

Dunnigan says Ford's celebration of religious diversity and the impact it has on culture can't be measured in financial terms alone: The Muslim repre-sentative "doesn't have to worry about where he'll go for his midday prayers. He thinks it makes him more loyal. Another man affiliated with the evangeli-cal Christian group told me he wouldn't want to work anywhere else because of Ford's welcoming environment. How do you put a dollar value on this?"

Nation of Believers

Religion remains integral to life in the United States, and religious practices are increasingly diverse. In a 2001 survey conducted by the Society for Human Resource Management (SHRM) and the Tanenbaum Center for Interreligious Understanding in New York, 36 percent of HR professionals reported an increase in the religious diversity of their employees during the previous five years. In SHRM's 2008 Religion and Corporate Culture: Accommodating Reli-gious Diversity in the Workplace survey report, 64 percent said their organiza-tions have some degree of religious or spiritual diversity.

Immigrants affiliated with various religions contribute to these numbers. In 1970, only 4.5 percent of the population was foreign-born; of those, 62 per-cent came from Europe and were overwhelmingly Christian. By 2000, 12 per-cent of the population was foreign-born but only 16 percent of that group shared European heritage. Many more came from Asia or Latin America and were Buddhists, Hindus, Muslims, Sikhs or members of other religions. Today, 78.4 percent of U.S. adults are Christian and about 5 percent are members of other religions; 16.1 percent are unaffiliated.

For some, religion and spirituality rest comfortably under the umbrella of "faith." For others, "religion" is a loaded, politically charged word.

"In the business community, many accept the notion that spirituality should be welcome at work, while religion is to be avoided," says Douglas Hicks, associate professor of leadership studies and religion and executive direc-tor of the Bonner Center for Civic Engagement at the University of Richmond in Virginia. "They contrast religion as dogmatic, rigid [and] tradition-bound, and spirituality as open, liberating, individualistic and creative."

Diversity's Forgotten Child

To the chagrin of those who favor religious expression, the HR community has been reluctant to champion the cause. "At best, HR has ignored the issues and at worst, it has been hostile," says David Miller, director of the Princeton University

Faith & Work Initiative in New Jersey. "How can you say you stand for diversity and inclusion when you limit it to external characteristics and don't extend it to the inclusion of worldviews that include some kind of god or not?"

Until recently, religion and spirituality have been the bête noire of the diversity movement. People who have advocated for diversity in gender, race or sexual orientation have avoided speaking in support of religious expression in the workplace. Hundreds of senior executives are devout but silent, says Miller. "They think it would be career suicide to come forward."

Human resource professionals know that religious expression can lead to litigation or polarization. To avoid problems, "stay away," advises Robert Campbell, senior vice president of HR at NiSource Inc. in Merrillville, Ind., a Fortune 500 company whose 7,600 employees engage in natural gas and electric generation, transmission, storage and distribution.

"HR folks are too busy worrying about where the next lawsuit will come from instead of helping enable people to live the one life they are called to live through a business which has a higher purpose than just to make money," says Don Barefoot, president of C12 Group, a support group for born-again Christian CEOs and business owners, based in Greensboro, N.C. "They're the gatekeepers for society's fears and hang-ups."

But when HR professionals look objectively at the spiritual values of the major religions, they will be less concerned, says Michelle Knox, executive consultant with Novations Group Inc. in Boston. "The values are very similar— integrity, respect for oneself, altruistic behavior, putting others first."

HR professionals are "risk-averse about what can happen from a compliance standpoint, and I was, too," recalls Rod Nagel, senior vice president of human resource operations at Tyson Foods Inc. in Springdale, Ark. But "You'll realize the benefits go well beyond the risks," he says. The publicly traded company's core values literature includes this language: We strive to be a faith-friendly company. . . . We strive to honor God and be respectful of each other, our customers and other stakeholders. . . .

Out of the Shadows

While no data are available, many experts say the number of companies that promote or encourage religious expression is trending up. Georgette Bennett, president and founder of the Tanenbaum Center and a member of SHRM's Workplace Diversity Special Expertise Panel, attributes the trend in part to globalization and the politicization of religion. "With everyone from the [U.S.] president on down wearing their religion on their sleeve, it's not surprising that employers and employees are encouraged to assert their rights."

In fact, "We've reached a tipping point where the conventional wisdom that you keep your spiritual side at home is about to collapse," Miller says, adding that millennials and Gen Xers "want to live a holistic life" and that older workers tend to be interested in religion as well.

The Business Case

Miller says welcoming religious diversity gives recruiters an advantage.

When employers allow spirituality to be expressed, levels of employee commitment and engagement increase, Knox adds. "It allows for greater meaning and reduces stress. Whenever we subjugate something that makes [other people] different, it lessens their ability to be productive and satisfied in their work."

It's no coincidence that in SHRM's Religion and Corporate Culture survey, HR professionals said employee morale was most affected by companies granting religious accommodations, Bennett notes.

To faith-focused executives, byproducts of promoting spiritual expression, such as financial rewards, "are icing on the cake," Pettus concludes. "Don't say you'll get more productivity because people will see it as a ploy to extract more work from them. Do it because it's the right thing to do."

Legal Parameters

Of course, employers are obligated to make reasonable efforts to accommodate the sincerely held religious beliefs of all workers. Accommodation may include opportunities for prayer, respecting holidays—even proselytizing and the distribution of literature. Under Title VII of the Civil Rights Act of 1964, discrimination occurs if an employer fails to reasonably accommodate employees, or if employees are harassed by being required to abandon or adopt, or coerced into abandoning or adopting, a religious practice as a condition of employment (quid pro quo) or subjected to unwelcome statements or conduct based on religion so severe or pervasive that the person finds the work environment hostile or abusive.

Hence, employers must balance the obligation to accommodate religious views of one or more employees—an obligation that legal experts say is becoming more onerous—with the obligation to prevent harassment or creation of a hostile work environment for others. For example, unwelcome words or conduct, whether emanating from a fellow employee or the boss, may be permissible until the target of the communication or conduct objects. Even then, they may not constitute harassment unless considered pervasive or severe.

Navigating this terrain is dicey; hence, most employers opt for a hands-off approach wherever possible.

More Than Meets the Eye?

Religious discrimination charges filed with the U.S. Equal Employment Opportunity Commission (EEOC) more than doubled from 1992 to 2007. Still, the EEOC received just 2,880 charges in 2007, a relatively small number compared to charges filed for other reasons. Of the EEOC claims filed in 2007, the agency found "no reasonable cause" in almost 60 percent. Claims cost businesses $6.4 million that year. Yet, only 2 percent of respondents to SHRM's 2008 Religion and Corporate Culture survey said their organization has been named as a defendant in a lawsuit related to religion in the past 12 months.

But these figures may underrepresent the problem, with many instances unreported or resolved. For example, in a 1999 employee survey by the

Tanenbaum Center, 66 percent of respondents said they had seen indications of religious bias at work. Of those who were targets, only 23 percent reported it.

In an April survey of 278 organizations by the Institute for Corporate Productivity (i4cp) in Seattle, nearly one-third of HR executives said they have seen personal clashes in the workplace linked to religion. Thirty-one percent said unsolicited sharing of religious views has been a problem.

In faith-focused organizations, employees sometimes quit, saying they felt "marginalized because the ethos was too Christian," Hicks says. "Many leave without formally complaining, making it difficult to assess the scope of the problem. Workers are vulnerable, unwilling to risk their jobs by coming forward or speaking out. Often, the cultures from which these workers come teach them to 'keep your head low—don't complain.' Also, they don't understand what their rights are."

Frank Manion, senior counsel at the American Center for Law and Justice in Washington, D.C., says people come forward reluctantly; "They don't want to offend anyone."

This can be problematic for employers that run into constructive discharge claims after employees leave. Seemingly, the burden rests on the worker to request that offensive conduct cease, yet Manion envisions scenarios where the conduct is so overt that the burden may rest with the employer. And, don't overlook the possibility that some individuals or groups may set traps that could lead to litigation. "I wouldn't be surprised if people in civil rights groups start sending out 'salts' to test the impartiality of employers," says employment lawyer Michael Homans of Falster/Greenberg PC in Philadelphia. "People aren't required to disclose their religion when they apply, but if the information is volunteered or an applicant displays a cross [or] Star of David or wears the head covering of a Muslim, for example, the potential for a discriminatory response arises."

Almost one-third of 580 HR executives told i4cp researchers that religious discrimination was a workplace concern. "They see it as an issue, but not as one that affects them personally," says Anne Lindberg, i4cp research analyst. "People who have faced discrimination claims have handled it in-house. There's not a lot of news about people being dinged for thousands of dollars in lawsuits. But we're only at the beginning. Once you get some big judgments, the popular media will get on board, and then watch out."

Following Chosen Paths

According to the Pew Forum on Religion & Public Life in Washington, D.C., two-thirds of the population affiliated with a religious tradition hold an inclusionary view, accepting that their chosen path is not the only road to salvation. One-third think their way is the only way and may be obligated by their beliefs to reach out. For example, data from The Barna Group, a research organization in Ventura, Calif., reveal that three-quarters of the nation's 1 million born-again Christians believe they "personally have a responsibility to tell other people about their religious beliefs."

The challenges presented by proselytizing grow large when supervisors deliver the message.

For instance, Brad Thompson, CEO at Columbia Forest Products in Greensboro, N.C., says leading his company by biblical principles is an opportunity to live his faith. "My goal is that people will sense something different about me. Once they do and want to know where it's coming from, I'll tell them. The best thing I can do is model Christian principles and let people come to me." Thompson identifies a dividing line "between an invitation and a push. I can't see any harm if I invite anyone to attend a religious event or prayer meeting with me. [But] I can't push anyone to the point that I make them uncomfortable."

Although Thompson seems to be within the law, some observers worry. "Because of the unequal power relationship, there should never be a situation where a supervisor is making any kind of religious overtures to a subordinate," Bennett insists.

Managers should not proselytize, agrees Campbell. "You don't want to give anyone the false impression that you'll make a work decision based on your preference. The potential for lawsuits—meritorious or not—is undeniable. If someone has been rewarded or punished for any reason, it's not hard to put a case together attributing the action to religious bias."

Making It Happen

Regardless of the perceived benefits of religious expression in the workplace, employment lawyers counsel caution and following a course that will minimize conflict. That means, regarding religion, less is better. "The suppression by private employers of religious speech at work generally does not create legal exposure for the employer so long as the employer 'reasonably accommodates' religion," Homans says. "Keep references to religious values and God out of written policies and practices; instead, describe your values in the secular language of ethics."

Campbell says even voluntary activities that aren't objectionable under the law—such as joining hands and saying prayers—may prove divisive and stressful, "so the person who is uncomfortable winds up going along."

Still, the growing number of successful faith-friendly and faith-based employers serves as testament that religion and spirituality can flourish in the workplace. Implementation remains key: If it is done carefully, faith-friendly employers may choose to celebrate religious and spiritual inclusiveness even if some people would prefer a secular environment. And faith-focused employers may pursue what critics perceive as "stealth agendas" of conversion, so long as they stick to the law that requires tolerance and equal treatment of all views. "You have to create a culture of openness that says, 'We'll open our conference room or message board on an equal basis to all faith groups; we'll have a brown-bag series where people can talk about their faith.' It should be employee-driven," advises Hicks.

Policies and Training Gap

Whether an employer is faith-friendly, faith-focused or faith-frosty, the issues, rights and responsibilities of workers, supervisors and executives are complicated and call out for detailed policy and training. So far, however, many employers have been slow to act. Of the respondents to SHRM's Religion and Corporate Culture survey, nearly half reported having no policy on religion. Only 2 percent reported having a formal separate policy. The remainder included religion under diversity or antidiscrimination umbrellas.

"The mere inclusion of religion in a list of protected classes in the boilerplate diversity policy does not address the critical issue of accommodation," Bennett argues. The best practice? "Adopt a distinct religious diversity policy," she says.

Miller suggests the following definition of faith-friendly as groundwork for a policy: "As a faith-friendly employer, we recognize the importance of faith to many people, that a spiritual grounding is what makes them tick, and so long as one's practices are compatible with our company's value and mission, we welcome it."

Only half of the 540 HR professionals responding to the SHRM survey said religious issues were part of training for managers and supervisors; 37 percent said they were part of training for employees.

In the end, it seems likely that HR professionals will spend more time with religion and spirituality in the future. Faith-frosty employers will have more accommodations to deal with as workers and managers learn more about the extent of their rights to express their faith. Regardless of motivation, employers who see advantages of actively incorporating faith into the workplace now have advice, guidelines and examples.

But the devil is in the details: "I agree with what the lawyers say about maintaining a nondiscriminatory environment," says Pettus. "Faced with all the do's and don'ts, a normal HR guy would probably hold up his hands and say, 'Golly, if I've got to do all that, I better not do anything and just make sure we don't get into trouble.'" . . .

Robert D Ramsey   **NO**

When Religion and Work Clash

Abstract (Summary)

America is known for freedom of religious expression, and most business leaders endorse and support religious tolerance. Increasingly, employers are being asked to make accommodations in the workplace for myriad forms of religious expression, including some controversial and confrontational practices. Accommodating wide-ranging forms of religious expression in the workplace and brokering the resulting conflicts of interest seems to call for divine intervention. The following advice from veteran human resources experts has helped many middle managers resolve problems regarding religion in the workplace. These suggestions will not answer all your questions, but they do provide a framework for developing your own solutions for the issues that occur in your particular work environment: 1. Deal with the rights, needs and attitudes of all workers, not just the ones requesting concessions. 2. Be sure the request is legitimate. 3. Do not make decisions based on personal bias or prejudice or simply what is easiest or the most popular thing to do.

> "What the church should be telling the worker is that the first demand religion makes on him is to be a good workman."
>
> —Dwight D. Eisenhower, US President

America is known for freedom of religious expression, and most business leaders endorse and support religious tolerance. But what happens when the workers' right to practice their religion clashes with the requirements of the job? Who wins? Who loses? Who decides?

These aren't just hypothetical or rhetorical questions. They are real live, in-your-face issues throughout the business world today.

Increasingly, employers are being asked to make accommodations in the workplace for myriad forms of religious expression, including some controversial and confrontational practices. Is there any limit? Is there a line, which should not be crossed? Where is it? Who gets to draw it?

If your answer to the last question was the supervisor or foremen in charge, you are probably right. Often it is up to middle management to define how far the organization will go in permitting religious practices on the job.

From *Supervision*, September 2007, pp. 13–15. Copyright © 2007 by National Research Bureau. Reprinted by permission.

More than anyone else, supervisors have to reconcile the employee's right to religious expression with the employer's right to get the job done and to meet the needs of customers.

Accommodating wide-ranging forms of religious expression in the workplace and brokering the resulting conflicts of interest seems to call for divine intervention. Yet flesh and blood foremen and managers have to deal with it every day. If you haven't been confronted with such issues in your factory, shop or office, it could happen tomorrow—or even yet today.

A Growing Problem

As the proliferation of diverse religious groups grows in our society, the incidence of conflict between religious practice and job performance becomes stickier, more complex and more challenging for supervisors in all fields. Examples are all around if you're paying attention.

Just within the last year, the media has reported cases where—

- Workers from many minority faiths have asked for time off to observe their religious holidays and special events.
- Islamic women workers have insisted on wearing traditional clothing on the job despite objections regarding safety and security.
- Muslim employees have demanded time and private space to accommodate mandatory prayers during the duty day.
- Jewish workers have lobbied for the addition of kosher food to vending machines and employee cafeteria menus.
- Muslim employees have requested facilities for foot-washing while at work. (At least one Minnesota college has already made this concession.)
- Somali cab drivers have refused to drive fares carrying liquor, which is banned by their religion or fares accompanied by a dog (even a seeing eye or other service dog) because Muslims view dogs as "unclean."
- Some Muslim grocery store cashiers and sackers have refused to handle pork products and have requested that other employees or the customers themselves check and bag these items.

The list could go on. The examples keep piling up and we probably haven't seen anything yet.

It's the Law

Unfortunately, denial is not an option. Making concessions and allowing greater latitude in bringing religious practices into the workplace is not merely a matter of exercising tolerance or simply being nice. It's also a legal requirement.

State and federal anti-discrimination statutes require businesses to make reasonable accommodations for religious practices on the job. "Reasonable" is the operative word.

The law does not require employers to make adjustments that cause undue harm or hardship to the business. Sometimes the workers have to make the allowances or accommodations.

Remaining fair, juggling opposing needs, satisfying the law and maintaining a competitive business edge all at the same time is tricky business. Decisions about mixing religion and work are never easy and each case is different. It's uncharted territory for most managers.

Tips and Guidelines

The good news is that some help is available. The following advice from veteran human resources experts has helped many middle managers resolve problems regarding religion in the workplace. They may assist you as well.

These suggestions won't answer all your questions, but they do provide a framework for developing your own solutions for the issues that occur in your particular work environment:

- Remember that the best and most universal criteria for accepting or rejecting requests to permit certain religious practices in the workplace is still simply, "What would a reasonable person do?"

Model tolerance every day. Building an overall culture of openness and acceptance is the best way to prevent contentious squabbling over isolated religious practices.

- Deal with the rights, needs and attitudes of all workers, not just the ones requesting (or demanding) concessions.
- Weigh the impact of possible accommodations on all employees—and especially on customers.
- Be sure the request is legitimate. Find out if it really is required by the religious doctrine. Some workers may request accommodations that are not considered mandatory by the majority of their faith community.
- Be deliberate. Don't be bullied or stampeded into making a snap decision. Every accommodation granted sets a precedent the organization may have to live with for years to come.
- Don't make decisions based on personal bias or prejudice or simply what's easiest or the most popular thing to do. Always have a bona fide business or legal reason for your action, and always explain your rationale to all those involved or affected by your decision.
- Educate yourself about the practice in question. Learn what it entails, what it means and why it is important to the followers of that particular faith. The greater your understanding, the better your decision will be.
- Find out what others in the industry are doing about similar requests. That's what networks are for. Someone else may have better insight regarding the issue. It's okay to steal good ideas from others—even the competition. There is no copyright on wisdom.
- Be fair and consistent. Anything less sets you up for litigation.
- Always seek the least intrusive or disruptive accommodation.
- When in doubt, don't be afraid to get legal counsel.
- Respect each worker's individual faith or religion even if you have to deny specific requests.
- When all else fails, try praying over the issue. That's one religious practice that not even a supervisor, manager or foreman can deny.

Religious practices and business practices are occasionally at odds with each other. Sometimes business has to bend a little to accommodate personal religious expressions. Sometimes religion has to pull back a bit to allow essential business to be conducted.

And sometimes a compromise can be reached. For example, if excusing employees for a special religious day or event creates a hardship for the employer, an accommodation might be to excuse a limited number of the faithful each year on a rotating basis.

Of course in other cases, no compromise is possible. When Somalian cab drivers in Minneapolis refused to serve paying customers because they were carrying liquor, the employers felt they had no choice but to impose suspensions and to threaten termination for repeated offenses.

I'm reminded of a Board of Directors I once worked for which had a majority of Jewish members and routinely rejected requests from Jewish employees for time off during their holy days. As the Board Chair (a Jew himself) explained, "Sometimes you have to pay a price for your religion."

Granting some accommodations. Refusing others. Compromising when possible. It's all in a day's work for effective supervisors.

The Bottom Line

All Americans are entitled to their personal religious beliefs and to practice and express their faith freely, but they are not necessarily entitled to bring their religious practices to work in someone else's business. Religious freedom is guaranteed by the Constitution. Holding a specific job is not.

If a particular religious practice makes it impossible to fulfill essential job functions or interferes with necessary business transactions, it's probably time for the worker to seek other employment.

As a supervisor and business leader in a democratic society, you are required to make appropriate accommodations to permit individual religious practices by employees. But you are not required to allow employees' religious expressions to drive away customers, to lose business or to go out of business.

Defining when, how or how much to accommodate religious expressions in the workplace involves both decisiveness and flexibility. Different situations demand different solutions. It's not a crapshoot. It's a balancing act. Fortunately, that's what good supervisors and managers do best. . . .

POSTSCRIPT

Should Employees Be Allowed to Wear Symbols of Faith to the Workplace?

The country is becoming increasingly a nation of immigrants who are bringing with them their rich and diverse religious backgrounds. To accommodate this diversity, many organizations are proactively embracing an environment that encourages employees to express or wear their symbols of faith to the workplace. Some organizations are even changing their mission statement to indicate that they are accepting of diverse spirituality. Further, increased globalization has made organizations realize that having a diverse religious work environment might possibly enhance business opportunities overseas. It might also be a very good business decision to be accepting of various religions and correspondingly their symbols of faith, as court cases of religious discrimination have increased dramatically since the 1990s. In 2007, there were 2,880 court cases, and religious claims cost organizations $6.4 million. Some organizations openly encourage employees to have their prayers at the workplace and also discuss core values of their religion. Employees feel complete knowing they can express the religious values that define their core personality. Experts also caution that if organizations decide to allow employees to express their faith, they should accommodate all religious faiths in their organization to do so.

On the other hand, opponents of a faith-friendly approach reiterate that business priorities supersede employees' requests for expression of their faith. They insist that organizations should make sure that their business strategy and business profits are not diminished due to any forms of religious expression. A case in point is when cab drivers refused to drive customers who had dogs or liquor because it was against their religion. In business lexicon, the customer's need is the ultimate regardless of any religious beliefs. Several organizations also follow a strict dress code either for the safety of their employees or to promote a very professional image. This might go against some religions that mandate a certain type of dress code. Some religions might also endorse certain grooming practices that might not be conducive to the work environment. Disney was in a lawsuit because one of its employees refused to follow the grooming code of not having facial hair. A recent 2008 court case illustrating the constant battle between religion and dress code is that of Nadia Eweida, a British Airways check-in staff member. She is a practicing Christian who wore a silver cross regularly to work. The company had a dress policy that stated employees could not wear any visible signs of jewelry. When she refused to remove her silver cross, she was fired by British Airways. Do organizations have the right to tell their employees how to dress or groom?

Suggested Readings

P. Dreier, "Good Jobs, Healthy Cities," *The American Prospect* (vol. 20, no. 8, pp. A10–A13, 2009).

Gillian Flynn, "Gray Areas in Controlling Employee Lifestyles," *Workforce* (vol. 82, no. 2, pp. 64–65, February 2009).

Mary-Kathryn Zachary, "Body Piercings and Religious Discrimination," *Supervision* (vol. 66, no. 3, pp. 23–26, March 2005).

Disney World Sued over Dress Code/Religious Discrimination: http://thedisneyblog.com/2008/06/14/disney-world-sued-over-dress-codereligious-discrimination.

Sikh Sues Disney over Worker Dress Code: http://www.sikhnet.com/daily-news/sikh-sues-disney-over-worker-dress-code.

U.S. Clinic Denies Muslim Doctor Right to Wear Hijab: http://www.presstv.com/classic/detail.aspx?id=110135&sectionid=3510203.

Debate over Religious Symbols Divides France: http://www.msnbc.msn.com/id/4106422/.

Eweida vs. British Airways Plc: http://www.personneltoday.com/articles/2008/12/08/48653/eweida-v-british-airways-plc.html.

Internet References . . .

Top Twenty-Five Social Networking Sites

David Wilson, co-owner of Braveheart Design Inc, has transformed social media optimization Web sites by merging traditional media, search engine marketing, and social marketing.

http://social-media-optimization.com/2009/02/top-twenty-five-social-networking-sites-feb-2009/

The Journal of Computer-Mediated Communication (JCMC)

The Journal of Computer-Mediated Communication (JCMC) is a web-based, peer-reviewed scholarly journal. Its focus is social science research on computer-mediated communication via the Internet, the World Wide Web, and wireless technologies.

http://jcmc.indiana.edu/vol13/issue1/boyd.ellison.html

Pros and Cons of Using Personality Tests in Personnel Assessment

This site is maintained by the International Congress on Assessment Center Methods. Here you will find two prominent psychologists discussing the arguments for and against using personality tests in personnel assessment in general and assessment centers in particular.

http://www.assessmentcenters.org/2004/gen_pros_cons.asp

What Test Should I Use Today? Pros and Cons for Recruiting Managers

HRM Guide publishes articles and news releases about HR surveys, employment law, human resource research, HR books, and careers that bridge the gap between theory and practice.

http://www.hrmguide.co.uk/recruitment/recruiting-assessment.htm

Ezine Articles

EzineArticles.com brings real-world experts and publishers together. Expert authors and writers are able to post their articles to be featured within the site. The searchable database includes hundreds of thousands of quality original articles. This particular article discusses the pros and cons of a background check.

http://ezinearticles.com/?The-Pros-and-Cons-of-a-Background-Check&id=1318646

HR Hero

HRhero.com provides legal information, training, and compliance tools on state and federal employment law, supervisor training, and employee management for human resources and other business professionals. HRHero.com is supported by the Employers Counsel Network (ECN), a select group of attorneys from top law firms in all 50 states, Washington, DC, and Canada.

http://www.hrhero.com/q&a/070105-background.shtml

Talent Acquisition

*W*here to hunt for the best talent? How to identify the brightest? Organizations have made recruitment and selection practices their top HRM priority. The quality of any product or service is reflected through the talent of the company's employees. How to ensure the applicants are not lying about their past work accomplishments? This section addresses some critical aspects of staffing practices. The current trend of getting job applicants through social networking sites is examined. Personality tests help identify critical work-related characteristics relevant in today's job market. Background checks have become imperative as society witnesses an increase in delinquent behavior. Can these staffing practices identify qualified talent?

- Are Social Networking Sites Good Recruitment Sources?

- Are Personality Tests Good Predictors of Employee Performance?

- Would Mandatory Background Checks for All Employees Reduce Negligent Hiring Lawsuits?

- Is Cognitive Ability Testing a Good Predictor of Work Performance?

ISSUE 5

Are Social Networking Sites Good Recruitment Sources?

YES: Jamie Eckle, from "Get Social, Get a Job," *ComputerWorld* (August 2009)

NO: David J. Solove, from "The End of Privacy?" *Scientific American* (September 2008)

ISSUE SUMMARY

YES: Jamie Eckle, former Managing Editor of ComputerWorld, suggests that social network sites are excellent ways to begin an informal recruiting dialogue with applicants. Informal recruiting approaches may provide more realistic job-related information so that applicants self-select themselves, saving recruiters a lot of time and money.

NO: Dr. David Solove, law professor at George Washington University and author of several books on topics related to privacy, asserts that online information is not an accurate and honest source for recruiters. Gen-Yers are more likely to post incorrect information when personal and business relationships become unpleasant.

Social networking sites (SNS) can be defined as Web services that allow individuals to connect with each other worldwide and provide their social and employment profiles. These profiles provide personal information and work-related information, and many times include photos that can be shared with others. These sites allow individuals to network professionally and also share their personal lives.

A historical background suggests that the first social network site, Six Degrees.com, began in 1997. It was established to allow individuals to connect with classmates and family members. However, this service did not do very well and closed in 2000. In 2003, the launching of MySpace revolutionized the online social landscape dramatically. Teenagers flocked to these Web sites to publicly to share their personal information and communicate endlessly with one another. This social site further allowed users to personalize their pages, providing their own personality and touch. MySpace has more than 100 million members, making it one of the most visited social Web sites.

In 2004, the world witnessed the debut of Facebook, which began primarily as an exclusive Harvard School social networking site. Subsequently, this elitism was expanded to include other university students but yet remained a college-dominated social networking site. In 2005, teenagers and professionals also were included, and, once again, the global community witnessed an exponential use of social networking. Facebook provides several marketing and recruiting initiatives for organizations that will allow them to use it as both a recruiting tool and a marketing tool. In 2003, social networking sites began to target niche communities such as professionals to capture an exclusive social platform for working individuals—this saw the origin of LinkedIn. LinkedIn allows professionals to share their education and work expertise, ask relevant business inquiries, and create job postings.

The main question is whether these interactive social Web sites are good recruitment sources. Career experts suggest that SNSs are wonderful ways to begin any recruiting dialogue because these sites have such high communication traffic among people and high membership. Further, companies can develop a huge applicant database that staffing departments can potentially contact. SNSs also allow you to identify passive applicants—prospective employees who are not actively looking for a job—and identify the most qualified talent. Do we not want to hire the best? For the younger generation, staying connected via social networking sites is an integral part of their lives. Recruiters should consider this a good hiring source for such talent. The younger generation also tends to trust information from SNSs more than traditional company Web sites. Finally, it is a very cost-effective recruiting method that can save organizations several thousands in third-party recruiter's fees.

On the other hand, opponents of SNSs suggest that organizations could be getting inaccurate information about individuals. Online malice has been reported on several occasions where individuals post incorrect information as business friendships and personal relationships become sour. Unfortunately, incorrect information posted on the Internet remains, creating an online reputation that haunts applicants forever. Further, individuals include personal information that is irrelevant to recruiters but would definitely cloud their judgment. Why would organizations want information irrelevant to the job?

Further, HR professionals might run into legal and privacy issues if they filter applicants based on online information. A Harvard Business case study "We Googled You" illustrates how an employee's online history looms even many years later. HRM professionals struggle with how to sift through the personal and professional clutter of information. Would you hire someone who has a negative online history?

Are other countries also socially wired like Americans? Around the same time the SNSs became prominent in the United States, international SNSs specific to various regions began to emerge. Orkut became synonymous with social networking in Brazil and India. In Japan, Mixi became a household name, with more than 15 million users, and online customers of Bebo surpassed that of MySpace in the United Kingdom. Facebook provides six different language versions in India to capture the multilingual population. Recruiters in these countries also use these SNSs to connect with applicants.

YES ↵

Jamie Eckle

Get Social, Get a Job

Abstract (Summary)

In an interview, Nina Buik, a careers expert and president of the Hewlett-Packard user group Connect, talked about using social networking. According to Buik, the easiest way for people to participate in social media venues is to really familiarize themselves with the site they want to utilize. She added that the most common and broad-based tools are sites such as LinkedIn, Facebook and Twitter, all of which have high membership numbers and can serve to start useful dialogues with company representatives as well as individuals. She noted that the great thing about user groups is that members can choose their own level of participation.

THE DISMAL ECONOMY has brought thoughts of the unemployment line to people in nearly every profession, and it has made many of them feel the need to constantly glance over their shoulders, notes Nina Buik, a careers expert and president of the Hewlett-Packard user group Connect. In this type of economic climate, everyone can begin to seem like a potential competitor, and some people will react by burrowing into their cubicles and keeping a low profile.

That's the wrong way to go, maintains Buik. Instead, she advises employees to connect with others both inside and outside of the office by joining a user group and using the tool of social networking. Buik spoke to contributing editor Jamie Eckle.

How can those whose social skills just aren't well developed participate in social networking? It's the same as with any new situation. The easiest way for people to participate in social media venues is to really familiarize themselves with the site they want to utilize. Look and listen to what's going on in the community. What are the conversations people are engaged in, and who are the participants? As they become more comfortable with the site, then It's probably a good time to start participating in other ways, such as adding content, commenting and beginning to cultivate relationships.

What are the best tools currently available? Of course, the most common and broad-based tools are sites such as LinkedIn, Facebook and Twitter, all of which have high membership numbers and can serve to start useful dialogues with company representatives as well as individuals. For a more targeted

From *ComputerWorld*, 43:26, August 17–August 24, 2009, p. 36. Copyright © 2009 by ComputerWorld. Reprinted by permission of The YGS Group.

approach, use sites that can serve as both a support system and resource for your personal brand. There are countless sites out there, so try to find one that caters to your needs and will give you more visibility and insight into your industry. For example, we just launched a social networking site on Connect called myCommunity. It's a place for the members of our organization to come together and post conversations, read blogs specific to HP technology and engage with each other. Another example of a niche social networking site would be something like Advogato, which is a forum for those interested in open-source software development. Additionally, sites such as Wikipedia and Mashable.com offer lists of popular social networking sites with brief descriptions that might be helpful in finding a site that is a good fit for you.

What about user groups? How active does one have to be in a user group for it to be truly beneficial? The great thing about user groups is that members can choose their own level of participation. In my personal experience with Connect, some of our users only participate when they have a question they feel other users might be able to heip address, and that's OK because our site is the perfect forum for this type of dialogue. On the other hand, many of our members use the site daily to keep abreast of what's going on in the industry, to foster and grow relationships or to contribute to conversations in the community. . . .

Daniel J. Solove → **NO**

The End of Privacy

Young people share the most intimate details of personal life on social-networking Web sites, portending a realignment of the public and the private.

He has a name, but most people just know him as "the Star Wars Kid." In fact, he is known around the world by tens of millions of people. Unfortunately, his notoriety is for one of the most embarrassing moments in his life.

In 2002, as a 15-year-old, the Star Wars Kid videotaped himself waving around a golf-ball retriever while pretending it was a lightsaber. Without the help of the expert choreographers working on the Star Wars movies, he stumbled around awkwardly in the video.

The video was found by some of the boy's tormentors, who uploaded it to an Internet video site. It became an instant hit with a multitude of fans. All across the blogosphere, people started mocking the boy, making fun of him for being pudgy, awkward and nerdy.

Several remixed videos of the Star Wars Kid started popping up, adorned with special effects. People edited the video to make the golf-ball retriever glow like a lightsaber. They added Star Wars music to the video. Others mashed it up with other movies. Dozens of embellished versions were created. The Star Wars Kid appeared in a video game and on the television shows Family Guy and South Park. It is one thing to be teased by classmates in school, but imagine being ridiculed by masses the world over. The teenager dropped out of school and had to seek counseling. What happened to the Star Wars Kid can happen to anyone, and it can happen in an instant. Today collecting personal information has become second nature. More and more people have cell phone cameras, digital audio recorders, Web cameras and other recording technologies that readily capture details about their lives.

For the first time in history nearly anybody can disseminate information around the world. People do not need to be famous enough to be interviewed by the mainstream media. With the Internet, anybody can reach a global audience.

Technology has led to a generational divide. On one side are high school and college students whose lives virtually revolve around social-networking sites and blogs. On the other side are their parents, for whom recollection of the past often remains locked in fading memories or, at best, in books, photographs and videos. For the current generation, the past is preserved on

From *Scientific American*, 299:3, September 2008, pp. 100–106. Copyright © 2008 by Daniel Solove. All rights reserved. Reprinted by permission of the author.

the Internet, potentially forever. And this change raises the question of how much privacy people can expect—or even desire—in an age of ubiquitous networking.

Generation Google

The number of young people using social-networking Web sites such as Facebook and MySpace is staggering. At most college campuses, more than 90 percent of students maintain their own sites. I call the people growing up today "Generation Google." For them, many fragments of personal information will reside on the Internet forever, accessible to this and future generations through a simple Google search.

That openness is both good and bad. People can now spread their ideas everywhere without reliance on publishers, broadcasters or other traditional gatekeepers. But that transformation also creates profound threats to privacy and reputations. The New York Times is not likely to care about the latest gossip at Dubuque Senior High School or Oregon State University. Bloggers and others communicating online may care a great deal. For them, stories and rumors about friends, enemies, family members, bosses, co-workers and others are all prime fodder for Internet postings.

Before the Internet, gossip would spread by word of mouth and remain within the boundaries of that social circle. Private details would be confined to diaries and kept locked in a desk drawer. Social networking spawned by the Internet allows communities worldwide to revert to the close-knit culture of preindustrial society, in which nearly every member of a tribe or a farming hamlet knew everything about the neighbors. Except that now the "villagers" span the globe.

College students have begun to share salacious details about their schoolmates. A Web site called Juicy Campus serves as an electronic bulletin board that allows students nationwide to post anonymously and without verification a sordid array of tidbits about sex, drugs and drunkenness. Another site, Don't Date Him Girl, invites women to post complaints about the men they have dated, along with real names and actual photographs.

Social-networking sites and blogs are not the only threat to privacy. As several articles in this issue of Scientific American have already made clear, companies collect and use our personal information at every turn. Your credit-card company has a record of your purchases. If you shop online, merchants keep tabs on every item you have bought. Your Internet service provider has information about how you surf the Internet. Your cable company has data about which television shows you watch.

The government also compromises privacy by assembling vast databases that can be searched for suspicious patterns of behavior. The National Security Agency listens and examines the records of millions of telephone conversations. Other agencies analyze financial transactions. Thousands of government bodies at the federal and state level have records of personal information, chronicling births, marriages, employment, property ownership and more. The information is often stored in public records, making it readily accessible to anyone—and the trend toward more accessible personal data continues to grow as more records become electronic.

The Future of Reputation

Broad-based exposure of personal information diminishes the ability to protect reputation by shaping the image that is presented to others. Reputation plays an important role in society, and preserving private details of one's life is essential to it. We look to people's reputations to decide whether to make friends, go on a date, hire a new employee or undertake a prospective business deal.

Some would argue that the decline of privacy might allow people to be less inhibited and more honest. But when everybody's transgressions are exposed, people may not judge one another less harshly. Having your personal information may fail to improve my judgment of you. It may, in fact, increase the likelihood that I will hastily condemn you. Moreover, the loss of privacy might inhibit freedom. Elevated visibility that comes with living in a transparent online world means you may never overcome past mistakes.

People want to have the option of "starting over," of reinventing themselves throughout their lives. As American philosopher John Dewey once said, a person is not "something complete, perfect, [or] finished," but is "something moving, changing, discrete, and above all initiating instead of final." In the past, episodes of youthful experimentation and foolishness were eventually forgotten, giving us an opportunity to start anew, to change and to grow. But with so much information online, it is harder to make these moments forgettable. People must now live with the digital baggage of their pasts.

This openness means that the opportunities for members of Generation Google might be limited because of something they did years ago as wild teenagers. Their intimate secrets may be revealed by other people they know. Or they might become the unwitting victim of a false rumor. Like it or not, many people are beginning to get used to having a lot more of their personal information online.

What Is to Be Done?

Can we prevent a future in which so much information about people's private lives circulates beyond their control? Some technologists and legal scholars flatly say no. Privacy, they maintain, is just not compatible with a world in which information flows so freely. As Scott McNealy of Sun Microsystems once famously declared: "You already have zero privacy. Get over it." Countless books and articles have heralded the "end," "death" and "destruction" of privacy.

Those proclamations are wrongheaded at best. It is still possible to protect privacy, but doing so requires that we rethink outdated understandings of the concept. One such view holds that privacy requires total secrecy: once information is revealed to others, it is no longer private. This notion of privacy is unsuited to an online world. The generation of people growing up today understands privacy in a more nuanced way. They know that personal information is routinely shared with countless others, and they also know that they leave a trail of data wherever they go.

The more subtle understanding of privacy embraced by Generation Google recognizes that a person should retain some control over personal information that becomes publicly available. This generation wants a say in how private details of their lives are disseminated.

The issue of control over personal information came to the fore in 2006, when Facebook launched a feature called News Feeds, which sent a notice to people's friends registered with the service when their profile was changed or updated. But to the great surprise of those who run Facebook, many of its users reacted with outrage. Nearly 700,000 of them complained. At first blush, the outcry over News Feeds seems baffling. Many of the users who protested had profiles completely accessible to the public. So why did they think it was a privacy violation to alert their friends to changes in their profiles?

Instead of viewing privacy as secrets hidden away in a dark closet, they considered the issue as a matter of accessibility. They figured that most people would not scrutinize their profiles carefully enough to notice minor changes and updates. They could make changes inconspicuously. But Facebook's News Feeds made information more widely noticeable. The privacy objection, then, was not about secrecy; it was about accessibility.

In 2007 Facebook again encountered another privacy outcry when it launched an advertising system with two parts, called Social Ads and Beacon. With Social Ads, whenever users wrote something positive about a product or a movie, Facebook would use their names, images and words in advertisements sent to friends in the hope that an endorsement would induce other users to purchase a product more than an advertisement might. With Beacon, Facebook made data-sharing deals with a variety of other commercial Web sites. If a person bought a movie ticket on Fandango or an item on another site, that information would pop up in that person's public profile.

Facebook rolled out these programs without adequately informing its users. People unwittingly found themselves shilling products on their friends' Web sites. And some people were shocked to see their private purchases on other Web sites suddenly displayed to the public as part of their profiles that appeared on the Facebook site.

The outcry and an ensuing online petition called for Facebook to reform its practices—a document that quickly attracted tens of thousands of signatures and that ultimately led to several changes. As witnessed in these instances, privacy does not always involve sharing of secrets. Facebook users did not want their identities used to endorse products with Social Ads. It is one thing to write about how much one enjoys a movie or CD; it is another to be used on a billboard to pitch products to others.

Changing the Law

Canada and most European countries have more stringent privacy statutes than the U.S., which has resisted enacting all-encompassing legislation. Privacy laws elsewhere recognize that revealing information to others does not extinguish one's right to privacy. Increasing accessibility of personal information, however, means that U.S. law also should begin recognizing the need to safeguard a degree of privacy in the public realm.

In some areas, U.S. law has a well-developed system of controlling information. Copyright recognizes strong rights for public information, protecting a wide range of works, from movies to software. Procuring copyright protection does not require locking a work of intellect behind closed doors. You can read a copyrighted magazine, make a duplicate for your own use and lend it to others. But you cannot do whatever you want: for instance, photocopying it from cover to cover or selling bootleg copies in the street. Copyright law tries to achieve a balance between freedom and control, even though it still must wrestle with the ongoing controversies in a digital age.

The closest U.S. privacy law comes to a legal doctrine akin to copyright is the appropriation tort, which prevents the use of someone else's name or likeness for financial benefit. Unfortunately, the law has developed in a way that is often ineffective against the type of privacy threats now cropping up. Copyright primarily functions as a form of property right, protecting works of self-expression, such as a song or painting. To cope with increased threats to privacy, the scope of the appropriation tort should be expanded. The broadening might actually embody the original early 20th-century interpretation of this principle of common law, which conceived of privacy as more than a means to protect property: "The right to withdraw from the public gaze at such times as a person may see fit . . . is embraced within the right of personal liberty," declared the Georgia Supreme Court in 1905. Today, however, the tort does not apply when a person's name or image appears in news, art, literature, or on social-networking sites. At the same time the appropriation tort protects against using someone's name or picture without consent to advertise products, it allows these representations to be used in a news story. This limitation is fairly significant. It means that the tort would rarely apply to Internet-related postings.

Any widening of the scope of the appropriation tort must be balanced against the competing need to allow legitimate news gathering and dissemination of public information. The tort should probably apply only when photographs and other personal information are used in ways that are not of public concern—a criterion that will inevitably be subject to ongoing judicial deliberation.

Appropriation is not the only common-law privacy tort that needs an overhaul to become more relevant in an era of networked digital communications. We already have many legal tools to protect privacy, but they are currently crippled by conceptions of privacy that prevent them from working effectively. A broader development of the law should take into account problematic uses of personal information illustrated by the Star Wars Kid or Facebook's Beacon service.

It would be best if these disputes could be resolved without recourse to the courts, but the broad reach of electronic networking will probably necessitate changes in common law. The threats to privacy are formidable, and people are starting to realize how strongly they regard privacy as a basic right. Toward this goal, society must develop a new and more nuanced understanding of public and private life—one that acknowledges that more personal information is going to be available yet also protects some choice over how that information is shared and distributed.

Key Concepts

- Social-networking sites allow seemingly trivial gossip to be distributed to a worldwide audience, sometimes making people the butt of rumors shared by millions of users across the Internet.
- Public sharing of private lives has led to a rethinking of our current conceptions of privacy.
- Existing law should be extended to allow some privacy protection for things that people say and do in what would have previously been considered the public domain.

Fast Facts

- Every day people post more than 65,000 videos on YouTube.
- In 2006 MySpace surpassed [a] million profiles.
- Since 1999 the number of blogs has grown from 50 to 50 million.
- More than 50 percent of blogs are written by children younger than 19. . . .

The Internet Never Forgets

A Public Life

A post on YouTube can provoke global ridicule with the press of a return key. When a young man applied for a job at a U.S. investment firm, he sent along a video with his resume. Called Impossible Is Nothing, it showed the student engaging in a variety of physical feats, from bench-pressing 495 pounds to doing a ski jump to breaking bricks with a karate chop. Throughout the clip, the student bragged about his athletic accomplishments and his overall success in life.

Needless to say, the video was not particularly appropriate for the job he was seeking, and his arrogance was so over the top that the video was quite funny. Apparently, someone at the investment firm leaked the video, and it was posted online. It became an instant hit and has been viewed hundreds of thousands of times. Throughout the Internet, the student has been mocked and parodied. His job prospects have diminished substantially. Although he certainly made a mistake and may have learned a lesson, his youthful bravado and misjudgment are now forever preserved in cyberspace. . . .

POSTSCRIPT

Are Social Networking Sites Good Recruitment Sources?

SNSs predominantly started out as Web services to reconnect old friends and family. Most of these social sites have privacy controls allowing users to monitor what they want to make publicly available. Some SNSs started out as exclusive sites but broadened their user base to include everyone. Today this industry has more than 170 million global subscribers, with LinkedIn suggesting that it adds a subscriber every second.

SNSs have provided recruiters a different approach to hiring applicants. Proponents argue that it is very cost-effective, identifies qualified applicants, and allows online dialogues with applicants even before they are hired. Online dialogues allow applicants to understand both the positives and negatives of any job—referred to as a realistic job preview. Therefore, applicants self-select themselves, which saves recruiters a lot of time and money. Gen Y or millennials spend a lot of time being connected with others through such sites—a trait that recruiters should not ignore.

Further, several organizations are adopting specialized versions of SNSs to help gain organizational specific talent. Pfizer, the pharmaceutical giant, has launched its own version of Facebook, called PFacebook, to leverage and identify global talent. HP has identified its own SSN with MyCommunity, which allows employees to share positive and negative experiences of their jobs and also identify potential areas of work interest. LinkedIn, a professional SNS, has 8 million global users with organizations scouting for almost 25 percent of their applicants through their networking resource. LinkedIn's International Director suggests that leveraging global talent has been one of the company's very specific recruiting advantages because of its universal visibility.

But such cost-effective recruiting comes with a price. Employers have to be wary of information obtained from cyberspace, as online misrepresentation is quite rampant. Dr. Solove, law professor at George Washington University, indicates that the "Internet never forgets," as there is evidence of applicants who have posted information on YouTube and have had negative consequences in hiring. Further, he argues in a country where privacy is so deeply valued, having recruiters scout both personal and professional applicant information could lead to either lawsuits or some potential changes in privacy acts.

Suggested Readings

D. M. Boyd and N. B. Ellison. "Social Network Sites: Definition, History, and Scholarship," *Journal of Computer-Mediated Communication* (vol. 13, no. 1, art. 11, 2007).

L. Leader-Chivée, B. Hamilton, and E. Cowan, "Networking the Way to Success: Online Social Networks for Workplace and Competitive Advantage," *People and Strategy* (vol. 31, no. 4, pp. 40–46, 2008).

Social Networking Tip: The Pros and Cons of Social Networking Sites: http://hubpages.com/hub/Pros-and-Cons-of-Social-Networking-Sites.

Social Networking Technology Boosts Job Recruiting: http://www.npr.org/templates/story/story.php?storyId=6522523.

Should You Recruit on Social-Networking Sites? http://www.hrworld.com/features/Should-you-012408/.

Using Social Networking Sites for Hiring: http://www.expresscomputeronline.com/20080317/technologylife01.shtml.

LinkedIn Skyrockets as Job Losses Mount: http://www.workforce.com/section/00/article/26/22/59.php.

ISSUE 6

Are Personality Tests Good Predictors of Employee Performance?

YES: Ira Blank, from "Selecting Employees Based on Emotional Intelligence Competencies: Reap the Rewards and Minimize the Risk," *Employee Relations Law Journal* (December 2008)

NO: Erin White, from "Theory and Practice: Personality Tests Aim to Stop 'Fakers'; Some Say Tool's Accuracy Could Be Improved to Make Misrepresentations Harder," *Wall Street Journal* (Eastern Edition) (November 6, 2006)

ISSUE SUMMARY

YES: Ira Blank, litigation attorney, suggests that personality tests are excellent predictors of job performance because they identify several critical work-related skills needed in today's team and multicultural environment.

NO: Erin White, reporter for the *Wall Street Journal,* cites the studies of Dr. Griffith, which state that student always fake their personality when they realize the outcomes are different. Questions on these tests are so transparent that it is easy to manipulate the answers.

Personality tests help organizations profile personality characteristics. Researchers have identified the "Big Five" personality characteristics: extroversion, adjustment, agreeableness, conscientiousness, and inquisitiveness. Personality traits, such as conscientiousness, have been demonstrated to be good predictors of job performance. About 35 percent of U.S. organizations use personality tests during their hiring process. Daniel Goleman championed the concept of emotional intelligence, which has very similar dimensions to that of the Big Five. The main concepts of emotional intelligence are self-awareness, self-management, social awareness, and relationship management. These dimensions can be measured by personality tests such as the Emotional and Social Competency Inventory (ESCI) or the Emotional Competency Inventory (ECI).

Traditional selection practices usually identify technical competence, work experience, education, and cognitive skills to predict superior job performance. However, organizations are realizing that as employees are increasingly working in a team environment, either domestically or internationally, emotional intelligence plays a very critical role in determining their success. Who will deny that a collaborative work spirit is an asset in organizations today? Emotional intelligence helps identify skills such as leadership, change agent, negotiation, adaptability, and integrity, among several others.

Several studies indicate promising results in the use of emotional intelligence as a predictor of job performance. Retail managers with high emotional intelligence scores have demonstrated superior success in terms of store profits. Further, managers with a higher score of emotional intelligence handled the unpredictable buyers' retail environment much better. Sales employees who received higher scores of emotional intelligence had higher sales records and also lower attrition levels. Superior scores on emotional intelligence also have shown enhanced performance for global executives who constantly need to interact, coordinate, and collaborate among various cultures. Expatriates—employees who work overseas—who score high on emotional stability and openness to experience have shown very positive work results. Studies from the U.S. Army also demonstrate that individuals who score high on personality characteristics were much more successful at their jobs than those who got lower scores on such tests.

Opponents of personality testing suggest that the biggest pitfall of these tests is that applicants can fake their answers. Dr. Griffith of the Florida Institute of Technology suggests that applicants frequently fake their responses on personality tests. Applicants fake answers to get positive scores and also to provide answers that are deemed socially correct. For instance, questions such as "are you deeply motivated?" will definitely bring out positive responses because the results of such answers are very transparent. Dr. Griffith demonstrated students faking in personality tests in a class study. The first time the students took the test, they were told it was a class-administered personality test. The second time the students took the same test, they were told recruiters were giving the test. The results indicated that 30 percent of the students faked their answers when they thought recruiters were providing the test so that they could get higher scores.

Apart from applicants' honesty about their answers, legal staffing experts are also concerned that some questions in personality tests may be considered invasive. Applicants might question how such questions are related to the job. Therefore, the validity or meaningfulness of such tests is an important concern for organizations while adopting such tests in any hiring process. Organizations should ensure that the questions on the personality tests have a direct relation to the job.

International perspectives suggest personality tests are used predominantly in some cultures because workplace harmony and personal relationships are very important. Kolbe personality tests that identify four distinct categories are increasingly used in the Mexican workplace. Psychometric tests are used by about 25 percent of the Indian organizations during the hiring process. Many of the tests that other cultures use are usually adopted from the United States, and HRM experts caution that such tests may not be tapping actual important personal traits relevant to the culture.

YES

Ira Blank

Selecting Employees Based on Emotional Intelligence Competencies: Reap the Rewards and Minimize the Risk

Abstract (Summary)

When evaluating candidates for an open position, an employer has a strategic business decision to make: hire the individual whose skills, work experience, and education most closely match what the employer believes it takes to do the job, or hire the superior performer. Unfortunately, too many employers are confident they can identify and select the former, but they are less confident that they can recognize and hire the latter. Traditionally, employers have looked to work experience, technical skills, cognitive skills, and education as predictors of successful job performance. Testing, moreover, has been met with legal challenges. The most prevalent forms of employment tests have been cognitive tests and personality tests. In recent years, researchers have found that emotional intelligence competencies are predictors of superior job performance. The business case for emotional intelligence is made by numerous studies that show that individuals who have particular emotional intelligence competencies add significant value to their organizations.

> Emotional intelligence is an effective predictor of successful job performance. Emotional intelligence competency-based employee selection can be accomplished in a manner that minimizes legal risk and adds substantial value to the organization.
> The ability to make good decisions regarding people represents one of the last reliable sources of competitive advantage, since very few organizations are very good at it.
>
> —Peter Drucker

When evaluating candidates for an open position, an employer has a strategic business decision to make: hire the individual whose skills, work experience, and education most closely match what the employer believes it takes to do the job, or hire the superior performer. Unfortunately, too many employers

From *Employee Relations Law Journal*, 34:3, Winter 2008, pp. 77–85. Copyright © 2008 by Wolters Kluwer Law & Business. Reprinted by permission.

are confident they can identify and select the former, but they are less confident that they can recognize and hire the latter.

Traditional Selection Process

Traditionally, employers have looked to work experience, technical skills, cognitive skills, and education as predictors of successful job performance. Employers have used employment applications, resumes, and interviews, and, in some cases, tests to establish those data points. However, although factors such as skills, experience, and education may predict adequate or average performance in a job, they do not identify the outstanding performers.[1]

Testing, moreover, has been met with legal challenges. The most prevalent forms of employment tests have been cognitive tests and personality tests. Cognitive tests are individualized assessment measures of an individual's general mental ability or intelligence. There are generally two forms of cognitive tests: aptitude tests and general intelligence tests.

Aptitude tests are designed to assess an applicant's ability to perform specific tasks.[2] Such tests purport to measure a variety of capabilities, including cognitive skills, verbal skills, and numerical skills.[3] Intelligence tests are designed to measure overall intelligence levels.

However, some standardized general aptitude and intelligence tests have been found to disproportionately disqualify applicants of a particular class (typically race or gender). If the use of any such test or other employment practice has an adverse impact on a segment of the workforce or applicant pool, such as African Americans, women, or individuals who are 40 years of age or older, such use may violate the anti-discrimination laws.[4] There is not a common definition of "disparate impact." The US Supreme Court has spoken of it as substantial disproportionate impact; the Equal Employment Opportunity Commission, on the other hand, defines "adverse impact" as the selection rate for any race, sex, or ethnic group as less than 80 percent of the rate for the group with the highest rate.[5] If the test or other selection procedure has an adverse impact on a particular race, sex, or ethnic group, the employer can justify its use by showing that it is valid.[6]

The law recognizes three types of validation:

1. Criterion-related validation (a statistical demonstration between scores on a selection procedure and the job performance of a sample of workers);
2. Content validation (a demonstration "that the content of [a] selection procedure is representative of important aspects of [job] performance"); and
3. Construct validation (measurement of an underlying human trait or characteristic that is important to job performance).[7]

Criterion-related validation is established when there is a significant positive correlation between comparative success on the test and comparative success on some measure of job performance. Content validation is established when the test itself closely approximates the tasks to be performed on the job. Construct validation is established when there is a significant relationship between the test and the identification of some trait, such as "intelligence" or "leadership," which is required in the performance of the job.[8]

While general aptitude tests and intelligence tests may present the risk of disparate impact claims, tests that require an applicant to perform actual job tasks (such as word processing or typing tests) present a minimal risk of disparate impact.[9]

Personality tests purport to assess an individual's psychological profile. Like other standardized tests such as aptitude and intelligence tests, personality tests present the risk of disparate impact on minority groups.[10] Moreover, when a personality test asks questions that could reveal a mental disability, such as depression, the test could be found to be an unlawful pre-employment medical examination under the Americans With Disabilities Act (ADA).[11] In one such case,[12] a federal appellate court concluded that the Minnesota Multi-Phasic Personality Inventory (MMPI), the most widely used test of adult psychopathology, was a "medical examination" under the ADA that screened out, or had the effect of screening out, job applicants with disabilities. Accordingly, the court held that employers could not lawfully use the MMPI as a preemployment screening and selection tool.

Emotional Intelligence Competencies

In recent years, researchers have found that emotional intelligence competencies are predictors of superior job performance. Emotional competencies and the emotional intelligence on which they are based became widely recognized as a result of the work of Daniel Goleman.[13] As Goleman points out, intelligence was thought of historically in terms of cognitive skills, such as language and math skills.[14] Emotional intelligence, though, describes noncognitive abilities that are distinct from, but at the same time complementary to, cognitive intelligence.[15]

Emotional intelligence is the capacity for recognizing our own feelings and those of others, for motivating ourselves, and for managing emotions well in ourselves and in our relationships.[16] Intellectual intelligence, measured by IQ, changes little after our teen years.[17] Emotional intelligence, on the other hand, is not fixed genetically, and it does not develop only in our formative years. Rather, emotional intelligence is, for the most part, learned.[18]

An emotional intelligence competency is an individual characteristic (or combination of characteristics) that can be measured reliably and that distinguishes superior from average performers, or effective from ineffective performers, at levels of statistical significance.[19] So what are the emotional intelligence competencies? Goleman's emotional intelligence model identifies four emotional intelligence domains and 19 associated competencies,[20] as follows:

Personal Competence: these capabilities determine how we manage ourselves.

1. Self- Awareness
   - Emotional self-awareness: Reading one's own emotions and recognizing their impact; using "gut sense" to guide decisions;

- Accurate self-assessment: Knowing one's strengths and limits; and
- Self-confidence: A sound sense of one's self-worth and capabilities.

2. Self-Management
   - Emotional self-control: Keeping disruptive emotions and impulses under control;
   - Transparency: Displaying honesty and integrity; trustworthiness;
   - Adaptability: Flexibility in adapting to changing situations or overcoming obstacles;
   - Achievement: The drive to improve performance to meet inner standards of excellence;
   - Initiative: Readiness to act and seize opportunities; and
   - Optimism: Seeing the upside in events.
   - Social competence: These capabilities determine how we manage relationships.

1. Social Awareness
   - Empathy: Sensing others' emotions, understanding their perspective, and taking active interest in their concerns;
   - Organizational awareness: Reading the currents, decision networks, and politics at the organization level; and
   - Service: Recognizing and meeting follower, client, or customer needs.

2. Relationship Management
   - Inspirational leadership: Guiding and motivating with a compelling vision;
   - Influence: Wielding a range of tactics for persuasion;
   - Developing others: Bolstering others' abilities through feedback and guidance;
   - Change catalyst: Initiating, managing, and leading in a new direction;
   - Conflict management: Resolving disagreements;
   - Building bonds: Cultivating and maintaining a web of relationships; and
   - Teamwork and collaboration: Cooperation and team building.

While no one individual has strengths in every one of the emotional intelligence competencies, outstanding performers typically are strong in around six such competencies.[21]

The Business Case for Emotional Intelligence Competencies

The business case for emotional intelligence is made by numerous studies that show that individuals who have particular emotional intelligence competencies add significant value to their organizations. For example, the US Air Force found that recruiters who had high scores in the emotional intelligence competencies of assertiveness, empathy, happiness, and emotional self-awareness were three times as successful as the recruiters who did not score well in those competencies.[22] In a retail chain, the ability to handle stress, another emotional competence, was a characteristic of each successful store manager. The most successful store managers—with success measured in net profits, sales per square foot, sales per employee, and per dollar inventory investment—were those best able to handle stress.[23] In another company, sales agents selected on the basis of certain emotional competencies outsold those salespeople selected using the company's old selection procedure.[24] At a national furniture retailer, salespeople hired based on emotional competence had half the drop-out rate during their first year.[25] Another study found that the main reasons that executives did not succeed in their careers involves deficits in emotional competencies—specifically, difficulty in handling change, not being able to work well in a team, and poor interpersonal relations.[26]

Measuring Emotional Intelligence Competencies

Because emotional intelligence competencies have been found to be predictive of successful performance in positions in many organizations, the question is: can emotional intelligence be measured? The answer is yes. Several test instruments measure emotional intelligence itself; that is, a person's ability to recognize and use emotion. Other test instruments measure emotionally competent behavior, because it is the emotional competencies of the star performers that add economic value to the organization.[27]

Among the test instruments that measure emotional intelligence are the Multifactor Emotional Intelligence Scale (MEIS) and the Mayer-Salovey-Caruso Emotional Intelligence Test (MSCEIT). The MEIS has evidence of validity and reliability. Cherniss and Goleman conclude that there is no reliability evidence and little validity evidence for the tasks constituting the MSCEIT.[28] Employers who are considering the use of the MSCEIT should, from the standpoint of mitigating legal risk, seek written assurance from the test publisher that the test does not have a disparate impact on minorities or insist upon a written representation as to the test's validity.

The Emotional Quotient Inventory (EQ-i) is a self-report measure of emotionally competent behavior that provides an estimate of the test subject's emotional intelligence. The EQ-i is supported by validity evidence.[29] The Emotional Competence Inventory (ECI) is a 360-degree assessment that develops self, subordinate, peer, and supervisory ratings on 20 emotional and social competencies. The ECI is supported by validity evidence.[30]

A word of caution about using tests to measure emotional intelligence competencies for selection decisions. Emotional intelligence has been described as amounting to something of a rainbow of competencies that may or may not be relevant to a particular job.[31] Accordingly, any test used to measure emotional intelligence for selection purposes should not be a generic measure of emotional intelligence competencies. Rather, the test should be designed to measure the specific competencies that actually predict success in the particular position. When considering whether to use tests of emotional intelligence for selection purposes, attention should be given to whether any particular test or group of tests is sufficiently job related to predict job success.

Implementing an Emotional Intelligence Competency-Based Selection Process

So why should employers use emotional intelligence competencies to recruit, hire, train, and promote employees? For several reasons. First and foremost, numerous studies show that emotional intelligence competencies are predictive of outstanding performance in most jobs. Hiring individuals with higher levels of emotional intelligence and training employees to be more emotionally intelligent adds substantial value to their respective organizations.[32]

Second, emotional intelligence is a matter of risk management. Employees lacking in certain emotional intelligence competencies may present a greater risk of bad behavior, such as theft and sexual harassment.[33] Selecting employees based on emotional intelligence competencies may enhance the likelihood that a "trouble maker" will not be hired.

That said, what are the costs, risks, and benefits of using assessment tools in emotional intelligence competency-based employee selection and development? The cost of an assessment tool, including administration time and any fee paid for using the test instrument may range from $25 to $200 per use.[34]

If and only if an emotional intelligence competency-based test has significant disparate impact based on race or other protected bases, the test must be professionally validated to ensure that the test is predictive of, or significantly correlates with, important elements of the employee's performance.[35] There is little evidence that the more widely used emotional intelligence tests result in adverse selection of minorities.

The Equal Employment Opportunity Commission, as part of its E-RACE initiative, has identified employment and personality tests as an area of concern and has indicated that new guidance on race discrimination in written employment tests will be forthcoming.[36] Therefore, employers should make a point of tracking the results of its emotional intelligence test(s) to ensure that the test(s) do not have an adverse impact, thereby minimizing the risk of a disparate impact claim. In an abundance of caution, the employer should consider going further and ask the test publisher to provide its validity study as evidence of validity. Be aware, though, that the fact that a test is supported by a validity study in itself means little. The validity study should meet the requirements of the Uniform Guidelines on Employee Selection Procedures as they pertain to the professional standards for validity studies. Reputable test publishers will state in writing that the procedures used in validating their particular test were consistent with generally accepted professional standards such as those described in the "Standards for Educational and Psychological Testing."[37] Employers should accept nothing less.

Selection based on interviews without the use of tests necessarily involves the use of subjective criteria to make employment decisions, which in and of itself is not unlawful.[38] However, although a selection process that depends almost entirely on the subjective evaluation of interviewers presents the potential for an adverse impact claim, that risk can be minimized by building objective guidelines into the interview and selection process.[39]

There are advantages to using job-related emotional intelligence tests as part of the selection process. First, when used in tandem with the interview, the test can improve the odds of hiring a superior performer. Second, a test that is validated minimizes the risk of discrimination litigation and liability.

To implement emotional intelligence competency-based selection of employees, with a minimum of risk, an employer can take the following steps:

For each job, perform a job analysis. Identify the job functions, the skills, knowledge, and experience necessary to perform the job, and the competencies that are critical for success.

Develop a job description, incorporating the job functions, the necessary characteristics, and the critical competencies.

Identify the methods that will be used to measure and evaluate applicants' characteristics and competencies and differentiate between the applicants who meet the minimum requirements and those who are likely to be the superior performers. Specifically, decide whether to use emotional intelligence competency tests. If yes, have the test publisher provide you with written confirmation (i.e., the relevant studies) that the test is reliable and valid.

Develop and implement behavioral interviewing using structured interview questions that are valid and relevant. The interview content should be legally defensible. Train the interviewers on accurate, effective, legal interviewing. The interviewer asks the applicant competency-based questions that are designed to elicit detailed information about situations in which the applicant has demonstrated the specific competency in the past. The applicant would typically be asked the following: (a) what was the situation in which you were involved?; (b) what task did you have to accomplish?; (c) what action did you take?; and (d) what results did you achieve?

Select candidates who are strong in the core emotional intelligence competencies that predict successful job performance.

Track and evaluate the economic value added by the superior performers.

Notes

1. Cary Cherniss and Daniel Goleman, The Emotionally Intelligent Workplace, 160 (2001).

2. Herbert G. Heneman and Robert L. Heneman, Staffing Organizations, 358 (1994).

3. Id. at 359.

4. Griggs v. Duke Power Co., 401 U.S. 424 (1971) (disparate impact claim under Title VII of the Civil Rights Act of 1964, 42 U.S.C. § 2000c, et seq. Employer can prevail by showing business necessity and no alternative practices that would not have an adverse impact); Smith v. City of Jackson, 544 U.S. 228 (2005) (disparate impact claim cognizable under Age Discrimination in Employment Act of 1967, 29 U.S.C. § 621, et seq. Employer can prevail by showing that the practice was reasonable); 42 U.S.C. § 12112(b)(1) ("discriminate" within the meaning of the Americans with Disabilities Act includes actions that cause adverse impact on the disabled).

5. Washington v. Davis, 426 U.S. 229, 246–247 (1976); 29 C.F.R. § 1607.4.

6. 29 C.F.R. Part 1607 (Uniform Guidelines on Employee Selection Procedures).

7. 29 C.F.R. § 1607.5B.

8. Sims v. Montgomery County Comm'n, 890 F. Supp. 1520, 1526, and ns. 8, 9 (M.D. Ala. 1995); see also Gillespie v. Wisconsin, 771 F. 2d 1035, 1040 and n. 103 (7th Cir. 1985).

9. Cynthia D. Fisher, et al., Human Resource Management, 321 (3d ed. 1996).

10. Donald H.J. Hermann, III, "Privacy, the Prospective Employee, and Employment Testing: The Need to Restrict Polygraph and Personality Testing," 47 Wash. L. Rev., 73, 109 (1971).

11. 42 U.S.C. § 12101 et seq.

12. Karraker v. Rent-A-Center, Inc., 411 F.3d 831 (7th Cir. 2005).

13. Daniel Goleman, Emotional Intelligence (1995).

14. Id. at 42.

15. Daniel Goleman, Working with Emotional Intelligence, 317 (1998).

16. Id.

17. Id. at 7, 317.

18. Id. at 7; Daniel Goleman, et al., Primal Leadership, 38 (2002).

19. Gary Cherniss and Daniel Goleman, The Emotionally Intelligent Workplace, 47 (2001).

20. Daniel Goleman, et al., supra at 39.

21. Id. at 38.

22. Cary Cherniss, "The Business Case for Emotional Intelligence,". . . .

23. Id.

24. Id.

25. Id.

26. Id.

27. Cary Cherniss and Daniel Goleman, supra at 85.

28. Id. at 100, 106–107.

29. Id. at 114–115.

30. Id. at 92.

31. The Blackwell Handbook of Personnel Selection, 213 (Arne Evers, et al., eds. 2005).

32. The Handbook of Emotional Intelligence, 434 (Reuven Bar-On and James D.A. Parker eds., 2000).

33. "Emotional Intelligence and Employment Practices Liability Part I: The Nature and Importance of Emotional Intelligence,". . . .

34. "Emotional Intelligence and Employment Practices Liability Part II: The Legality and Effectiveness of Employee Assessment Tools,". . . .

35. See 29 C.F.R. § 1607.3A ("The use of any selection procedure which has an adverse impact on the hiring, promotion, or other employment or

membership opportunities of members of any race, sex, or ethnic group will be considered to be discriminatory and inconsistent with these guidelines, unless the procedure has been validated in accordance with these guidelines, or the provisions of section 6 below are satisfied."); 2 EEOC Compliance Manual, § 15-VI.

36. . . .

37. The 1999 Standards for Educational and Psychological Testing are a set of testing standards developed jointly by the American Educational Research Association, the American Psychological Association, and the National Council on Measurement in Education. The 1999 Standards are the third revision of the joint standards. A fourth revision was begun in 2008. The Standards are recognized as sound principles of accepted psychometric practice.

38. See Millbrook v. IBP, Inc., 280 F.3d 1169, 1176 (7th Cir. 2002) (use of subjective criteria for selection decision did not constitute race discrimination).

39. See EEOC v. Rath Packing Co., 787 F.2d 318, 322, 328 (8th Cir. 1986) (hiring practices that lacked selection guidelines but were based on "getting the right person for the job," had an adverse impact on women).

Erin White

➡ NO

Theory and Practice: Personality Tests Aim to Stop "Fakers"; Some Say Tool's Accuracy Could Be Improved to Make Misrepresentations Harder

Abstract (Summary)

About 30% of respondents change their answers to achieve significantly higher scores. Faking "substantially harms the ability of the test to predict" people's performance, Dr. Richard Griffith says. (The students are later told it's a research project.)

Test makers analyze a job for the personality traits that would make workers successful, and then design questions to detect those traits, Dr. Griffith says. The right answer depends on what the employer is looking for; what's good for one job could be bad for another. The tests are designed to reveal an applicant's behavior patterns, not necessarily what someone would do in any particular situation, he adds. "For any given instance, I wouldn't bet a dime" that the assessment would necessarily predict a person's actions, he says.

CraftSystems, Bradenton, Fla., works with Dr. Griffith and has conducted studies to weed out questions that lend themselves to fake answers. Statements such as "I am highly motivated to achieve outstanding results" and "I am more outgoing than shy" were deemed too transparent. Respondents could tell what the question was looking for and answered accordingly.

PSYCHOLOGY PROFESSOR Richard Griffith is on a mission to stop "fakers."

To Dr. Griffith, of the Florida Institute of Technology, fakers are people who misrepresent themselves on personality tests increasingly used to screen applicants for entry-level jobs at call centers, retail stores and other customer-service positions. The tests typically ask candidates to agree or disagree with statements about their character and personality traits, hoping to shed light on how the job applicants approach tasks and problems.

Researchers such as Dr. Griffith say it's too easy to lie on some of these tests, because applicants try to predict the "right" answer, which can vary depending on the job. Applicants can also research employment tests on the Web and ask friends who have taken them previously.

In his research, Dr. Griffith collects personality-test responses from community-college students twice, about six weeks apart. The first time, the students' instructor administers the test and tells students to answer honestly. The second time, Dr. Griffith or his graduate assistants pose as recruiters, and distribute tests containing many of the same questions.

About 30% of respondents change their answers to achieve significantly higher scores. Faking "substantially harms the ability of the test to predict" people's performance, Dr. Griffith says. (The students are later told it's a research project.)

Despite the tests' flaws, Dr. Griffith says pre-employment tests are generally more reliable predictors of performance than an interview alone. But he says they could be more accurate.

Test makers analyze a job for the personality traits that would make workers successful, and then design questions to detect those traits, Dr. Griffith says. The right answer depends on what the employer is looking for; what's good for one job could be bad for another. The tests are designed to reveal an applicant's behavior patterns, not necessarily what someone would do in any particular situation, he adds. "For any given instance, I wouldn't bet a dime" that the assessment would necessarily predict a person's actions, he says.

Facing the perennial challenge of hiring the right applicant, more employers have adopted prehire tests in recent years, thanks in part to the Internet making distribution cheaper and easier. About 70% of entry- and midlevel jobs at big companies now include testing, says Scott Erker, a senior vice president at Development Dimensions International, a Bridgeville, Pa., human-resources consultancy.

Sherri Merbach, senior director for organizational development for Orange Lake Resorts, which sells time shares in Florida, says prehire personality tests are especially helpful in hiring salespeople. Sales applicants are usually able to make a good impression—and thus interview well—but sometimes offer answers that don't display great urgency, another quality that Orange Lake is seeking in its sales force.

Ms. Merbach has used bad test scores to dissuade colleagues from offering jobs to some suave candidates. "You're less likely to make a bad hiring decision," she says.

Employers and testing companies are aware that some applicants give misleading answers. So they include questions designed to weed out fakers. But Dr. Griffith says some of these tactics can backfire.

One common question designed to trap fakers asks applicants whether they have or haven't done something common but frowned upon, such as "I have never looked at a dirty book or magazine." In theory, liars are more apt to say they never have, while honest people admit the behavior.

But savvy applicants know to confess. "They fake those in the reverse direction," says Dr. Griffith. Another problem: Applicants who answer truthfully that they've never looked a naughty magazine can be labeled liars.

Ms. Merbach, from the time-share company, says the test she uses, by CraftSystems Inc., is sophisticated enough to reduce the likelihood of faking and is a good predictor of job performance.

CraftSystems, Bradenton, Fla., works with Dr. Griffith and has conducted studies to weed out questions that lend themselves to fake answers. Statements such as "I am highly motivated to achieve outstanding results" and "I am more outgoing than shy" were deemed too transparent. Respondents could tell what the question was looking for and answered accordingly.

Some employers say tests are useful, but need to be used together with other ways of judging applicants. Steve Suggs, president of sales at Sales Manage Solutions LLC, a Knoxville, Tenn., consulting firm, advises clients to use assessments to help make hiring decisions. But he cautions clients not to base hiring decisions solely on the test, because the answers don't always reflect all of an applicant's characteristics.

For example, he says test results may suggest that an applicant is cold and self-centered. In person, though, the applicant may demonstrate that he's learned to control these tendencies and could be effective. In a hiring decision, "there are other factors that come into play," Mr. Suggs says.

POSTSCRIPT

Are Personality Tests Good Predictors of Employee Performance?

Personality tests are quite controversial when used as a hiring practice in the workplace. Proponents suggest that traditional hiring practices might not bring out many personality characteristics that are very critical to the current workplace. Global collaboration, team management, and project management are some of the hallmarks of today's organizations that require comprehensive hiring practices. Relationship management, inspiring leadership, team-building spirit, and adaptability are critical in today's workforce, which cannot be tapped from traditional hiring practices. Several financial organizations have adopted personality tests to significantly enhance team performance.

Personality tests, whether they determine emotional intelligence or the Big Five, help detail employees' personality profiles and provide important work-related characteristics. Research has proven that applicants with higher scores on personality tests do perform superiorly at work whether it is retail, sales, or finance. Companies have also demonstrated higher retention for employees who get high scores on personality tests, therefore providing a return on investment on these staffing practices. Personality tests are relatively inexpensive and can be obtained from multiple sources. Proponents also argue that though faking may be a concern of such testing, test authorities can administer methods to identify "fakers."

Opponents suggest that the possibility of faking responses is the most important drawback of these tests. What is the point of adopting such tests when you know that there is a possibility that applicants are going to lie? Most questions on personality tests are very obvious so that applicants know how to provide the answers that the organizations are looking for. Further, applicants will usually avoid providing answers that society holds as ethically wrong regardless of applicants' actual opinions or experiences. Legal experts also caution that some questions on these tests might be considered an invasion of privacy against federal acts such as the Americans with Disabilities Act (ADA). For instance, personality testing used for managerial positions in a national rental car chain was deemed inappropriate by the court of law because it seemed more like a medical exam asking specific questions related to applicants' mental health.

It is very important that organizations do not purchase generic personality tests that do not tap or identify knowledge, skills, and abilities (KSAs) congruent to their work or industry environment. Also, these tests should not demonstrate adverse impact, where certain ethnic groups are unintentionally discriminated against. Organizations will find it helpful to work with industrial psychologists to understand the validity (meaningfulness) and reliability (consistency) of these personality tests to their work environment.

Suggested Readings

Victoria Knight, "Personality Tests as Hiring Tools," *Wall Street Journal* (Eastern Edition) (p. B.3A, March 15, 2006).

Edwin P. Morrow, "Enhance Your Staff EQ," *Financial Planning* (vol. 136, January 2002).

Ilya Adler, "Workplace Referee," *Business Mexico* (vol. 14, no. 3, p. 15, March 2004).

The Pros and Cons of Personality Testing in the Workplace: http://www.thefreelibrary.com/The+pros+and+cons+of+personality+testing+in+the+workplace.-a0160104861.

Pros and Cons of Psychological Testing: http://articles.techrepublic.com.com/5100-10878_11-5025293.html.

Psychometric Tests in India Are Faulty: http://www.mid-day.com/news/2009/jan/230109-Milind-Joshi-psychometrics-tests-HR-process-Maersk-HR-consultancy-D-G-Deshpande-mental-asylum.htm.

ISSUE 7

Would Mandatory Background Checks for All Employees Reduce Negligent Hiring Lawsuits?

YES: **Lessing Gold**, from "Get a Background Check," *SDM* (October 2007)

NO: **Chad Terhune**, from "The Trouble with Background Checks: Employee Screening Has Become a Big Business, But Not Always an Accurate One," *BusinessWeek* (June 2008)

ISSUE SUMMARY

YES: Lessing Gold, attorney and writer, contends that organizations have a liability in checking the background references of both their permanent or temporary applicants. He indicates how applicants with criminal records emerge back into the work environment with false records, potentially putting customers and co-workers in jeopardy.

NO: Chad Terhune, senior writer for *BusinessWeek,* asserts that information from background checking companies is so inaccurate that it is very unfair to several whose employment records have become blemished. He feels that the unregulated nature of this industry could be one of the main reasons for such employment errors.

Negligent hiring occurs when an employer hires an applicant without checking his or her background, and subsequently, the applicant causes harm to either co-workers or customers. The employer would be accused of negligent hiring for failing to take reasonable care to check on an applicant's background, which could have minimized danger or violence.

Lessing Gold suggests that organizations should get a thorough background check on employees whether the position requires it or not. He describes a court case in which a customer was kidnapped at gunpoint by a promotional representative of a security company. The assailant had a track record of committing a felony and kidnapping. However, the security company had failed to conduct a background check on the applicant, which would have revealed his past criminal record.

This court case was in fact appealed and reversed in the court of law due to legal definitions specific to this case. The company's senior employees argued that background checks were not performed on promotional sales representatives because they were considered independent contractors. Further, the company's general manager stressed that promotional representatives were not allowed to enter customers' houses. Also, the company officials added that the kidnapping act was not committed during the stipulated work hours of the security company. Should organizations not be responsible to provide a safe environment to their customers and co-workers regardless of their employees' status or company policies?

The main contention in this case is that if the organization had exercised reasonable care and performed a background check, the company would have uncovered the employee's criminal past. Further, performing a background check would save organizations millions of dollars in attorney fees and also reduce the impact of a negative reputation. In legal terms, the burden to provide a safe environment is squarely on the organization.

Some suggest that background checks are really not as authentic as they claim to be. Background checking has become a very lucrative business, with several companies mushrooming to create an unregulated environment with intense competition. Most of these organizations are relying on sources that might not be very accurate and therefore provide incorrect information about applicants. Organizations are able to provide detailed portfolios describing applicants' work histories, educational backgrounds, credit histories, personal lives, and also drug or alcohol addiction for a reasonable fee ($60–80 per applicant).

Several cases point to the inaccuracy of information provided by background check organizations. Pendergrass, a supervisor at Rite Aid, was fired in 2006 for stealing and not accounting for store merchandise properly. The employee denied the allegation and was later proved innocent at a court hearing. However, Rite Aid, as a routine legal procedure, submitted the supervisor's complete work record to a background check database. Pendergrass was unable to get subsequent jobs at retail stores, completely tarnishing his work and professional reputation. Another case is that of Carter, a truck driver, who was fired in 2006 for violating company policy. The truck driver complained about the safety of his vehicle, which the company, Martin Transport, viewed negatively. Though Carter won a court case against the company, he feels his work image has been completely destroyed because no trucking company would hire him subsequently. The employment database for transport companies, DAC (Drive-A-Check), has a permanent record of his dismissal from Martin Transport. Mr. Carter had to borrow from his retirement savings to support his family.

An international perspective suggests that local laws and host culture play an important role in completing background checks. In the United Kingdom, it is impossible for background checking firms to get any criminal records from the police without the consent of the recruiting firm and applicant. Further, the process can take as long as 40 days. In China, before conducting background checks, organizations need to get the applicant's government work number, which the Chinese government assigns to employees. In India, to verify an applicant's educational background, organizations need to have an applicant's "seat number" or admission number for the university to release such records.

YES ↵

Lessing E. Gold

Get a Background Check

In a recent case in the State of Georgia, a kidnap victim brought a negligent hiring action against a security company and its authorized dealer after she was kidnapped by the dealer's salesman. The trial court ruled against the plaintiff kidnap victim and granted summary judgment to the security company.

The victim appealed. The victim was kidnapped at gunpoint by a convicted violent felon who had once worked for the alarm company as a "promotions representative" selling home security systems door to door. The alarm company did not perform a background check before hiring the sales person, which would have revealed that he had been convicted of burglary and kidnapping in another state in 1979, sentenced to life in prison, and paroled in 1995. On appeal, the Appellate Court reversed the decision of the trial court.

The president of the defendant security company at deposition testified no background checks were performed on promotions representatives because they were considered independent contractors and not employees.

The general sales manager of the company testified that members of the promotions team were not authorized to enter a prospective buyer's home absent a background check; they were advised that background checks were not required unless the worker was entering a home.

The plaintiff, in her deposition, said she wrote her name, address and telephone number on a form which inquired whether she was interested in having someone contact her about installing a security alarm system. The representative called on the plaintiff on two or three separate occasions. The plaintiff declined to allow the representative into her home. Subsequently, the representative came to the plaintiff's home, where the kidnap occurred.

The issue before the court was whether the alarm company owed a duty to the plaintiff and whether the alarm company breached the duty. The Appeals Court said a jury must decide these questions of fact. The court said the jury must decide whether the defendant has a duty to exercise ordinary care not to hire or retain an employee the employer knew or should have known posed a risk of harm to others, where it is reasonably foreseeable from the employee's "tendencies" or propensities that the employee could cause the type of harm sustained by the plaintiff.

The court further pointed out that the act was not committed within working hours. Therefore, there was an issue as to whether or not the abduction was committed "under the color of employment"—and that also should be determined by the jury, said the court. Therefore, the matter was reversed and remanded to trial.

The bottom line is that companies are advised to obtain a background check on each agent hired to represent the company, whether mandated or not.

Chad Terhune

➜ **NO**

The Trouble with Background Checks: Employee Screening Has Become a Big Business, But Not Always an Accurate One

Abstract (Summary)

Background screening has become a highly profitable corner of the HR world. At the screening division of First Advantage, profits soared 47% last year, to $29 million; revenue grew 20%, to $233 million. HireRight reported that earnings jumped 44%, to $9 million, last year on revenues of $69 million. Screening often goes far beyond the familiar checking of public criminal records. Just by dint of their heft and permanence, the proprietary data caches they compile can seem authoritative, even though the information sometimes contains errors, innuendos, or outright falsehoods. Lester Rosen, a veteran in the industry and president of Employment Screening Resources, says that, essentially, it's the Wild, Wild West. It's an unregulated industry with easy money and not a huge emphasis on compliance or on hiring quality people to do the screening.

Theodore Pendergrass was shocked in November, 2006, when the Walgreens pharmacy chain rejected his application for a store supervisor job. The company told him a background-screening firm called ChoicePoint reported that a past employer had accused him of "cash register fraud and theft of merchandise" totaling $7,313. "I wanted to cry," Pendergrass says. The $4 billion business of background screening is booming. Companies large and small are sorting mostly mid- and lower-level job applicants based on information compiled by ChoicePoint, its major rivals, and hundreds of smaller competitors. Some employers have grown more vigilant about hiring since the September 11 terrorist attacks. Others like the efficiency of outsourcing tasks once handled by in-house human resources departments or bosses who simply picked up the phone themselves. Whatever their motives, employers are becoming more dependent on mass-produced background reports that rely heavily on anonymous, and sometimes inaccurate or unfair, sources.

Pendergrass' difficulties stemmed from a previous job at Rite Aid. By late 2005, when he was 25 years old, he had reached the first rung of management as a shift supervisor in a Rite Aid store in Philadelphia. His bosses trusted him to oversee cashiers, bank deposits, and merchandise deliveries. Then, in January, 2006, a store official accused him of stealing goods and underpaying for DVDs. He denied the accusations, but the official said police were waiting outside to arrest him if he did not confess. Pendergrass wrote a statement but wouldn't admit to theft. He was soon fired anyway.

Later, at a hearing for unemployment compensation, Pendergrass was vindicated. A state labor referee ruled that Rite Aid had not proved its allegations and awarded him nearly $1,000 in benefits. But Rite Aid had already submitted its theft report to a database used by more than 70 retailers and run by ChoicePoint, the largest screening firm for corporate employers in the U.S. Based in a leafy Atlanta suburb, ChoicePoint says it checks applicants for more than half of the country's 100 biggest companies, including Bank of America, UnitedHealth Group, and United Parcel Service. Because of Pendergrass' tainted ChoicePoint file, retailers CVS Caremark and Target also rejected him for jobs.

Pendergrass, now 27, makes lattes at a Starbucks in Philadelphia. The coffee chain doesn't use a screening firm for entry-level hires. Pendergrass earns $17,000 a year, or 30% less than he did at Rite Aid, and fears his career has been derailed. "I worked hard in that store, and none of this stuff was true," he says. "I would be locked up somewhere if I stole $7,000."

Rite Aid declines to comment. A ChoicePoint spokeswoman says the company's background report merely conveyed information provided by a former employer.

Fat Profits

Background screening has become a highly profitable corner of the HR world. At the screening division of First Advantage, based in Poway, Calif., profits soared 47% last year, to $29 million; revenue grew 20%, to $233 million. HireRight, based in Irvine, Calif., reported that earnings jumped 44%, to $9 million, last year on revenues of $69 million. To grab a piece of this growing market, Reed Elsevier Group, the Anglo-Dutch information provider, agreed to acquire ChoicePoint for $4.1 billion in February—at a 50% premium to its stock price.

Industry surveys show why Reed Elsevier was eager to expand its screening business. In a 2004 study by the Society for Human Resource Management, 96% of personnel executives said their companies conduct background checks on job candidates, up from 51% in 1996. Two-thirds of larger companies say they outsource screening, and many now vet current employees in addition to applicants.

Screening often goes far beyond the familiar checking of public criminal records. For $60 to $80 per applicant, ChoicePoint and its rivals assemble digital dossiers of educational degrees and credit histories as well as interviews with friends, past bosses, and colleagues. Call-center workers wearing headsets inquire about work habits, personal character, and drug or alcohol problems. Just by dint of their heft and permanence, the proprietary data caches they compile can seem authoritative, even though the information sometimes contains errors, innuendos, or outright falsehoods.

"You won't believe what people tell you," says Mary Beth Gotshall, who has done interviews since 1999 at Employment Background Investigations, a midsize firm in Owings Mills, Md. She and colleagues have collected comments from a father who said he would never rehire his son because he had missed so much work at a family business. Another former boss accused an applicant of stealing and demanded Employment Background help find him. (The firm declined.) "We put everything in there," Gotshall says while juggling employment checks for retailer Ikea, a Pittsburgh medical clinic, and a Texas engineering firm. Her boss, Richard Kurland, chief executive of Employment Background, says the company goes to great lengths to be accurate. "We have a huge responsibility to mankind," he adds.

But Lester Rosen, a veteran in the industry and president of Employment Screening Resources in Novato, Calif., says: "Essentially, it's the Wild, Wild West. It's an unregulated industry with easy money and not a huge emphasis on compliance or on hiring quality people" to do the screening.

Theron Carter, a 61-year-old unemployed truck driver in Middleville, Mich., is waiting for his name to be cleared in a database used widely in the transportation business. In May, 2006, a U.S. Labor Dept. administrative law judge ruled that Carter was wrongly terminated by Marten Transport for making legitimate complaints about the safety of his 18-wheel truck. He had hauled loads for the Mondovi (Wis.) company for only two weeks before being fired in June, 2005. The judge awarded him more than $31,000 in damages and back pay and ordered Marten Transport to delete "any unfavorable work record information" in a report compiled by USIS, a large screening company in Falls Church, Va. Once an arm of the federal Office of Personnel Management, USIS was privatized in 1996. It still screens government workers and runs an employment-history database used by 2,500 transport companies called Drive-A-Check, or DAC.

Despite his legal victory, Carter's DAC report still says Marten Transport dismissed him for "excessive complaints" and a "company policy violation." "No one will hire me," says Carter, who withdrew $50,000 from retirement savings to support his wife and himself. Trucking company J.B. Hunt Transport Services "told me I had excessive complaints and wouldn't hire me. I told them I won my case." Hunt declines to comment.

Marten Transport has appealed the Labor Dept. ruling. A company attorney, Stephen DiTullio, says it would be "fraudulent" for the carrier to remove the reference to excessive grievances from Carter's DAC file. "That was an accurate portrayal of what led to his termination," DiTullio says. Marten Transport has addressed Carter's safety concerns, he adds.

John Griffith, 47, won a similar Labor Dept. ruling in October, 2003, against his former employer, Atlantic Inland Carrier. The administrative law judge ruled that the company wrongly fired Griffith in December, 2001, for complaining about the safety of his truck and ordered Atlantic Inland to remove unfavorable information from his DAC record.

Someone at Atlantic Inland—it's not clear who—had told DAC that Griffith was terminated and not eligible to be rehired because of his grievances. The company eventually deleted that information in January, 2004—more than two years after it was posted. During that time, Griffith says, it was hard to find trucking work. The Aiken (S.C.) resident turned to lower-paying odd jobs, although he recently got back behind the wheel making deliveries for a nursery. "Truck drivers live and die by DAC," he says. "They can ruin a driver's career with a few clicks of their mouse."

Living in Fear

USIS declines to comment on any specific cases. Gripes about its database have made "DAC" a popular verb in the industry, with drivers lamenting they have "been DAC-ed." Responding to the anxiety surrounding the database, USIS officials have defended their methods on radio interview shows aimed at truckers. They argue that screening is legally required, generally accurate, and keeps bad drivers off the road.

But Kristen Turley, director of market development and communications at USIS' commercial-services unit in Tulsa, concedes that no system is immune to mistakes and misuse. "There is a chance somebody who holds a grudge will put negative information in the database," she says. "We are not trying to blackball drivers or ruin their chance to get a job." When a driver disputes a background report, USIS asks its sources for proof supporting negative comments, she says. USIS doesn't seek such evidence up front. "Ideally that would be a good solution," Turley says, but it could dissuade past employers from submitting information in the first place.

The federal Fair Credit Reporting Act covers background screeners, but it hasn't been aggressively enforced. The law says screeners must use "reasonable procedures" to ensure "maximum possible accuracy." It also requires employers to give a copy of background reports to rejected applicants. An applicant can dispute the information, but the Federal Trade Commission has said employers must wait only five business days before hiring someone else, meaning that objections frequently become moot. Lately the agency has focused more on identity theft than on screening, Rebecca Kuehn, assistant director for privacy and identity protection, says.

ChoicePoint has run into trouble because of how it has disseminated personal data. A 1997 spin-off from credit bureau Equifax, the company stumbled in 2004, when it offered a $40 software package at Sam's Club stores that allowed small businesses to obtain personal information on applicants. The company dropped the product after privacy advocates pointed out that it wasn't verifying whether users had a business license and a legitimate purpose for searching, as opposed to snooping on a neighbor or old boyfriend.

Then, in 2005, it came to light that ChoicePoint had given identity thieves pretending to be small business clients seeking background checks access to people's addresses, Social Security numbers, and dates of birth. ChoicePoint agreed in 2006 to pay a $10 million civil penalty to the FTC and $5 million more to compensate 160,000 consumers whose information had been compromised.

Luring Consumers

Today, ChoicePoint bills itself as the gold standard in screening. "The big issue for us is making sure we're doing things as accurately as possible," says Bill Whitford, a senior vice-president. The company conducts 10 million background checks annually and estimates it has about 20% of the U.S. market. "The number of complaints vs. transactions is very low," says Katherine Bryant, vice-president for consumer advocacy. The FTC has logged 695 complaints against ChoicePoint since 2005, some of which related to the identity-theft episode. USIS had the second-highest total, with 89.

ChoicePoint now is trying to draw consumers as clients. It sells a preemployment self-check to people who want a preview of what an employer would learn about them. These reports cost from $24.95 to as much as $75, depending on how customized they are. Savvy consumers can save themselves some money: Under federal law, individuals are entitled to a copy of any background report compiled by a screening company for a minimal fee, generally $10 or less.

Along with price, screening firms compete on speed. HRPLUS, in Evergreen, Colo., offers five reference interviews within 72 hours. At Employment Background Investigations, a whiteboard hanging on a cubicle wall recently celebrated the clearing of 1,025 applicants in one week by a group of about two dozen screeners, a company record.

Screening firms say their services are vital. In many industries, they argue, employers don't seek prosecution of minor infractions but are willing to report them to employment databases. USIS says its retail records have identified more than 30,000 applicants with histories of theft in just the past few years. All theft reports are re-verified with the employer that submitted them before being shared with an inquiring company, USIS says. But mistakes occur, and once a worker is flagged, it can be nearly impossible to work again in retail.

Two screening companies got it wrong in the case of Ingrid Morales. In 2001, Morales, then 26, was fired after only a month as a makeup artist at a Saks Fifth Avenue store in Boca Raton, Fla. Saks cited a report supplied by a retail database, now owned by USIS, and a smaller Florida screening firm, Merchants Security Exchange. The screeners said she had been terminated from a Burdines department store in 1995 for "unauthorized taking of merchandise" valued in the hundreds of dollars. Morales denied the theft allegations. But it wasn't until she sued Burdines and the screening firms in federal court later in 2001 that the information was corrected. USIS deleted the negative reference, and Merchants Security changed her file so that it noted merely a company "policy violation" in connection with her use of an employee-discount card.

A judge dismissed her suit in 2003, ruling that she had not been defamed by Burdines, a part of what is now Macy's, and that the screening firms hadn't violated the law. A spokesman for MAF Background Screening, previously known as Merchants Security, says that "mistakes do happen" and that the Morales case illustrates why applicants should review their background reports. USIS and Macy's decline to comment.

Morales, now 33 and the mother of three children, says that her firing and inability to find work again at store cosmetics counters put her family in a financial bind for several years. Her husband's construction business has since taken off, and she helps manage it from home. But she's still bitter about the background report. "It ruined my whole career, and I felt very humiliated," she says. "They can put whatever they want in your file, and you can't get work." . . .

POSTSCRIPT

Would Mandatory Background Checks for All Employees Reduce Negligent Hiring Lawsuits?

Researchers and practitioners suggest that organizations must use a lot of caution when hiring applicants by thoroughly investigating their backgrounds. Though this process might be an additional step in the hiring process, it can save organizations a lot of liability and most importantly ensure a safe working environment for employees and customers. Several court cases indicate that sexual offenders, kidnappers, and criminals try to conceal their background and transition smoothly back to the workplace. Unfortunately, their past wrongful acts haunt them, and they commit those harmful crimes again. A case in point, Avis was sued in 1979 for negligent hiring when an employee raped a co-worker. Subsequently, it was learned that the employee had a history of violence and a criminal record that the company had failed to unearth because it did not conduct a background check. The female co-worker was awarded $750,000.

Organizations have a liability in checking applicants' backgrounds to ensure a safe workplace. Regardless of the type of the job, organizations should bear the burden of thorough applicant checking. Organizations that fail to do background checks can tarnish their image by improper hiring and, of course, pay heavy lawsuits. For employees to prove there is negligent hiring, the plaintiff must prove the following factors: 1) existence of an employment relationship, 2) the employee's incompetence (who committed the act), 3) the employer's awareness of such incompetence, and 4) the employer's omission of checking on an employee's (who committed the act) work background.

However, organizations that do conduct background checks have become such an unregulated industry that it is very difficult to verify the accuracy of the information coming from such sources. Several industry cases report that employees are wrongfully reported while their work records have actually been clean. Therefore, employees have struggled to get employment because their professional images have been stigmatized forever. Another case in point is that of Ingrid Morales, who was a retail employee working for a Saks Fifth Avenue store in 2001 and was fired when background checks revealed that she had a past record of stealing merchandise. Morales denied such accusations and sued the company for improper defamation. It came to light that the background checking organization had made a mistake. However, for several years after that, Morales and her family were under severe financial stress because her work record always seemed to have that blemish.

Suggested Readings

Ron Lashier, "Background Screening Can Diminish Hiring Mistakes," *SDM* (vol. 36, no. 10, pp. 93–94, October 2006).

Pamela Babcock, David Marino-Nachison, "Foreign Assignments," *HR Magazine* (vol. 50, no. 10, pp. 91–92, 94, 96, 98, October 2005).

K. Morris, "Don't Forget the Background Check," *Hotel and Motel Management* (vol. 223, no. 10, p. 8, June 2008).

Judy Greenwald, "Employers Must Exercise Caution with Background Checks," *Business Insurance* (vol. 41, no. 18, pp. 4, 80, April 2007).

S. Wells, "Ground Rules on Background Checks," *HR Magazine* (vol. 53, no. 2, pp. 47–48, 50, 52, 54, February 2008).

Negligent Hiring in Illinois: http://www.illinoislawyerblog.com/2009/02/negligent_hiring_in_illinois_1.html.

Corporate Liability: Sharing the Blame for Workplace Violence: http://www.apasecurity.net/news.htm.

How Reliable Are Online Background Checks?: http://ezinearticles.com/?How-Reliable-Are-Online-Background-Checks?&id=791570.

ISSUE 8

Is Cognitive Ability Testing a Good Predictor of Work Performance?

YES: Martha J. Frase, from "Smart Selections," *HR Magazine* (December 2007)

NO: Rangarajan (Raj) Parthasarathy, from "Emotional Intelligence and the Quality Manager: Beauty and the Beast?" *The Journal for Quality and Participation* (January 2009)

ISSUE SUMMARY

YES: Martha Frase, freelance writer, suggests that cognitive ability tests are excellent predictors of work performance because they are objective, valid, and reliable. Further, these tests can be administered to a variety of job categories from entry to executive levels.

NO: Raj Parthasarathy, process improvement manager, states that emotional intelligence is the best predictor of job performance because it involves critical components of self and relationship management. Researchers are paying increasing attention to emotional intelligence (EI) as its components have positive consequences on job performance.

$\mathbf{A}$lfred Binet, French psychologist, introduced cognitive ability testing in 1905 to distinguish intelligence levels in school children. Over the decades, this method of distinguishing intelligence levels became specialized and was adopted at organizations as well. Today several tests are available off the shelf that cater to specific job environments. The results of cognitive ability testing are used to identify the intelligence quotient (IQ).

Cognitive ability, referred to as "g", by psychologists, is considered an excellent predictor of job performance for any job occupation. Primarily, people with higher cognitive abilities are able to apply learned information effectively. Second, people with higher "g" levels are able to learn and process information much faster. Therefore, such higher intelligence levels help employees perform their jobs more effectively. Further, cognitive ability tests are considered cost-effective because they can be provided to multiple applicants at the same time. Finally, they can be objectively and numerically scored. However, cognitive ability tests create adverse impact or unintentional discrimination against certain ethnic groups.

Cognitive ability testing has become very specialized today and can be used to cater to specific organizational levels. Executive cognitive ability testing is one such area that has received significant attention as executives direct and manage their organizations. Executives usually have to perform diverse tasks of integrating information, analyzing critically, and solving business problems. Cognitive ability testing helps identify such higher-order thinking skills. Further, executives are usually expected to perform quickly once they have been hired. Such mental ability testing becomes a useful tool to identify talent that will perform at such superior levels quickly.

Practitioners also suggest that "g" testing provides a sense of exclusiveness because it identifies superior talent. This also provides a sense of elitism to the hired applicants. Many high-profile organizations such as Microsoft and Google adopt such cognitive ability testing to identify their talent. Organizations that adopt such exclusive methods of recruitment emphasize a performance-driven culture.

On the other hand, practitioners and scholars applaud the concept of emotional or social intelligence (or EI). Daniel Goleman introduced this concept to businesses in the 1990s, and it has slowly gained tremendous importance. EI can be identified with two distinct components—"self" and "social." Self-management includes how well people are aware of their emotions and are cognizant of their levels of motivation. Social components involve how people manage professional relationships and collective interactions.

People with high EI demonstrate high motivation levels, superior team skills, and excellent stress-management skills. Research has shown that in organizational settings, high scorers on EI tend to provide inspiring leadership. They are highly self-motivated and sensitive to listen to the concerns of others. They are able to provide clear rational decisions based on careful and thoughtful decision-making processes. Why would companies not want to hire employees with such profiles.

While researchers debate over the nature versus nurture role (heredity versus environment) on cognitive intelligence, EI is considered largely a developed trait. Over the years, individuals shape their personal and social competences of EI based on the unique experiences and opportunities they encounter. Developing EI is considered a repetitive process—similar to that of building blocks—building one component of EI leads to developing another.

Today's business world abounds with global frameworks, intense competition, and economic downturns, placing a lot of emphasis on self and relationship management. Organizations are seeking to get talented individuals who can distinguish themselves in the crowded marketplace. Recruiting and hiring employees in organizations therefore has become a strategic priority for firms as they navigate in this complex business world.

An international perspective suggests that many countries adopt the method of testing (cognitive and emotional) to identify talent. Scholars also suggest that countries that have a strong uncertainty-avoidance (a cultural orientation for elaborate procedures and policies) tend to have more psychometric testing in their staffing process.

YES ↵

Martha J. Frase

Smart Selections

Intelligence tests are gaining favor in the recruiting world as reliable predictors of future executive performance.

In the complex process of selecting talent for executive posts, it's common to have candidates take tests designed to measure various characteristics—behavior, for example, or personality, attitudes, integrity or "emotional intelligence."

Lately, a less common type of test—one that measures pure cognitive ability—has been gaining ground among recruiting professionals, particularly those in executive hiring.

"There is a movement to convince companies to do mental ability tests," says Frank L. Schmidt, Ph.D., the Ralph L. Sheets Professor in the Department of Management and Organizations at the University of Iowa in Iowa City. "Academic research is driving this, as evidence is accumulating that mental ability is the best way to measure predicted job performance."

Schmidt has been doing much of that research. His decade-long work suggests that general cognitive ability influences job performance largely through its role in the acquisition and use of information about how to do one's job. People with higher levels of cognitive ability acquire information faster and more easily, and are able to use that information more effectively.

Concerns at the Start

Certainly, some HR professionals question the usefulness and even the fairness of administering intelligence tests in connection with candidate selection. A major concern is that intelligence tests discriminate against certain groups.

Linda Bond has had serious doubts. About 15 years ago, when she was director of human resources at GTE's Management Development Center in Norwalk, Conn., she was concerned that minorities were at a disadvantage because of culturally biased questions and differences in academic exposure, and there was little evidence at the time to prove otherwise.

But in the years since, the science of assessing general cognitive ability—known to psychologists as "g"—has evolved, alongside strong evidence that rigorously designed and executed intelligence tests are not culturally biased.

So Bond has altered her position. "Executive intelligence testing now tends to be more situational, and it has a place and a value," she says. "There appear to be tools to measure and assess critical thinking and leadership skills."

Bond, who left GTE and earned a law degree, represents employers in employment and labor cases for Rumberger, Kirk and Caldwell PA, in Tallahassee, Fla. Now, she says, as she looks at the use of intelligence testing in candidate selection "from a legal perspective, I say, go for it, as long as you can prove it does not have a discriminatory impact and that there is a legitimate business reason for the testing." She adds that in her more than 10 years of legal practice, she has never seen a discrimination case based on intelligence testing.

Qualified Support

Intelligence testing for executive candidates is, for some, a useful tool but not an exclusive one. "In the hiring process, it's important to gather as much information about candidates as possible that relate to the job criteria," says Lori A. LePla, Ph.D., a consultant in organizational development and personnel assessment for Plante & Moran, a global certified public accounting and business advisory firm based in Southfield, Mich.

"G" can be used as a baseline screening at lower levels, she says, but in filling executive-tier posts, "it's another piece of data we have to predict future performance."

In her consulting practice, LePla uses a variety of standardized tests, including intelligence tests. "In general, we find that it's one component of a best-practice selection system that would have several components. As organizations become more progressive, they incorporate more of these best practices."

Not everyone accepts "g" as a necessary selection criterion, however. "It's not wide enough as an indicator to be leaned on really heavily," says Lester Levine, senior director of human capital management for Day & Zimmermann, a Philadelphia-based global provider of engineering, security, and other business services with 23,000 employees. "But if you are looking to have the complete picture—say, trying to select between two really qualified people—it's another arrow in the quiver."

Levine says that while "g" may be "a very good test of potential and has been used that way, people who are selecting senior-level employees are looking for those who have applied that potential."

In other words, why test executive candidates for intelligence when you already know that they are smart? After all, Levine says, "you are picking from people who have been very successful or they wouldn't be on your radar screen. That's fairly good documentation that you have to be pretty smart to get there in the first place."

Justin Menkes, managing director of New York-based Executive Intelligence Group, who provides executive talent assessment to clients, agrees that past performance is the acid test of an executive's potential for success. "But measuring this can be really rough," he says. "It's hard to collect numeric data when you are relying on a candidate's descriptions, truthfulness, and information that is sometimes hard to pull out. An intelligence test makes somebody figure out the right answer in front of you, in the moment, showing their facility for problem-solving."

In fact, intelligence testing can work as a marketing tool for the hiring company, Menkes says. "Executives can't stand the dog-and-pony [show]—the popularity contest of the interviewing process. Anyone at their level can tell a good story, and doing that can be tiresome." But a chance to show their off-the-cuff problem-solving skills in an intelligence test can get them fired up about the job and the company, he says.

Indeed, although it might seem as though senior executives would bristle at a requirement to take tests of their brain power, most candidates actually like such tests, according to industrial and organizational (I/O) psychologists who use cognitive testing. Schmidt says candidates often view the tests as an opportunity to show their mettle. "The job then means more to the successful candidate because not just anyone could have gotten it."

Targeted Applications

Different hiring circumstances lend to the usefulness of intelligence tests, LePla says. "If a candidate has a prior history of on-the-job learning, has had great mentors, has tried-and-tested solutions in his or her toolkit, and is applying for a position that is very similar to previously held positions in which they've had proven success, then intelligence tests will not give us much unique information.

"But if you know the candidate will need to face a steep learning curve or will be making decisions outside of [his or her] area of expertise, the intelligence test can be helpful in predicting how quickly and effectively the candidate will perform."

Schmidt offers another possible reason for intelligence tests for proven executives: the politics of internal hiring. "Sometimes, you are in the position of selecting among internal candidates who are already part of the top management team," he says. "No matter who is chosen, they will have to work together, and it can be a touchy position to have to promote one over another.

"Intelligence testing can provide a more objective, quantifiable way to predict which candidate will be best for this particular job."

Menkes notes that some companies give a classic IQ test to every candidate because "they want to be a culture of academic excellence. They want book-smart people; they don't care if the IQ cutoffs are a turnoff" to candidates.

Beyond the No. 2 Pencil

Intelligence testing was developed by French psychologist Alfred Binet in 1905, initially to identify schoolchildren who needed special instruction. "It was never intended to be a holistic measure of intelligence," says Menkes. "The classical Stanford-Binet IQ test is a powerful predictor of how well someone will do in school, but it becomes less predictive in other applications."

So unless you are promoting a Mensa-type culture, Menkes says, look for an instrument that measures what he calls "executive intelligence." Such instruments can evaluate skills such as the ability to identify flawed assumptions, recognize unintended consequences, evaluate the quality of data, or identify the core issues in a conflict—all in a format that more accurately emulates the real business environment," he says.

There are hundreds of established intelligence tests on the market, so if you are committed to establishing an assessment program, you might want to try a few to find one that fits your business.

Marni Dorman, SPHR, corporate director of human resources at the Scott McRae Group, an automotive sales company based in Jacksonville, Fla., uses both the Hogan Personality Profile and the Watson Glaser Aptitude Assessment. "We use these in the selection process for all levels of management in our auto dealerships and in our Auto Credit Finance Division as well," Dorman says. Test results do not eliminate candidates, she says, "but these assessments seem to be right on target for predicting success in our industry."

The two tests are used together, Dorman explains, to determine both a candidate's leadership style and his or her ability to acquire new skills. Some auto dealership managers have been dictatorial in the past, she says. "We're striving to get away from this, and also to get insights into candidates' capacity to learn." It was the company's in-house I/O psychiatrist, she continues, who decided that "this particular one-two punch is the best for us."

Menkes prefers to sidestep "fill in the bubble" standard instruments; he conducts intelligence tests as structured 30-minute interviews in which candidates consider practical situations that are germane to the position. Usually, the interview is carried out by an HR professional or an I/O psychologist. All interviewees are asked the same questions, and their responses are scored. "You are looking for them to get to one or two 'right' answers," he says, so that results can be measured and compared with those of other candidates.

Deciding on a Test

Most publishers offer off-the-shelf tests and have experts who can tailor a version to your business needs. The advantage of an off-the-shelf test, Menkes says, is that it comes with a large pool of results that you can use to compare your candidates' performances with others who have taken the same test.

Typically, tests are sold as individual units for use by one candidate, starting at $10 for each off-the-shelf test. If you decide to construct your own test or to tailor an off-the-shelf exam to your needs, it's essential that you work with an I/O psychologist to ensure that the test can be validated, say assessment experts such as John W. Jones, Ph.D. While it may seem like a time-consuming step, it's necessary "to avoid test misuse," he explains. "You need to verify your instrument with qualified people. The end product must be properly constructed and validated so there is no impact against protected groups."

Jones, president and senior I/O psychologist for IPAT Inc., a developer of assessment tools and strategies for employee selection and coaching in Savoy Ill., says it is always more complicated to do it yourself than to use an off-the-shelf product, but "a lot of companies have in-house industrial psychologists who can develop a scorable interview that presents intellectual scenarios and hypothetical simulations that skew toward intelligence and mental ability."

If you don't have an in-house expert, Jones suggests, check with the Society for Industrial and Organizational Psychology "to see if there are I/O psychologists in the neighborhood or at the local university, so you can ask them questions about what's appropriate for your selection needs." He also notes that the American Psychological Association "has rigid professional standards that guide testing and use."

In addition, Jones recommends contacting the Association of Test Publishers (ATP), which represents providers of tests and assessment tools and services related to assessment, selection, screening, certification, licensing, and educational or clinical uses. "Their members are committed to only turning out scientific, legally sound instruments," he says.

Jones advises contacting several ATP members, telling them about your business needs and seeing how they respond. Your I/O expert can then evaluate the responses to help you pick the top three publishers so you can ask them to present a formal proposal. "You want to make sure they send you all relevant research on the instruments they use," he says.

Use your I/O expert to help you make a final choice of publisher and test. "It's better when you have a psychologist as a second opinion, but make sure to pick someone without a bias or business relationship with any publishers," Jones says.

Assessing the Results

Once candidate testing is completed, Jones suggests, bring back your I/O expert for a day to do a comprehensive assessment and to compile a short list of about three candidates for review.

"Hiring managers often do see actual scores," says Schmidt, and they can get a lot of information this way. But some companies prefer to mask numeric scores "by using a simple code that puts candidates into a range, like green, yellow, red."

But there is nothing wrong with letting candidates see their own results, Menkes says. "This is a great tool for feedback." He concludes that intelligence testing, "if you do it right, will bring a positive reaction from executive candidates. They get to demonstrate their problem-solving [skills] in a job-relevant way. They respect that, and it leaves an impression of a business culture that cares about excellence. That's not a bad message when you are recruiting."

Online Resources

For more information on intelligence testing in executive hiring, see the online version of this article . . . for links to

- An article on using standardized tests in hiring
- SHRM research on selection tests
- The Society for Industrial and Organizational Psychology
- The Association of Test Publishers
- The American Psychological Association's Testing Information Clearinghouse

Rangarajan (Raj) Parthasarathy　　　　　　　➡ **NO**

Emotional Intelligence and the Quality Manager: Beauty and the Beast?

$\mathbf{T}$he world of quality has undergone several transformations over the years. The 1960s and '70s focused on quality control (a reactive approach) rather than on quality assurance (a proactive approach). A quality manager in this era monitored various metrics and calculations in a bid to correct the process and prevent future problem occurrences.

In the '80s, radical reforms occurred in quality management, and the concept of total quality management gained popularity. During this period, the focus of the quality manager was split between quality control and quality assurance. The quality manager of the '80s was required to focus not just on the current process, but also on the design phase that dictated the process to use and also on planning for quality. Engineering schools began to teach a course titled "design for manufacturability," which emphasized that product design must facilitate manufacturing of parts with acceptable quality.

The '90s saw quality assurance and defect prevention take precedence over quality control. The word "defects" was replaced by "nonconformities." A new viewpoint emerged—by working proactively it was possible to produce products that conform to specifications. The concept of Six Sigma was popularized by Motorola and adopted enthusiastically by GE and other companies. With the goal of Six Sigma set at 3.5 or fewer defects per million opportunities, the role of the quality manager became complex, requiring interaction with all departments of the organization including purchasing, design, production, and fulfillment.

The quality buzzword of the present decade is Lean Six Sigma, a combination of the best practices of Six Sigma and Lean manufacturing. The quality manager of this decade is required to be a dynamic and multi-faceted individual with excellent interpersonal skills and breadth of knowledge. To succeed in this environment, the quality manager of today needs to have not only intelligence, but also emotional intelligence in good measure.

What Is Emotional Intelligence?

The term emotional intelligence was used for the first time by renowned psychologist Daniel Goleman. He emphasized two key domains in emotional intelligence: the personal competence domain (self-awareness and

From *Journal for Quality and Participation*, vol. 31, issue 4, January 2009, pp. 31–34 (refs. omitted).

self-management) and the social competence domain (social awareness and relationships management). Self-awareness includes emotional self-awareness (recognizing the impact of emotions on decision making), self-assessment (knowing the strengths and weaknesses of oneself), and self-confidence (knowledge of self-worth and capabilities). Another important aspect of emotional intelligence is relationship management, which includes traits such as inspirational leadership, conflict resolution capability, and capacity for teamwork.

Carter summarized emotional intelligence as self-awareness, self-motivation, empathy, management of relationships, and management of one's emotions. Craig described emotionally intelligent people as those who can maintain their course and stay calm in the face of pressure and disagreement from the important people in their lives. We may conclude from these definitions that an emotionally intelligent individual does not make decisions based on emotions alone or without considering all the facts of the situation at hand. Instead, he/she makes decisions objectively and dispassionately, with due consideration given to the facts, while emotions based on prejudice and stress are discounted.

An emotionally intelligent quality manager will listen to the viewpoints of representatives from all departments of the company and consider them dispassionately when making decisions impacting product quality and quality assurance. He/she is then able to communicate the rationale behind the decision to personnel at all levels in the organization and work with them to assure product quality without precipitating unnecessary conflicts and without breeding antagonism. In addition, such a manager is able to achieve a good balance between work life and personal life, even in the face of increasing workload and pressures. Last but not the least, such a manager is able to motivate and energize his/her direct reports to achieve optimal outcomes.

Intelligence Versus Emotional Intelligence

Cognitive intelligence (or intelligence as it is normally described) is the ability to perform a task by applying technical or non-technical education acquired using analysis, reasoning, and logic. Clearly, cognitive intelligence does not include relationship management and non-emotion-based decision making in the way emotional intelligence does. Emotional intelligence, by contrast, has very little to do with formal education or analytical skills. Emotional intelligence has everything to do with relationship management and the ability to get along with others, as well as the ability to make sound decisions in an atmosphere of stress, emotions, and pressure.

An individual, therefore, can have a very high level of cognitive intelligence with little or no emotional intelligence and vice-versa. There is no doubt that technical jobs still require a threshold level of cognitive intelligence, whether this is acquired through education or experience; however, all jobs in today's corporate world require emotional intelligence. Cherniss and Goleman emphasized the importance of emotional intelligence in the workplace. Research by Feist and Barron concluded that social and emotional abilities (emotional intelligence) are four times as important as intelligence quotient (a measure of cognitive intelligence) in determining professional success. Singh argues that although cognitive intelligence is important, it is emotional intelligence that decides one's success in the long term.

Emotional Intelligence: Acquired or Developed?

Craig refers to "development spurs" in life, which are transformational in nature. As individuals encounter such development spurs, their behavior and attitudes change; thus, two individuals who start out with identical psychological dispositions will react differently to the same situations based on the specific development spurs they have encountered with the passage of time. We can conclude that emotional intelligence is not acquired overnight, but rather develops over time based on one's experiences and development spurs.

Damasio found that the thinking side of the brain does not work in isolation from the emotional side of the brain. It is believed that human beings developed from monkeys, and monkeys have a well developed emotional brain. The emotional brain seems to be more primitive than the thinking brain and is usually the first to spring into action either for defense or in the face of a stressor. This is consistent with Selye's description of the "fight or flight response" of humans when encountering a stressful situation. The ultimate response to stress in this situation consists of the following phases: alarm reaction, resistance, and exhaustion. It is interesting to note that the final outcome of such a reaction is exhaustion.

An emotionally intelligent individual will not react in either of the above ways to a stressful or an emotionally-charged situation. Instead, an emotionally intelligent individual will have conditioned his/her thinking brain to work in close association with the emotional brain to temper the situational response in the most appropriate way. It is conceivable that such an individual also will apply the same conditioned response in a stressful situation, minimizing or avoiding the fight or flight syndrome referred to by Selye. As emotional intelligence is a conditioned response, it not only can be developed, but also honed, over time to encompass various situational horizons including personal tragedies and shocking situations. The development of emotional intelligence also has an "iterative effect" because as one develops a certain amount of emotional intelligence, this helps the person become more emotionally intelligent, increasing the overall rate of developing emotional intelligence.

Leadership Without Emotional Intelligence

According to Davis and Newstrom, leadership is the process of encouraging and helping others to work enthusiastically toward objectives. Fiedler's contingency model of leadership suggests that the effectiveness of a leader depends on the favorability of a given situation to the leader and states that "leader-member relations," "task structure," and "leader position power" are the three key aspects influencing leadership success. Hersey and Blanchard's situational leadership theory evaluates leadership effectiveness based on compatibility with the maturity level of the employees.

It follows from the above definitions of leadership that a leader needs to be emotionally intelligent to succeed. Stated differently, the leader's degree of success is directly proportional to the level of emotional intelligence attained by the leader. A leader has to work with and influence co-workers. This is nothing more than the relationship management domain of emotional intelligence. Also, as the popular saying goes, "It can be lonely at the top." A leader must be able to make decisions individually as well as in a group setting. Juran and Gryna refer to rewarding individualism as much as rewarding collectivism in an organizational setting as both have their place in the organization.

The buck usually stops at the leader's desk, so leaders should have the ability to make non-emotional and objective decisions, which is possible with emotional intelligence. When a leader has to criticize, it should be through constructive criticism, aimed at bettering an employee or a situation, and never destructive criticism. In the face of opposition, a leader must have the emotional intelligence to hold his/her ground and explain his/her decision objectively. If the outcome proves that the decision was a mistake, a leader must have the humility to accept the mistake and move forward. The leader must learn from the mistake so it is not repeated. Only by displaying these qualities can a leader hope to earn the respect of co-workers and colleagues. Since these leadership traits are part and parcel of emotional intelligence, a leader without emotional intelligence is likely to be a failure in both professional and personal terms.

Achieving Success With Emotional Intelligence

Emotional intelligence helps an individual deal efficiently and effectively with his/her personal and professional life, without getting into emotion-based decision making. The world is becoming increasingly complex due to the social, political, technological, and economic changes. Individuals without emotional intelligence react to pressures from these changes in undesirable ways, producing unpalatable or even illegal outcomes. Such individuals not only bring harm to themselves but also to any professional organization with which they are associated. Organizations naturally seek to hire individuals who possess a high degree of emotional intelligence. These individuals will help their employers in tangible and intangible ways by displaying aspects of emotional intelligence such as unyielding motivation, effective conflict resolution, and dedication to the task at hand.

Charles Darwin's theory of "survival of the fittest" is truer today than ever. Emotional intelligence enables an individual to adapt to the environment at hand without giving up his/her basic principles or losing ground. Emotional intelligence has a lifelong impact on individuals and enables them to face the trials and tribulations of life with self-confidence and realism.

An individual with emotional intelligence definitely will be a part of the fittest of this complex world and will have the ability to survive its ups and downs with dignity and grace, while successfully adding value in his/her professional and personal life.

Conclusion

The lack of emotional intelligence can break or significantly slow a professional's career progression in today's complex world. This is especially true for the quality manager because he/she must interact successfully with employees at all levels in the organization and with suppliers and customers from all cultures. The presence of emotional intelligence in the employees of a company (including the quality manager) will have an impact on improving profitability and productivity. Although today's manufacturing world is complicated, the manufacturing world of the future will be even more so. By developing and utilizing emotional intelligence in work life and in personal life, the quality manager (or for that matter, all employees and managers) will be a "beauty" to his/her environment instead of being the "beast!"

POSTSCRIPT

Is Cognitive Ability Testing a Good Predictor of Work Performance?

Organizations are constantly seeking the best talent and adopting different hiring practices to get the right applicant. Cognitive ability and emotional intelligence testing are applauded by their eclectic researchers for various reasons. Bill Gates, founder of Microsoft, made a dramatic statement in the late 1990s when he openly stated that his company uses a lot of cognitive testing as he wanted "brains in his office." Several researchers resonate similar thoughts that higher levels of IQ lead to superior levels of job performance.

Further, psychologists and researchers today can modify cognitive tests to cater to distinct work environments. This has made this method of testing, initially developed for school children, available to a wider audience in both the academic and corporate environment. The intelligence tests can also be scored objectively minimizing any favoritism that could blur objectivity in staffing. Employees with higher levels of intelligence learn work quicker, assimilate information faster, and process ideas better creating a much superior work environment.

On the other hand, researchers suggest that higher levels of EI create superior work performance. Individuals with higher levels of EI demonstrate a greater understanding of their own personalities and also in managing their relationships with others. Also, in work environments, they exhibit inspiring leadership skills to their professional peers. Such individuals are also driven by their own sense of achievement and motivation and they frequently raise their bar for performance.

Daniel Goleman, from his extensive research on 200 large companies, suggests that testing for EI definitely will have positive consequences in the workplace. For instance, high scores on self-management result in employees who are confident, realistic, motivated, and open to change. High scores on the social component help employees build relations with customers, develop coherent teams, and become visionary leaders.

The debate over whether cognitive or emotional intelligence is a better predictor of job performance continues as researchers, practitioners, and psychologists devise novel methods to test employees. Why is cognitive testing frowned upon by organizations but a necessary criterion for any university admission (SAT, GMAT, GRE)? Why is EI not tested for in universities and schools? Such questions will continue to concern both practitioners and researchers alike.

Suggested Readings

Cognitive ability tests: http://www.opssc.wa.gov.au/recruitment/3_select/tools/cognitive.htm

Cognitive ability tests: http://apps.opm.gov/adt/Content.aspx?page=3-04&AspxAutoDetectCookieSupport=1&JScript=1

Daniel Seligman, "Brains in the Office," *Fortune* (vol. 135, no. 1, p. 38, 1997).

"Digits," *Wall Street Journal* (Eastern Edition) (p. B.3, 2004).

EI Definitions Comparison Table: http://eqi.org/comp_tab.htm

Emotional Intelligence: Issues and Common Misunderstandings: http://www.eiconsortium.org/reprints/ei_issues_and_common_misunderstandings.html

Jane Simms, "Powered by Emotions," *Supply Management* (vol. 8, no. 17, pp. 20–24, 2003).

Lin Grensing-Pophal, "Plays Well with Others . . . ," *Credit Union Management* (vol. 21, no. 5, pp. 52–54, 1998).

Internet References . . .

Women Face Glass Ceiling in Hiring

About.com is a Web property that is part of The New York Times Company and frequently publishes current debatable events. This article addresses the different paths that women are sometimes required to take when building their career while men with the same qualifications are often allowed to skip over these same steps. You will also find related links at this Web site.

http://careerplanning.about.com/od/forwomenonly/a/glass_ceiling.htm

Are Women Happy under The Glass Ceiling?

Forbes is an international business magazine that publishes the latest business and economic activities. The article found here discusses the invisible barrier between women and men in the workforce.

http://www.forbes.com/2006/03/07/glass-ceiling-opportunities--cx_hc_
0308glass.html

Women in Business

Here you will find several articles and links discussing women in business and the challenges they face and overcome.

http://womenshistory.about.com/od/business/tp/women_business_leaders.htm

Women Leaders and Organizational Change

Harvard Business School Working Knowledge is a forum for innovation in business practice, offering readers a first look at cutting-edge thinking and the opportunity to both influence and use these concepts before they enter mainstream management practice. In this article, the authors call for fundamental changes to transform organizations. They discuss how merely expanding the number of women in leadership roles does not automatically induce organizational change.

http://hbswk.hbs.edu/item/3796.html

Women in Corporate Levels

*H**ave women reached the corporate levels they really want to? Do they enhance business profits? For several decades, women seemed to struggle for an equal footing in employment, and this section addresses these questions on the role of women in the American workplace. Women have traditionally faced an unspoken barrier in corporate circles. Scholars and critics have applauded women for their leadership characteristics that could augment or decrease business goals. How do corporate women perform today?*

- Does the Glass Ceiling Still Exist in U.S. Organizations?
- Do Women Make Better Business Leaders?

ISSUE 9

Does the Glass Ceiling Still Exist in U.S. Organizations?

YES: **Jessica Marquez**, from "Gender Bias Found to Start Early in Career," *Workforce Management* (June 2009)

NO: **Anonymous**, "Breaking the Glass Ceiling," *Black Enterprise* (February 2009)

ISSUE SUMMARY

YES: Jessica Marquez, journalist at *Workforce Management,* suggests that women face a glass ceiling, possibly because their careers generally begin much later and they have more career interruptions due to family commitments.

NO: *Black Enterprise* journalists state that women do occupy top-notch positions. The effort is in finding the right universities and organizations that will actively support such diversity initiatives.

The term "glass ceiling" appeared in the *Wall Street Journal* in 1986 in a discussion on corporate women and their career growth. The *glass-ceiling* concept can be defined as any promotional barriers women face to attaining higher positions or higher pay in organizations. Women traditionally have a difficult time trying to reach the upper levels of any institution because these levels have been stereotypically held by men. However, federal acts such as Title VII, Affirmative Action, and the Equal Pay Act have provided women a sense of equality at the workplace.

In 1970, women were 38 percent of the workforce, but today they represent almost 47 percent of the workforce. More than half of the college graduate degrees today are awarded to women. Women in the United States compete for the highest political position and also hold Supreme Court positions. Yet the path to the top seems to be a road less travelled by women.

Proponents suggest that statistics are misleading as women still face invisible barriers to become leaders in their field. Women are consistently misrepresented at every management level with the distinction becoming very stark in the upper echelons. A gender study indicated that women began to feel the discrimination even at the first level of management, where the representation of men exceeded women by 28 percent. This difference in gender representation increased to 50 percent, with men holding executive level positions half the time more than women. Another study on *Fortune* 500 companies suggests that women hold just 16 percent of corporate executive positions and constitute about 6 percent of top earners at *Fortune* 500 companies. Despite federal interventions, gender-biased pay patterns continue as women are still paid lower than men. In 2002, male CEOs of nonprofit organizations earned $147,085, while their female counterparts earned $98,108.

There are many reasons why women face such invisible barriers. Family obligations impede women from pursuing a linear career path as they tend to be the main caregivers. Women generally take career breaks to raise their children and support other family responsibilities. At the workplace, women usually do not participate in the "old boys'" network, an informal method of socializing, which helps employees become more visible to climb the corporate ladder. Women are not asked to frequently relocate as often as men are, possibly due to family commitments. Such opportunities usually provide promotional or developmental benefits. Many organizations do not provide work-life balance and a supportive environment conducive to women's corporate success.

Opponents feel women have inched their way into the corporate boardrooms. Their way to the top has been through the support of organizations that actively recruit and promote diversity, colleges that endorse protected groups, and women's networks that support active career planning. Organizations such as Macy's and Kellogg's, promote corporate diversity by having women in visible leadership positions. For instance, 75 percent of Macy's workforce is made up of women with about 66 percent in supervisory positions. Kellogg's promotes employee resource groups, such Women of Kellogg (WOK), which actively help women reach their highest professional levels through internal networking. Dell has women representing about one-third of its global employees and actively promotes women into leadership positions by encouraging all managers to be informal mentors to women. Colleges that actively promote protected groups (such as women and African Americans) help students find the best transition to organizations that would promote their careers. Women also find that they are able to plan and develop their careers better if they are a part of women's support groups that proactively have a career agenda. Women are also becoming entrepreneurs and therefore business leaders of their field. In a study of women and business types, women choose to launch their businesses as sole proprietorships instead of corporations, suggesting they want to be their own bosses.

The glass-ceiling experience exists in other countries also and is usually exacerbated by cultural and traditional gender stereotypes. Several cultures do not accept female business leaders, making the glass-ceiling concept even more obvious. However, politically, women make great strides. New Zealand appointed its first woman prime minister in 2000, the World Health Organization (WHO) appointed its first female director-general in 2002, and Mexico appointed its first female governor for the state of Yucatan in 2007. Why is there a discrepancy between political and corporate boardrooms?

YES

Jessica Marquez

Gender Bias Found to Start Early in Career

Abstract (Summary)

Despite discussion regarding women hitting the glass ceiling once they reach the executive level, discrimination starts much earlier in their careers, according to a recent paper by Development Dimensions International (DDI). Their data suggests that when you look at the things that would help people develop in their careers, women wouldn't get the same opportunities as men did, says Ann Howard, DDI's chief scientist. Many companies don't track how many women participate in high-potential programs, which also adds to this problem, says Jan Combopiano, VP and chief knowledge officer at Catalyst, a New York-based organization dedicated to helping businesses build inclusive workplaces for women.

Discrimination

Despite discussion regarding women hitting the glass ceiling once they reach the executive level, discrimination starts much earlier in their careers, according to a recent paper by Development Dimensions International.

"Holding Women Back," which is based on responses from 12,800 leaders in 76 countries, found that women face gender discrimination from the very beginning of their careers.

"Our data suggests that when you look at the things that would help people develop in their careers, women wouldn't get the same opportunities as men did," says Ann Howard, DDI's chief scientist.

One of the main areas where employers fail to include women is in their high-potential programs, where they identify those employees who managers believe could make strong leaders someday.

According to the study, there were 28 percent more men than women in high-potential programs at the first level of management and 50 percent more men than women in such programs at the executive level.

The problem with many companies' high-potential programs is that there is often no standard procedure to identify candidates, Howard says. Usually it is up to the managers to choose candidates, she adds.

From *Workforce Management*, 88:7, June 22, 2009, p. 8–9. Copyright © 2009 by Workforce Management. Reprinted by permission.

"I'm not saying that there is some evil plot here," Howard says. "It's just that managers might think about future executives as men because that is the traditional norm at the company."

Many companies don't track how many women participate in high-potential programs, which also adds to this problem, says Jan Combopiano, vice president and chief knowledge officer at Catalyst, a New York-based organization dedicated to helping businesses build inclusive workplaces for women.

"It's really important that there is accountability tied to these programs," Combopiano says. "It's critical for overcoming gender stereotyping."

Another way to make sure that women have the same opportunities as men to advance their careers is by having a.formal succession planning program in place, Howard says.

"It sets the same objective standards for everyone," she says.

Companies need to pay attention to all leadership development programs and make sure gender stereotypes don't get in the way of advancing women, Howard says.

"Employers need to have objective performance management standards in place," she says.

Too often a company will say that there aren't women in management roles because they took time off to have babies, but that often doesn't explain the issue, Howard says.

"The bottom line is that women are just as capable as men and if you have objective standards in place, women can show their stuff," she says.

Anonymous

→ **NO**

Breaking the Glass Ceiling

Abstract (Summary)

Tie past year will go down as a time of contrasts for African American women: While the very greatest advances made headlines, the numbers as a whole showed that things hadn't changed much for the broad majority—particularly in the executive ranks of the American economy. A study released last year found that whites are more often perceived as leaders than people of color. That said, a number of factors transform the "glass" ceiling that blocks women from entering the highest levels of corporate management into a concrete barrier that excludes African Americans. First, role models—African American women who have made it to the boardroom—are few and far between. A few specific steps in the year ahead could help any company make inroads in breeching the concrete ceiling. They include: 1. appointing a watchdog, 2. putting teeth in diversity, and 3. making mentorship count.

There's no way to sugarcoat the overall numbers: When it comes to bringing African American women into the boardroom, Corporate America still has its work cut out-and quite a lot to do by most indications.

The past year will go down as a time of contrasts for African American women: While the very greatest advances made headlines, the numbers as a whole showed that things hadn't changed much for the broad majority—particutarly in the executive ranks of the American economy. Yes, Barack Obama was elected president and Hillary Clinton mounted what was arguably the strongest challenge a woman has yet made for the nation's top political office. . . .

The greatest challenge, of course, is to find ways to make meaningful change, especially at a time when companies are cutting back, retrenching, or calling it quits altogether. Progress is likely to stall while the global economy gropes for a way to dig out of last year's financial market collapse. "In an economic environment like this people are under stress, and under those circumstances it's not uncommon to see them turn to their natural inclinations and to become more conservative," says Katherine Phillips, a professor at Northwestern University's Kellogg School of Business. A study released last year that was co-authored by Phillips, a director of Northwestern's Center on the Science of Diversity, found that Whites are more often perceived as leaders than people of color. "In this environment it's going to be difficult for African Americans and women—and African American women in particular." Katherine Giscombe of Catalyst says there were signs that gender stereotyping was "alive and well," before 2008's hardships, particularly the notion that women are not as capable in problem solving.

In some ways, the numbers reflect a long-standing disparity in the American workplace. The last generation has seen women make great strides— Census Department figures from the last nationwide headcount show that women made up 47% of the U.S. personnel headcount, up from 38% in 1970. According to the same database, women are now more than half the employees in major occupations such as sales and office jobs, as well as in service and professional positions. Yet, despite these gains the Census Bureau's 2006 calculations show that women on average earned 77 cents for every dollar men take home.

That said, a number of factors transform the "glass" ceiling that blocks women from entering the highest levels of corporate management into a concrete barrier that excludes African Americans. First, role models—African American women who have made it to the boardroom—are few and far between. "We see that a major area of concern is the lack of connection to 'influential others'," says Giscombe. "Women of color have the same percentage of mentors, but the lack of a connection to someone who wields true influence or decision making power is quite telling."

Additionally, Catalyst studies have shown that women of color feel diversity and inclusion programs have been ineffective for them. Often, African American women complain that they are falling through the cracks. Giscombe says past Catalyst surveys have found that African American women create smaller in-company networks and often communicated informally within smaller company circles than their peers.

The good news? Experts say that for all of the turmoil that 2008 brought to the global economy, 2009 does not have to go down as a lost year in the push to include all women in the ranks of company directors, especially among the Fortune 500 elite. A few specific steps in the year ahead could help any company make inroads in breeching the concrete ceiling.

They include:

- Appointing a watchdog. Phillips says corporate diversity efforts have to be given more punch. One step is to move responsibility out of human resources and to put it in the hands of an executive with direct access to the board and CEO.
- Putting teeth in diversity. Giscombe and Phillips agree that financial incentives can move things along as well. "Companies have to put in place a strong sense of accountability," says Gicombe, "Everyone who oversees the initiative has to know that there is positive or negative reinforcement to back it up. Employees will support the effort more if they see that there's a positive impact to the bottom line."
- Making mentorship count. In some ways opening the door to greater numbers of African American women could act as precedent to prod other solutions into motion. According to Giscombe, bringing more

African American women into the boardroom will help keep progress on track by making mentorship more meaningful. "It's a signal that is very clear," she says, "Making sure there is variety in the senior levels always sends a strong message companywide." . . .

Macy's

Macy's, Inc's long-standing commitment to diversity and inclusion is reflected in its recognition as a top company for women by the National Association of Female Executives, Latina Style, and Essence. Two of Macy's top ranked women executives speak to the company's commitment to recruit, develop, and retain its female executives of color:

Felicia Williams, Vice President, Treasury and Risk Management comments, "Macy's commitment to recruiting and retaining women of color is evident throughout all levels of the Company. In my former role as head of Internal Audit, I had the opportunity to travel and interact with many of these women. As a result, I've been able to personally support the Company's recruitment and retention goals by establishing formal and informal mentoring relationships with many professional women of color around the Company."

"Macy's commitment to ensuring women of color are given the opportunity to join us and advance is noteworthy," says Ann Munson Steines, Vice President, Deputy General Counsel, and Assistant Secretary. The number of women and women of color in our ranks speaks to Macy's recognition that to be successful, we need to reflect our customer base.

In Macy's Law Department, women of color are represented at different levels and stages of their professional careers. Notably, women of color run a number of our key legal functions. However, even with our achievement in this area, we believe that we need to stay focused on making even greater progress."

Macy's commitment is reflected in its workforce, which is overall 75% women, with women representing nearly two thirds of Macy's managers.

Kelloggs

Attribute to: Sherri Toney, vice president, diversity and inclusion.

At Kellogg Company, we have a strong tradition of diversity and inclusion. Our founder, W.K. Kellogg, was a pioneer in employing women in the workplace and reaching across cultural boundaries. Our company carries on his legacy by ensuring our diversity strategy remains a top priority for the organization.

With today's demographic shifts, technological advances and worldwide connectivity . . . we live in a global marketplace that moves 24/7 and changes daily. Kellogg is part of that change. Today, people from all backgrounds and walks of life enjoy our products. Our marketplace and our workplace is becoming more diverse than ever before. Our Diversity and Inclusion Strategy enables us to not only build a culture reflective of the consumer bases we serve, but provides the best opportunity to develop high performing teams who will develop tomorrow's innovation.

Our company's commitment to diversity and inclusion is evident throughout the organization as well as in the communities where we live and operate. For example, our Executive Diversity and Inclusion Council, led by CEO David Mackay, is a cross-functional team that serves as a catalyst for driving new ways to build a culture of inclusion. With more than 300 suppliers representing businesses owned by minorities, women, and disabled veterans, Kellogg's supplier-diversity program builds on the belief that partnering with diverse suppliers opens up a pipeline to new ideas and innovative solutions. We also encourage opportunities for minorities and women, including support for the 100 Black Men of America, National Black MBA Association, NAACP Law Fellows Program, and other scholarship programs.

With over 30,000 employees worldwide, products manufactured in 19 countries and marketed in 180 countries around the world—Kellogg truly is a multinational, multicultural company. "One recipe, many ingrethents" is a belief that has helped us grow as a company for more than 100 years and will continue to guide us in our vision to become the food company of choice.

Chaka Elam

Chaka Elam began her career with Archer Daniels Midland Company as a summer intern in 1996. Today she manages the day-to-day production of fuel grade ethanol as the Alcohol Superintendent for the Decatur Processing Plant.

"I was attracted to ADM because of my positive experiences as an intern here. I was really drawn to the hands-on, practical style of engineering at ADM. I believe it fortifies your engineering education and gives you a good base to build on." Chaka points out that she observes diversity each day at ADM and no two days are ever the same. There is also the opportunity for continuous learning that sets ADM apart.

There are a lot of great things about ADM. Our approach to diversity helps make ADM a place where world-class talent comes to do its best work every day. We define diversity broadly, in keeping with our perspective as a global business. We see diversity as a broad mix of talented people: different genders, ethnicities and races as well as varied backgrounds, styles, cultures, and skills. Through global and crossfunctional teams, we build on diverse perspectives to achieve better results. . . .

Diversity has helped to make us who we are . . . a company where potential has no boundary, a company where you can make your mark. ADM is committed to being the best company we can be, a diverse team of individuals making a positive difference in the world. For more information please visit us at: http://www.admworld.com/naen/about/diversity.asp.

POSTSCRIPT

Does the Glass Ceiling Still Exist in U.S. Organizations?

The term "glass ceiling" appeared in the American press in the mid-1980s to signify how women struggle to climb up the corporate ladder. Women traditionally receive less pay than men and also are not represented well enough in upper levels of management. Advocates of the glass-ceiling concept suggest that such misrepresentation begins early in women's careers and becomes pronounced at executive levels. The possible reasons could be that women generally take a hiatus to fulfill either maternal or caregiver obligations. Also, women may not participate in after-office social networks as often as men do, which might be informal methods of rising to the top.

On the other hand, opponents of the glass-ceiling concept suggest a supportive managerial environment is a definite way for women to reach upper-level positions. Current and past successful women leaders such as Meg Whitman (eBay), Carol Tome (Home Depot), and Andrea Jung (Avon) suggest corporate cultures as a predominating factor for their corporate success. Organizations that actively promote representation of women in executive levels through formal succession planning or mentorship contribute to promoting women leaders. Further, some women choose to become their own leaders by starting their own businesses and completely eluding the glass-ceiling concept. While they traditionally started becoming entrepreneurs in retail or service, today they are expanding into software and technology.

Suggested Readings

Dan Gilgoff, "Investing in Diversity: American Corporations Have Long Lacked Minorities and Women at the Top. But More Employers, Recruiters, and Business Schools are Working on It," *U.S. News & World Report* (vol. 146, no. 10, p. 72, November 2009).

A. Nancherla, "One Step Forward, Two Steps Back," *T + D* (vol. 63, no. 7, p. 24, July 2009).

Anne Donnellon, Nan Langowitz, "Leveraging Women's Networks for Strategic Value," *Strategy & Leadership* (vol. 37, no. 3, p. 29–36, 2009).

Thurmond Woodard, "Developing Women Leaders," *Leadership Excellence* (vol. 23, no. 9, p. 10, September 2006).

Nancy Lockwood, "The Glass Ceiling: Domestic and International Perspectives, *HR Magazine* (vol. 49, no. 6, p. R2–R9, June 2004).

"Women to Watch (A Special Report); The Journal Report Online," *Wall Street Journal* (Eastern Edition) (R.2, November 19, 2007).

J. Brusino, "Women Entrepreneurs Choose a Different Path," *T + D* (vol. 63, no. 9, p. 21, September 2009).

Bureaucracy, Glass Ceiling Queer Pitch for India's Women Scientists: http://www.livemint.com/2009/06/01002900/Bureaucracy-glass-ceiling-que .html?pg=3.

Women Business Leaders: http://www.woopidoo.com/profession/women/ index.htm.

ISSUE 10

Do Women Make Better Business Leaders?

YES: Ann Pomeroy, from "Cultivating Female Leaders," *HR Magazine* (February 2007)

NO: Herminia Ibarra and Otilia Obodaru, from "Women and the Vision Thing," *Harvard Business Review* (January 2009)

ISSUE SUMMARY

YES: Ann Pomeroy, senior writer for *HR Magazine*, illustrates how organizations have identified that women are better business leaders with an example from Safeway. She states that women have some innate characteristics that serve them well as leaders.

NO: According to the research studies of INSEAD Professor Herminia Ibarra and her doctoral student, Otilia Obodaru, women demonstrate low visionary skills. These business skills are very important for strategizing and understanding the dynamic environment.

The results of a 2004 study on gender issues and *Fortune* 500 companies indicated that having female senior leaders contributed to a substantial increase in organizational profits and shareholder's wealth. Safeway, a grocery company, demonstrated to the corporate world that having a predominant female leadership talent contributed to increased sales and earnings for the company. The grocery store chain has 200,000 employees and is a very profitable $40 billion company in the supermarket industry.

Studies indicate that women have certain personality characteristics that make them natural leaders. Women are known to be very intuitive, which is considered an excellent trait for discerning underlying business problems. Women also are very communicative, which can make them more conducive to team-based environments. Women are able to multi-task different corporate roles very well as their experience in balancing work and life has prepared them to do so. Expatriate women (women who are sent overseas on work assignments) demonstrate greater sensitivity to local practices and cultures than men and therefore are considered an asset in multinational organizations. Women are considered empathetic of employees and customer concerns, making them very communicative leaders. They also demonstrate a great sense of tenacity and resilience, which is an excellent business trait in a corporate world known for deadlines and uncertainty. Women also tend to be more assertive than men in the workplace, perhaps to minimize any stereotypical association of their gender.

Safeway championed the cause of increasing female leadership talent in its stores since 2000 through a program called Retail Leadership Development (RLD). The organization has seen wonderful results both in increasing profits and attracting customers. Realizing that 70 percent of their customers are women, Safeway launched a very proactive program to develop female talent through development and mentoring. Larree Renda, executive vice-president and one of the 50 most powerful women in the supermarket industry, dedicated her efforts to ensure that top leadership relentlessly supported this gender-based initiative. Today Safeway female managers have increased their representation substantially by 42 percent since the RLD program was launched.

On the other hand, INSEAD Professor Ibarra and her student emphasize that women still have not made great strides in the corporate ranks because they do not demonstrate a strong sense of visionary skills. Their longitudinal study with 2,816 executives from 149 countries over 5 years indicated that women outshone men on several business qualities. In this study, women were more detailed-oriented, interactive, and diligent. However, they did not seem to have high scores on visionary skills—the ability to recognize new business opportunities and promote a strategic orientation. Visionary skills help identify strengths, weaknesses, threats, and opportunities, and also strategize effectively in any business environment. Scholars suggest that a lack of envisioning is very detrimental because such leaders cannot foresee their business strategy and seize good opportunities quickly.

These researchers also offered three possibilities for why females scored low on visionary skills. Women frequently rely on the opinion and judgment of their peers, making them feel less concerned about any strategic opportunities or threats. Women have been observed to rely on hard data and input for making business decisions. Frequently, strategic visioning might entail taking a big leap in the dark. Second, women fail to observe the broader picture of their industry or business environment although they may be effective leaders within their own organizations. Women fail to articulate clearly their organization's position in the entirety of their competitors and customers. Finally, women may not view envisioning as a critical leadership competency and hence not develop it accurately.

In another global study of 1,000 executives from 9 countries, men were viewed as more effective business leaders. The results of this study indicated that the most important quality male leaders demonstrated was the quality to inspire others successfully. Experts suggest the ability to inspire or the skill to encourage and persuade others is a very critical competency of leadership.

A global perspective suggests that the representation of female business leaders in many male-dominated cultures is skewed disproportionately. In India, women comprise a mere 1 percent of the upper-level positions, and, in Mexico, women represent only 7 percent of the managerial positions. However, a Thunderbird research study of females and leadership positions suggested that Sweden and Switzerland have a predominant participation of females in upper-level positions, suggesting a more egalitarian approach to leadership.

YES

Cultivating Female Leaders

Abstract (Summary)

Some companies are making significant progress in stripping away stumbling blocks to gender diversity. One of those companies is Safeway, a Fortune 50 corporation that began focusing a decade ago on ways to identify promote and retain high-potential women. The diversity strategy includes effective communication of the business case for diversity and programs that focus on leadership development, mentoring and work/life balance. Communicating the business case effectively to the entire organization starts with visible leadership at the top. When the women's initiative was implemented in 2000, the Retail Leadership Development program began to focus particularly on women and people of color, and targets were established to increase the number of women and minorities who go through the training. Another resource for women interested in advancing into management is the women's leadership network, established 10 years ago as part of the women's initiative. Since 2000, the number of female store managers has increased by 42%.

Retail grocery giant Safeway is seeing the results from long-standing efforts to help women advance in the company.

The research is clear and dramatic: Female executives can help improve a company's bottom line. According to a 2004 study by Catalyst, a research and advisory organization that focuses on women's issues, Fortune 500 companies with the highest percentages of female corporate officers saw, on average, a 35.1 percent higher return on equity and a 34.0 percent higher return to shareholders than companies with the lowest percentages of female corporate officers.

Yet, despite this correlation, companies don't seem to be doing enough to promote greater gender diversity at the executive level. In fact, progress in this area has essentially ground to a halt.

Catalyst, which has tracked this issue for 10 years, says the results of its latest census, the 2005 Catalyst Census of Women Corporate Officers and Top Earners of the Fortune 500, were disappointing. While the number of women in top positions increased slightly, "the growth rate for the past three years is dramatically lower than the rates we have seen in the past." In other words, Catalyst concludes, "progress has almost come to a standstill."

From *HR Magazine*, February 2007, pp. 44–50. Copyright © 2007 by Society for Human Resource Management, Alexandria, VA. Reprinted by permission via the Copyright Clearance Center.

In spite of these discouraging statistics, some companies are making significant progress in stripping away stumbling blocks to gender diversity. One of those companies is Safeway, a Fortune 50 corporation that began focusing a decade ago on ways to identify, promote and retain high-potential women.

Here is what the company is doing—and how it has prospered as a result.

Helping Women Succeed

Ten years ago, Safeway began facing increasingly stiff competition from up-market specialty grocers on one end and cut-rate pricing on the other from big box stores such as Walmart and Target. To meet these market challenges, the company began exploring programs to attract, develop and retain its best talent, and to position Safeway as an employer of choice.

Since 70 percent of its customers are women, the retail grocery giant also wanted to broaden the diversity of its workforce to reflect the customer base. The company recognized that a diverse workforce would help it better understand and respond to the needs of its customers, and that would give Safeway a competitive advantage in the marketplace.

Male leadership has long been the norm in the retail grocery industry, so the new programs required a real culture shift. Kim Farnham, director of HR planning, says Safeway took a series of steps aimed at changing the corporate culture to "a culture of development," one that focused on helping women—including women of color—advance into management.

The foundation of today's diversity initiative was laid down in 1997, says Farnham. A diversity workshop to educate managers was designed, balanced workforce goals were created, and a system that holds managers accountable for meeting those goals was developed. Metrics to track their success were put in place.

The goal throughout the planning phase was "to do it right, not to be first on the block," says Farnham. The resulting women's initiative, "Championing Change for Women: An Integrated Strategy," was fully implemented in 2000 as the first piece of Safeway's overall diversity initiative.

The diversity strategy includes effective communication of the business case for diversity and programs that focus on leadership development, mentoring and work/life balance. A rigorous accountability system for measuring and tracking balanced workforce goals alerts the company to any potential problems.

Communicating the Business Case

Larree Renda, executive vice president, chief strategist and administrative officer, says communicating the business case effectively to the entire organization starts with "visible leadership at the top. You need executives who talk the talk and also walk the walk, and I think we've been very good at that."

For example, CEO Steve Burd talks regularly with employees about diversity issues in live discussions and at town hall meetings and conferences.

He also makes a point of discussing diversity via taped satellite broadcasts, part of a program of weekly broadcasts that are sent to store managers and that frequently cover diversity. Managers are expected to make the broadcasts available to their employees. The programs, which can spark discussions at staff meetings in each store, are shown on monitors in the staff break room. In addition, employees can view the broadcasts on their computers, Renda says.

Renda, who was responsible for developing the unique instore broadcast/interactive TV network for training and communication, says the system allows the company to quickly broadcast live or taped programs simultaneously to the approximately 1,800 stores in Safeway's 10 divisions.

When it comes to the taped programs, "diversity is expected to be a regular item on the agenda," she says.

Employees also have access to a series of diversity DVDs featuring interviews with successful Safeway women and people of color.

Developing Future Leaders

Safeway likes to promote from within and has traditionally focused on the retail level as a source of potential managers. Many current executives came up from entry-level positions in Safeway stores through the Retail Leadership Development (RLD) program, a formal, full-time career development program. Farnham estimates that 90 percent of the company's 1,800 store managers moved up through the company ranks this way, and all but one of the 10 division presidents began their Safeway careers working in one of its stores, often as grocery baggers or salesclerks.

When the women's initiative was implemented in 2000, the RLD program began to focus particularly on women and people of color, and targets were established to increase the number of women and minorities who go through the training. Employees who are interested in becoming store managers can apply for the program by taking an entrance exam that tests such basic retail knowledge as understanding gross margins. Applicants also write an essay explaining how they would solve a business problem.

Those who successfully complete the 26-week program are immediately assigned to a store as an assistant manager—a position that can lead to corporate-level jobs.

Safeway's efforts to encourage women to advance don't end there, however. Recognizing that women often need to coordinate work schedules with family responsibilities, the company ensures that all qualified employees—including part-timers and those who work flexible schedules—have the same opportunities for coaching, development and advancement as those who work more traditional hours.

The company also realized that frequent relocations didn't work for some employees, particularly women. As a result, Safeway modified the once-traditional requirement that employees seeking to move up should broaden their experience by doing stints at a variety of company locations. . . .

Development Networks

Another resource for women interested in advancing into management is the women's leadership network, established 10 years ago as part of the women's initiative. The group sponsors such events as the "Women's Road Show," a series of presentations at Safeway locations throughout the country that highlight the success of individual Safeway women and provide learning and networking opportunities.

Wherever the "Road Show" executives speak, they also meet with women in the area who've been identified as likely candidates for management positions and targeted for developmental opportunities in stores. In discussions with these high-potential women about their career interests, the executives suggest potential job opportunities and encourage them to apply for so-called "stretch positions" that can help them advance to the next level.

Today there are five network groups, including groups for blacks, Asians, Hispanics, and lesbian, gay, bisexual and transgendered employees. Each is open to all employees and regularly offers a variety of educational activities and events.

The Diversity Advisory Board, which includes representatives from each major operating and functional area of the organization, also sponsors events and seminars.

In addition to the corporate board, each Safeway geographical area has its own diversity advisory board to address local issues. Today there are 13 advisory boards and 14 network leadership groups throughout the company.

From One Mentor, Many

A strong mentoring program is critical to the success of the company's leadership development efforts. Every Safeway manager, from the CEO on down, is expected to mentor his or her own employees, plus several others.

Because there is a serious lack of female and minority mentors, says Renda, it is expected that a manager's first mentee should be a woman, the next a person of color of either sex, "and then you can have a [white] man, in that order."

Renda, whose responsibilities include retail operations, HR, public affairs, labor relations, government relations, industrial engineering, re-engineering and communications, is the company's top female executive and one of its five highest-paid officers. She's also the company's first—and so far only— female executive vice president, a statistic she would like to see changed. "There should be more of me," she says.

From a 16-year-old, working part time bagging groceries at her local Safeway store, Renda has spent 33 years building a high-powered career at the Fortune 50 company. In 2001 and again in 2002, she was named one of the 50 most influential women in business by Fortune magazine.

As she moved up the ladder, Renda says she was often the first woman to hold each successive new job. As a result, while she always had a mentor, "I've never had a female mentor," she says. She knows how difficult that can be for women, and she feels a special responsibility today to mentor women and to be a role model for the next generation of female leaders. . . .

Jewel Hunt, vice president for corporate deli food service, Starbucks and Jamba Juice, also "believes in mentorship." She has been fortunate to have mentor-managers throughout her career who helped her learn needed job skills as she advanced in the organization. Hunt, who started 25 years ago as a part time bakery salesclerk while she was attending college, recalls when she was promoted to director of marketing for the Northern California division. Her new boss, the chief financial officer at the time, helped her develop the software and complex math skills she would need in her new job.

In turn, Hunt strives to perform the same kinds of services for her mentees. For example, she remembers one mentee who had applied for a director position. Although she was very well qualified, says Hunt, the woman withdrew her application at the last minute. She said she lacked retail skills and was afraid she wasn't ready for the job.

"I knew she was the strongest candidate, so I encouraged her to go ahead and apply," says Hunt. "I promised that I or an associate would personally work with her in the stores if she got the job." The woman agreed, she did get the job, and "today she's a superstar."

Without Hunt's encouragement at the crucial moment, the woman "might have waited a couple of years to apply, and she had so much to add today."

Lori Raya, vice president of retail operations in Safeway's Northern California division, feels a real sense of mission about her responsibility to mentor other women. "My goal is to impact someone's life," she declares. "I love it when I get notes from former mentees who tell me about a promotion and say, 'Thanks for believing in me.'"

Raya says her first mentor at Safeway, who recognized her ability and took steps to keep her when Raya was ready to quit, has had a lasting effect on her life. Raya was in college, working part time and coaching high school girls' basketball, soccer and volleyball in the evening when a new female store manager asked her to change her hours.

Raya explained that the proposed schedule would conflict with her coaching job. "I was ready to walk out the door," she says, when the manager asked, "What would it take to keep you?" Undaunted when Raya said, "Well, your job looks kind of easy!" the woman encouraged her to apply for the RLD program and subsequently became her mentor.

Today Raya is the only female vice president among approximately 19 vice presidents in the retail division, and she is looking ahead toward the next step up—division president. "There is only one female division president today, and I hope to become the second."

Balancing Work and Home Life

Work/life issues tend to affect women more than men, and Safeway seems to have taken this fact into account in its efforts to help all women—regardless of their family status—ensure that they have a healthy work/life balance.

For example, Hunt faced significant work/life challenges as a single mom raising two sons while going to school and working full time.

Her sons, now 22 and 24, were 1 and 3 when she became a single parent. Although her former husband remained involved with the children, he lived in another state and couldn't participate in their day-to-day care. Hunt, who left college before graduation to marry and start a family, now had to raise her sons and finish her degree.

She says she has always had supportive managers at Safeway who helped her juggle school, work and child care. And Safeway's tuition reimbursement program helped pay for her degree.

"I've always been grateful that Safeway helped me with work/life balance" during that difficult time, she says.

In turn, she tries to do the same for the women she mentors today. She makes a point of working with them on the kinds of problems that are particularly relevant to women—the need to work flexible hours during some periods, for example, or to deal with child care or elder care responsibilities.

Safeway also makes a point of ensuring work/life balance for those who do not have children. For example, Dianne Lamendola, group vice president for information technology, has no children and does not plan to have any. She does, however, have an active life outside of work.

Lamendola spends many hours training for competitions in adventure racing, a demanding sport that combines running, kayaking, mountain hiking, navigation and orienteering. When Lamendola is in training, she does not hesitate to say she can't work late on a particular night. Since she throws herself into her work with the same kind of energy she devotes to adventure racing, Safeway knows she's a high performer for the company too.

In addition to her outdoor activities, Lamendola serves on the board of the San Francisco Bay Area Girl Scouts, participates in a book club, and enjoys spending time with her sister and her nieces and nephews.

Because she has so many outside interests, Lamendola says work/life balance has always been important to her. At Safeway, she has been able to pursue those interests while holding a very demanding job.

Accountability

Managers are responsible for driving the company's diversity efforts throughout the organization, so education and training begins with them. All new managers, starting at the top, attend the Managing Diversity Workshop, an eight-hour session cofacilitated by a line manager and HR. Farnham says she intentionally involves line managers to avoid the perception that the workshop is "just an HR program. It's integrated into the business," she says.

While each manager attends the workshop only once, "we recognize that diversity education is not complete in one eight hour session." Farnham says the education continues through events sponsored by the network groups and diversity advisory boards, through video productions such as a "Women in Management" DVD, and through regular diversity discussions in staff meetings. A toolkit designed to guide managers in incorporating diversity discussions into their staff meetings is available on the company intranet.

"Safeway is a data-driven company," says Farnham. "We track census data to identify the demographics of each geographic area," and this data is used to set each manager's specific targets for developing women.

Managers are evaluated on their success in meeting the diversity goals via balanced scorecard data and performance evaluations from their supervisors, employees and customers. And there are big incentives for managers to reach their diversity targets: High marks all around can increase a manager's bonus by up to 10 percent, and consistently high ratings are critical to advancement in the company.

Conversely, those who have trouble meeting their goals will be coached by senior leaders, and their bonuses can be reduced.

The Proof Is in the Pudding

The following metrics offer mounting proof of the success of the women's initiative programs. Since 2000, says Farnham, the number of female store managers has increased by 42 percent. Within that group, the number of white females rose 31 percent and the number of women of color shot up a whopping 92 percent.

She cites another statistic to corroborate the connection between these increases and the women's initiative strategies. During the past five years, says Farnham, the number of women who have qualified for and completed the RLD program rose 37 percent.

There is external validation of the initiative's success as well. Last year, Safeway's "Championing Change for Women: An Integrated Strategy" was honored with the highly coveted Catalyst Award, which is presented annually by the nonprofit research organization to outstanding companies that promote the career advancement of women and minorities.

In addition, Safeway's diversity efforts have garnered praise from global investment bank Lehman Brothers. A research report prepared by the bank's independent analysts points out that Safeway's diversity programs have not only "led to substantial advancement for women and minorities both at the stores and at the corporate office," but also increased the company's sales and earnings. (In an industry with razor-thin margins, Safeway today is a highly profitable $40 billion company with 200,000 employees throughout the United States and Canada.) "Diversity is good for business," concludes the report.

CEO Burd is fully aware of the value a diverse workforce brings to the company. In his acceptance speech at the Catalyst Award ceremonies last year, Burd told the audience that Safeway had approached the subject of diversity as a business issue, "just like we do any other important objective."

In fact, he said, "all we did was act in our own best self interest."

Herminia Ibarra and Otilia
Obodaru

→ **NO**

Women and the Vision Thing

Many believe that bias against women lingers in the business world, particularly when it comes to evaluating their leadership ability. Recently, we had a chance to see whether that assumption was true. In a study of thousands of 360-degree assessments collected by Insead's executive education program over the past five years, we looked at whether women actually received lower ratings than men. To our surprise, we found the opposite: As a group, women outshone men in most of the leadership dimensions measured. There was one exception, however, and it was a big one: Women scored lower on "envisioning"—the ability to recognize new opportunities and trends in the environment and develop a new strategic direction for an enterprise.

But was this weakness a perception or a reality? How much did it matter to women's ability to lead? And how could someone not perceived as visionary acquire the right capabilities? As we explored these issues with successful female executives, we arrived at another question: Was a reputation for vision even something many of them wanted to achieve?

A Brilliant Career

A leading services company CEO we'll call Anne Dumas typified in many ways the women we spoke with. The pillar of her leadership style was a principle taught to her 20 years ago by her first boss: Always stay close to the details. As she explained it: "I think strategy comes naturally from knowing your business and the forces that influence your market, clients, and suppliers—not at a high level but at a detailed level. Intermediaries kill your insight. You obviously can't monitor everything, but nothing should keep you from knowing in detail the processes on which your company runs—not supervising everything but understanding at a detailed level what is going on. Otherwise, you are hostage to people who will play politics. At best you don't have full information; at worst you're vulnerable to hidden agendas. My job is to go to the relevant detail level."

In her four years as CEO, Dumas had achieved some impressive results. She had doubled revenues and operating margins, given the company a new strategic direction, and undertaken a fundamental reorganization of the company's core processes and structures. More recently, she had turned her attention to developing her leadership team.

From *Harvard Business Review,* January 2009, pp. 62, 64–70. Copyright © 2009 by Harvard Business School Publishing. Reprinted by permission.

IDEA IN BRIEF

- Women outshine men in many areas measured by 360-degree assessments but score low on one key leadership capability: envisioning.
- Three theories could explain why. Women might use different processes than men for shaping the future. They might perceive that they have less license to go out on a limb. Or they might not buy into the value of being seen as visionary.
- Vision is a must-have for enterprise leadership, regardless of gender. Luckily, it's a capability that can be learned.

Yet Dumas knew she should somehow improve her communication effectiveness, particularly in her role as an executive member of her parent company's board. One challenge was her stylistic mismatch with her chairman, a broad-brush, big-picture thinker who often balked at what he perceived as excessive attention to detail. She found herself reluctant to favor "form over substance." She told us, "I always wonder what people mean when they say, 'He's not much of a manager but is a good leader.' Leader of what? You have to do things to be a leader." She went on to imply that so-called visionary behaviors might even be harmful. "We are in danger today of being mesmerized by people who play with our reptilian brain. For me, it is manipulation. I can do the storytelling too, but I refuse to play on people's emotions. If the string pulling is too obvious, I can't make myself do it."

Dumas's reluctance is not unusual. One of the biggest developmental hurdles that aspiring leaders, male and female alike, must clear is learning to sell their ideas—their vision of the future—to numerous stakeholders. Presenting an inspiring story about the future is very different from generating a brilliant strategic analysis or crafting a logical implementation plan, competencies on which managers like Dumas have built their careers.

Indeed, a whole generation of women now entering the C-suite owe their success to a strong command of the technical elements of their jobs and a nose-to-the-grindstone focus on accomplishing quantifiable objectives. But as they step into bigger leadership roles—or are assessed on their potential to do so— the rules of the game change, and a different set of skills comes to the fore.

Vision Impaired

Our research drew on 360-degree evaluations of 2,816 executives from 149 countries enrolled in executive education courses at Insead. As with most 360-degree exercises, these managers filled out self-assessments and invited subordinates, peers, supervisors, and other people they dealt with in a professional context, such as suppliers and customers, to evaluate them on a set of leadership dimensions. In total 22,244 observers participated. (See the sidebar "Critical Components of Leadership" for a description of the Global Executive Leadership Inventory, or GELI.)

As we looked for patterns within this data set, we focused on differences between the male and female leaders, both in terms of how they saw themselves and in terms of how the observers evaluated them. Certainly, there were plenty of data to work with, since 20% of the executives assessed and 27% of the evaluating observers were women. When analyzing the data, we controlled for the effects of the executives' age and level.

The first surprise for us, given prior published research, was that we found no evidence of a female "modesty effect." Quite the opposite: Women rated themselves significantly higher than men rated themselves on four of the 10 GELI dimensions we analyzed. And on the remaining dimensions, the women and men gave themselves ratings that were about the same.

Our analyses of how leaders were rated by their male and female associates—bosses, peers, and subordinates—also challenged the common wisdom. Again based on prior research, we'd expected gender stereotypes to lower the ratings of female leaders, particularly those given by men. That was not the case. If there was a gender bias, it favored female leaders: Male observers scored female leaders significantly higher than they scored male leaders on seven dimensions, and female observers scored them significantly higher on eight. (See the exhibit "Comparing the Ratings of Male and Female Leaders.")

Ratings on one dimension, however, defied this pattern. Female leaders were rated lower by their male observers (but not by women) on their capabilities in "envisioning." That deficit casts a large shadow over what would otherwise be an extremely favorable picture of female executives. The GELI instrument does not claim that the different dimensions of leadership are equal in importance, and as other research has shown, some do matter more than others to people's idea of what makes a leader. In particular, the envisioning dimension is, for most observers, a must-have capability.

Intrigued by this one apparent weakness, we looked more closely at the observers' ratings. Was a particular group responsible for bringing the envisioning scores down? Indeed one was. As shown in the exhibit "Who Says Women Aren't Visionary?" the male peers (who represented the majority of peers in our sample) rated women lower on envisioning. Interestingly, female peers did not downgrade women, contrary to the frequently heard claim that women compete rather than cooperate with one another. Our data suggest it's the men who might feel most competitive toward their female peers. Male superiors and subordinates rated male and female leaders about the same.

What It Means to Be Visionary

George H.W. Bush famously responded to the suggestion that he look up from the short-term goals of his campaign and start focusing on the longer term by saying, "Oh—the vision thing." His answer underlines vision's ambiguity. Just what do we mean when we say a person is visionary?

The distinction between management and leadership has long been recognized. Most agree that managing for continuous improvement to the status quo is different from being a force for change that compels a group to innovate and depart from routine. And if leadership is essentially about realizing

IDEA IN PRACTICE

When taking on more-strategic leadership roles, both men and women must come to grips with the vision thing. Here's a high-level plan for making that happen.

- **1. Get a vision test.** Undergo a 360-degree evaluation to explore the differences between how you see yourself and how others see you. Find out whether you have a vision gap to close and who perceives it. As Insead coaches say, if one person tells you that you have donkey ears, don't listen; if two people tell you, go buy yourself a saddle.

- **2. Gain a new respect.** Learn to appreciate vision as a matter of not just style but substance. It's not about meaningless mission statements but about strategic acumen and positioning know-how. Respect the size of the challenge you may face. If you pride yourself on your peo-ple skills, establishing the distance needed for a helicopter view may require reinventing your identity as a leader.

- **3. Leverage (or build) your network.** Strategic analysis demands a solid grasp of what is happening outside your group and firm. A good external network is the first line of defense against insular thinking. If you're like most executives we've studied, your network probably isn't strong enough to take you to the next level.

- **4. Learn the craft.** Much of envisioning can be learned the old-fashioned way: at the elbow of a master. Find role models and study how they develop and communicate strategic ideas. Then work with your leadership development organization or a good executive coach to identify training and tools to build your capabilities.

- **5. Beware of identity traps.** When you are very good at a needed task, the whole organization will conspire to keep you at it. Stop being so hands-on. Even if delivering on the details has always been your ticket to advancement, staying in the weeds is risky now.

- **6. Constantly communicate.** As your vision develops, find oppor-tunities to articulate it. Don't wait until it's perfect. Try out draft ver-sions along the way and even after the vision is mature. You'll never be seen as visionary if you don't get the word out.

- **7. Step up to the plate.** A vision doesn't come only from the outside; it comes from greater self-confidence. It is an internal presumption of competence: giving yourself latitude, believing in your ability, and assuming responsibility for creating a future for others.

change, then crafting and articulating a vision of a better future is a leadership prerequisite. No vision, no leadership.

But just as leadership is a question of what one does rather than what one is, so too is vision. It encompasses the abilities to frame the current practices as inadequate, to generate ideas for new strategies, and to communicate possibilities in inspiring ways to others. Being visionary, therefore, is not the same as being charismatic. It entails "naming" broad-stroke patterns and setting strategy based on those patterns. (See the sidebar "What Does It Mean to Have Vision?")

Visionary leaders don't answer the question "Where are we going?" simply for themselves; they make sure that those around them understand the direction as well. As they search for new paths, they conduct a vigorous exchange with an array of people inside and outside their organizations, knowing that great visions rarely emerge from solitary analysis. As "practical futurists," leaders also test new ideas pragmatically against current resources (money, people, organizational capabilities) and work with others to figure out how to realize the desired future. True strategists offer much more than the generic vision statements that companies hang on their walls; they articulate a clear point of view about what will transpire and position their organizations to respond to it. All of this adds up to a tall order for anyone in a leadership role. It's not obvious, however, why it should be a particular challenge for women.

Perception or Reality?

As we sought to understand why women fail to impress with their vision, research findings from prior studies were not much help. To begin with, most attempts to compare men's and women's styles have focused on how leaders are rated by subordinates. Yet, as we all know, leaders play a key role in managing stakeholders above, across, and outside their units. Moreover, the vast majority of studies ask participants either to rate hypothetical male and female leaders or to evaluate "the majority" of male or female leaders they know, rather than the actual, specific leaders they know well. Empirical studies of gender differences in leadership styles have often used populations of students, members of diverse associations, and nonmanagers, rather than the midlevel to senior business managers we are actually trying to understand.

We turned therefore to the experts who were living this reality every day: the women participating in our executive education programs. When we asked

---

CRITICAL COMPONENTS OF LEADERSHIP

The Global Executive Leadership Inventory (GELI) is a 360-degree feedback instrument developed at Insead's Global Leadership Center by Manfred Kets de Vries, Pierre Vrignaud, and Elizabeth Florent-Treacy. To identify significant dimensions of exemplary leadership, they interviewed more than 300 senior executives over the course of three years. The emerging questionnaire was then validated on an international sample of more than 300 senior executives and MBA students. The result, GELI, measures degrees of competency in these dimensions of global leadership, which it defines as follows[1]:

Envisioning
Articulating a compelling vision, mission, and strategy that incorporate a multicultural and diverse perspective and connect employees, shareholders, suppliers, and customers on a global scale.

Empowering
Empowering followers at all levels of the organization by delegating and sharing information.

Energizing
Energizing and motivating employees to achieve the organization's goals.

Designing and aligning
Creating world-class organizational design and control systems and using them to align the behavior of employees with the organization's values and goals.

Rewarding and feedback
Setting up the appropriate reward structures and giving constructive feedback.

Team building
Creating team players and focusing on team effectiveness by instilling a cooperative atmosphere, promoting collaboration, and encouraging constructive conflict.

Outside orientation
Making employees aware of outside constituencies, such as customers, suppliers, shareholders, and other interest groups, including local communities affected by the organization.

Global mind-set
Inculcating a global mentality, instilling values that act as a glue between the regional or national cultures represented in the organization.

Tenacity
Encouraging tenacity and courage in employees by setting a personal example in taking reasonable risks.

Emotional intelligence
Fostering trust in the organization by creating—primarily by setting an example—an emotionally intelligent workforce whose members are self-aware and treat others with respect and understanding.

1. GELI contains two additional dimensions, life balance and resilience to stress, which we did not analyze in our study, since many observers were unable to provide evaluations on them.

how they would interpret our data, we heard three explanations. First, several women noted that they tended to set strategy via processes that differed from those used by their male counterparts. This suggests that what may in fact be visionary leadership is not perceived that way because it takes a different path. Second, we heard that women often find it risky to stray away from concrete facts, analyses, and details. And third, many women betrayed negative attitudes toward visionary leadership. Because they thought of themselves as grounded, concrete, and no-nonsense, and had seen many so-called visionary ideas founder in execution, they tended to eye envisioning behaviors with some suspicion. Each of these interpretations invited serious consideration.

THEORY 1: Women are equally visionary but in a different way. Several of the women who had taken the GELI survey argued that it is not that women

COMPARING THE RATINGS OF MALE AND FEMALE LEADERS

In the 360-degree assessments of participants in Insead's executive education program, female leaders received higher ratings than male leaders in most dimensions of leadership. But in one dimension—envisioning—women were rated lower than men.

	Which leaders rated themselves higher?	Which leaders did male observers rate higher?	Which leaders did female observers rate higher?
Envisioning	Neither	Men	Women
Empowering	Neither	Neither	Neither
Energizing	Women	Women	Women
Designing and aligning	Women	Women	Women
Rewarding and feedback	Neither	Women	Women
Team building	Neither	Women	Women
Outside orientation	Women	Women	Women
Global mind-set	Neither	Neither	Neither
Tenacity	Neither	Women	Women
Emotional intelligence	Women	Women	Women

lack vision but that they come to their visions in a less directive way than men do. One executive put it like this: "Many women tend to be quite collaborative in forming their vision. They take into account the input of many and then describe the result as the group's vision rather than their own." Another said, "I don't see myself as particularly visionary in the creative sense. I see myself as pulling and putting together abstract pieces of information or observations that lead to possible strategies and future opportunities."

Vivienne Cox, CEO of BP Alternative Energy, is known for having an "organic" leadership style. She led a team that crafted a strategy for moving BP into alternative energy in a more unified and substantial way, by combining a set of peripheral businesses such as solar, wind, and hydrogen-fired power plants into one new low-carbon-powered unit that BP would invest billions in. Ask those involved how the new strategy came about, and the answer always involves multiple players working collaboratively. One of her key lieutenants described Cox's approach like this: "She thinks about how to create incentives or objectives so that the organization will naturally find its own solutions and structures. It encourages people to be thoughtful, innovative, and self-regulating." Cox herself claims that her role is to be a "catalyst." She consistently articulates a management philosophy in which the leader does not drive change but, rather, allows potential to emerge.

Interestingly, the processes these women describe do not hinge just on a collaborative style. They also rely on diverse and external inputs and alliances. At BP Alternative Energy, Cox spent much of her time talking to key people outside her business group and the company in order to develop a strategic perspective on opportunities and sell the idea of low-carbon power to her CEO and peers. Her ideas were informed by a wide network that included thought leaders in a range of sectors. She brought in outsiders who could transcend a parochial view to fill key roles and invited potential adversaries into the process early on to make sure her team was also informed by those who had a different view of the world. Our results hint at an interesting hypothesis: By involving their male peers in the process of creating a vision, female leaders may get less credit for the result.

THEORY 2: Women hesitate to go out on a limb.   Some women responded to our findings by noting that they need to base their marching orders on concrete facts and irrefutable analysis, not unprovable assertions about how the future will take shape. Here, two Democratic candidates for the 2008 U.S. presidential race offer an interesting parallel. Barack Obama was viewed as a visionary, a charismatic communicator offering a more hopeful if undetailed future. Hillary Clinton was viewed as a competent executor with an impressive if uninspiring grasp of policy detail. According to a recent *New Yorker* article by George Packer, Clinton as much as admitted that she does not inspire through rhetoric and emotion. She said: "A President, no matter how rhetorically inspiring, still has to show strength and effectiveness in the day-to-day handling of the job, because people are counting on that. So, yes, words are critically important, but they're not enough. You have to act. In my own experience, sometimes it's putting one foot in front of the other day after day."

Might women feel they have to choose between being seen as competent and in control or being visionary? Recall Anne Dumas, our services executive, and her pride in having a vast, detailed knowledge of what is happening in her firm. Often, she told us, she'd called on that reservoir of data to defend her position against challenges. The same attitude comes through in the observation of a management consultant who told us, "Men speak more confidently and boldly on an issue, with very little data to back it up. Women want to have a lot of data and feel confident that they can back up what they are saying."

A common obstacle for female leaders is that they often lack the presumption of competence accorded to their male peers. As a result, women are less likely to go out on a limb, extrapolating from facts and figures to interpretations that are more easily challenged. When a situation is rife with threat—when people, male or female, expect that they are "guilty until proven innocent"—they adopt a defensive, often rigid, posture, relying less on their imagination and creativity and sticking to safe choices.

The presumption-of-competence effect is compounded by gender stereotypes that lead us to expect emotional, collaborative women and rational, directive men. When men communicate from the heart or manage participatively, it's taken as evidence of range, an added plus. Women's emotional communication or inclusive process, by contrast, is implicitly viewed as proof of an incapacity or unwillingness to do otherwise, even if the situation calls for it.

THEORY 3: Women don't put much stock in vision. Do men and women really have different leadership styles? Certainly a lot of ink has been spilled on the question, but the answer provided by hundreds of studies, subjected to meta-analysis, is no. When other factors (such as title, role, and salary) are held constant, similarities in style vastly outweigh the differences. The occasional finding that women are slightly more people oriented and participative tends not to hold up in settings where there are few women—that is, in line positions and upper management. But put aside the science and ask individuals for their opinion on whether men and women have different leadership styles, and most women (and men) answer yes.

This can only complicate the solution to the vision deficit. It's one thing for a woman who suspects she is wrongly perceived to resolve to change certain behaviors in order to convey the competence and substance she has to offer. It's quite another thing when her own self-conception has become colored by the same biases.

Our interviews with female executives highlighted one potential difference in attitude between the genders that could explain women's lower ratings on envisioning. We suspect women may not value envisioning as a critical leadership competency to the same extent that men do or may have a more skeptical view of envisioning's part in achieving results. Over and over again in our discussions with women, we heard them take pride in their concrete, no-nonsense attitude and practical orientation toward everyday work problems. We were reminded of a comment made by Margaret Thatcher: "If you want anything said, ask a man; if you want anything done, ask a woman." Many of the women we interviewed similarly expressed the opinion that women were more thorough, had a better command of detail, and were less prone to self-promotion than men. Like Anne Dumas, they valued substance over form as a means of gaining credibility with key stakeholders. A pharmaceutical executive elaborated further: "I see women as more practical. Although the women in my organization are very strategic, they are also often the ones who ground the organization in what is possible, what can or cannot be done from the human dimension."

Making the Leadership Transition

Women may dismiss the importance of vision—and they may be reassured by the many claims made over the years about their superior emotional intelligence—but the fact remains that women are a minority in the top ranks of business organizations. Our findings suggest to us that the shortfall is in no small part due to women's perceived lack of vision.

The findings of a 2008 study by Catalyst researchers Jeanine Prime and Nancy Carter and IMD professors Karsten Jonsen and Martha Maznevski

WHAT DOES IT MEAN TO HAVE VISION?

Across studies and research traditions, vision has been found to be the central component in charismatic leadership and the essence of the oft-noted distinction between management and leadership. But what does it look like in action? As detailed by the Global Executive Leadership Inventory, behaving in a visionary way is a matter of doing three things well:

Sensing opportunities and threats in the environment
- simplifying complex situations
- foreseeing events that will affect the organization

Setting strategic direction
- encouraging new business
- defining new strategies
- making decisions with an eye toward the big picture

Inspiring constituents
- challenging the status quo
- being open to new ways of doing things
- inspiring others to look beyond limitations

concur. In it, more than 1,000 executives from nine countries (all alumni of executive education programs) were asked for their impressions of men and women in general as leaders. Both men and women tended to believe that the two genders have distinct leadership strengths, with women outscoring men on some behaviors, and men outscoring women on others. But here's the catch: When people were asked to rate the behaviors' relative importance to overall leadership effectiveness, the "male" behaviors had the edge. Across countries, "inspiring others"—a component of our envisioning dimension—landed at the top of the rankings as most important to overall leadership effectiveness. And what of the areas of leadership where men agreed that women were stronger? Let's take women's standout advantage: their much greater skill at "supporting others." That one ranked at the bottom of the list. As a component of overall leadership effectiveness, it was clearly not critical but merely nice to have.

We've seen how these priorities play out at close hand, in the personal stories of women we study. Particularly at midcareer, when senior management sizes up the leadership potential of competent managers, they take their toll. A manager we'll call Susan offers a cautionary tale. A strong performer, Susan rose through the functional ranks in logistics and distribution, thanks to her superior technical and people skills and belief in running a tight ship.

As a manager she prided herself on her efficient planning and organizing and her success in building a loyal, high-performing team. But her boss saw her capabilities differently. By this point in her career, he expected her to sense emerging trends or unexploited opportunities in the business environment, to craft strategy based on a view of the business as opposed to a view of her function, and to actively work to identify and bring on board stakeholders. Eventually a proposal came from outside her division calling for a radical reorganization of it. Still focused on making continuous improvement to the existing operation, Susan lacked the networks that would have helped her spot shifting priorities in the wider market and was blindsided by the idea.

It's often observed that the very talents that bring managers success in midlevel roles can be obstacles to their taking on bigger leadership roles. That was Susan's situation, and it's possible that it is a common trap for women. Having had the message drummed into their heads that they must be rational, nonemotional, and hyperefficient, they might actually place a higher value than men on knowing the details cold and getting the job done. That, in turn, makes their leadership transition more difficult, because they stick with what they know longer. Another woman we interviewed, this one an investment banker, captured the scale of the challenge. "It's like my whole basis for existence is taken away from me," she told us, "if I can't rely on the facts." Her words reminded us that an executive's accustomed approach and style define who she is as a leader. To walk away from them is to be left without a clear sense of identity.

The challenge facing women, then, is to stop dismissing the vision thing and make vision one of the things they are known for. In a senior leadership role, it's the best use of their time and attention. It's a set of competencies that can be developed. And of all the leadership dimensions we measured, it's the only thing holding women back.

POSTSCRIPT

Do Women Make Better Business Leaders?

Organizations such as Safeway have demonstrated that having a higher representation of women in leadership positions definitely contributed to the bottom line profits. Women have been shown to have some innate characteristics that help them navigate very well in leadership positions. Their characteristics such as intuitiveness, interpersonal skills, multi-tasking, feelings of empathy, and determination are identified as some excellent leadership qualities. Female leaders extol the diversity initiatives that Safeway implemented to ensure that women become leaders such as senior vice presidents of different functional capacities. As women have been traditionally underrepresented, it is only such aggressive organizational initiatives that can make women climb up the ranks. Women make up 50 percent of the managerial positions in the U.S. workforce and hold 14.6 percent of the corporate *Fortune* 500 positions.

On the other hand, scholars suggest that women may demonstrate a limitation of characteristics critical to leadership. International research has indicated that visionary skills are notably lower among female leaders versus male leaders. Visionary skills help leaders provide the big picture, generate new ideas, inspire across borders, and foresee the future, among several others. In business parlance, a parochial view might pose as a very insular business approach. Women might also underestimate the importance of these skills in managing a business environment. Research also suggests that leadership positions demand and consume an enormous amount of time that female leaders might not be able to commit due to work-life balance issues.

Male leaders have demonstrated high visionary skills or the ability to take a holistic view of business situations. This allows them to inspire others, plan strategically ahead, and also consider new business initiatives. The business world seems to be more aware of the Bill Gates, Warren Buffetts, and Steve Jobs than the Larree Rendas (Safeway vice president), Indra Nooyis (CEO Pepsi), and Anne Mulcahys (CEO Xerox). So the debate on whether men or women make better leaders continues.

Suggested Readings

"Power of Women: Or Should That Be Women of Power? It Doesn't Matter: At BT's Annual Event to Honor the Most Powerful Women in Indian Business, Both Were on Ample Display," *Business Today* (November 2008).

A. Houlihan, "It's a Woman's World: How Women Can Thrive in Any Industry," *Cost Engineering* (vol. 50, no. 8, pp. 8–9, 2008).

Carol Hymowitz, "Women Get Better at Forming Networks to Help Their Climb," *Wall Street Journal* (Eastern Edition) (p. B.1, November 19, 2007).

Gina Zabludovsky, "Women Managers and Diversity Programs in Mexico," *The Journal of Management Development* (vol. 20, no. 4, pp. 354–370, 2001).

Ed Frauenheim, "Bias Study Sees Few Gains for Female Leaders," *Workforce Management* (vol. 86, no. 15, pp. 12, 14, September 2007).

Qualities of Women Leaders; The Unique Leadership Characteristics of Women: http://womensissues.about.com/od/intheworkplace/a/WomenLeaders.htm.

Inspirational Women in Business: http://sbinformation.about.com/cs/development/a/womenbiz.htm.

Women as Business Leaders: Where Does Your Country Rank?: http://knowledgenetwork.thunderbird.edu/research/2009/07/10/women/.

Women Business Leaders in India: http://mindbodypolitic.com/2008/08/06/795/.

Women CEO for Fortune 500 companies: http://money.cnn.com/magazines/fortune/fortune500/2007/womenceos/.

Internet References . . .

History of E-learning

The E-learning Web site is a comprehensive resource and information guide on e-learning, online learning, and programs in different areas of study, including instructional design, accredited online distance education, online degrees, and colleges and universities in the United States and Canada.

http://www.about-elearning.com/history-of-e-learning.html

The High Impact Learning Organization

The Web site provides research, guides, case studies, and vendor analyses filled with practical best practices in enterprise learning and talent management. The research is based on detailed discussions with hundreds of companies implementing real-world learning and talent management solutions.

http://store.bersinassociates.com/governance.html

Electronic Gadgets Like Apple iPod—A Boon or Bane

The Articlebase Web site has established itself as one of the Internet's leading article directories and offers custom articles written by expert authors. The article here discusses life with technology today, how technology has made our lives more comfortable, and perhaps too comfortable.

http://www.articlesbase.com/technology-articles/electronic-gadgets-like-apple-ipod-a-boon-or-bane-513360.html

Some Advice for Handling Information Overload

This site outlines information overload problems that business people deal with. Some of these include spending time reading too many unimportant emails, participating in online chat groups, and the many publications that come across your desk. How do you determine what is needed and important to stay updated and effective? This site also provides suggestions for handling information overload.

http://lawprofessors.typepad.com/law_librarian_blog/2009/11/some-advice-for-handling-information-overload.html

Do Unions Work?

Fedgazette is a regional business and economic newspaper providing information on the latest business and economic news. This article discusses issues with union organizations and provides research results on the effectiveness and productivity of unions.

http://www.minneapolisfed.org/publications_papers/pub_display.cfm?id=2154

The Pros and Cons of Labor Unions

eHow.com is an online community dedicated to enabling visitors to research, share, and discuss instructional solutions that help complete day-to-day tasks and projects. The site debates the pros and cons of labor unions.

http://www.ehow.com/about_5097523_pros-cons-labor-unions.html

Employee Performance and Organizational Productivity

*W*hat HRM practices will enhance employees' performance? Do certain HRM practices dissuade employee performance? Organizations are constantly seeking practices to enhance employee performance and therefore increase their business profits. The digitized world today allows for continuous learning, which organizations are taking advantage of to enhance knowledge capital. The information overload that employees experience with increased dependence on technology has brought such practices into question. The collaborative efforts of unions are seen both in a positive and negative light. Can these HRM practices augment organizational performance?

- Does E-Learning Actually Promote Employee Learning and Development?

- Does Increased Dependence on Laptops, Cell Phones, and PDAs Hurt Employee Productivity?

- Do Unions Help Organizational Productivity?

ISSUE 11

Does E-Learning Actually Promote Employee Learning and Development?

YES: Steve Allison, from "The Role of Social Learning," *E.learning Age* (October 2007)

NO: Penny Reynolds, "Yearning for E-Learning? The Pros and Cons of the Virtual Classroom for Your Call Center," *Customer Inter@ction Solutions* (June 2008)

ISSUE SUMMARY

YES: Steve Allison, technical consultant for Adobe Connect, believes that e-learning provides excellent opportunities for employees to learn at their own pace. Businesses also profit because e-learning is very cost-effective compared to traditional methods.

NO: Penny Reynolds, trainer and consultant, implies that e-learning training methods are not for everyone because the lack of interaction might impede learning. Also, most e-learning initiatives pack in too much content, which hinders mastery of the subject matter.

E-learning refers to learning (training and development) provided to employees via any electronic medium such as the Internet, intranet, satellite TV, video, or CDs/DVDs. The global e-learning market is predicted to surpass $52.6 billion by 2010, with North America having the lion's share of this market. As of today, about 60 percent of U.S. organizations actively promote e-learning to train their employees.

Several employee and business advantages have been identified with this learning method. Employees can learn at their own pace as learning styles vary greatly among individuals, and as their schedule permits. Further, from a learning standpoint, a Web training program tends to be more consistent or standardized than instructor-based learning. E-learning training does not have to follow a calendar format, once again suggesting the incontestable option in flexibility. Often employees opt to not participate in learning and development programs because it may conflict with their regular work or family schedules. Finally, employees can augment their learning and development on any subject matter from a pool of global experts.

E-learning is very cost-effective and provides a positive return on investment. IBM suggests that the company saves $50,000 for every 1,000 classroom training days being replaced with e-learning. In contrast, for classroom training, the instructor's fees, employees' travel expenditures to training sites, and the cost of training rooms make it very expensive. Businesses always seek to maximize their profits by implementing management practices that provide economical gains. Further, logistically, e-learning is very conducive to businesses that want to provide learning and development to a multitude of employees in geographically dispersed locations. As the world is becoming a global marketplace, e-learning allows for such international learning among working professionals.

On the other hand, practitioners and scholars have also pointed out several disadvantages of e-learning. This learning method requires a lot of discipline and self-direction from the employees. The collaborative and interactive spirit of classroom training cannot be replicated by an online medium. Employees may not seek to clarify their area of concerns or doubts immediately as they would do in classroom environments. Therefore, employees may not actually master the subject content. Many e-learning programs try to cram too much content into their learning modules, which may hinder learning. E-learning does not facilitate easy learning for content material that is new and subject matter that requires a lot of knowledge sharing. In contrast, classroom training provides clarification of immediate doubts and also provides opportunities for class discussions that enhance learning. Also, the start-up costs for establishing e-learning may be very prohibitive for small and medium-sized companies to even pursue these learning avenues. Opponents also suggest that the e-learning approach may be personality-specific or generation-specific. Employees that are technology-savvy and are independent learners may thrive better on e-learning.

Proponents of e-learning acknowledge that solitary learning may impede mastery over the content material. They suggest methods to include the social aspects of learning that are so vital to trainees. A blended approach allows for both solitary and online social learning (either with subject experts or peers) so that employees can enhance their learning of subject matter with relevant discussions. It is very important to determine what kind of learning styles employees prefer, even for e-learning.

An international perspective suggests that Europe, Asia, and Latin America lag behind the United States in adopting e-learning practices. The reason could be either cultural or economical. Many cultures support a very interactive and participative learning method. Further, some cultures prefer to have an authority disseminate learning and knowledge to enhance the power and status of such employees. E-learning seems very isolating because it does not provide for such collaborative interactions. Many countries also do not have the infrastructure to support e-learning because of low Internet usage in comparison to the United States.

YES

The Role of Social Learning

Abstract (Summary)

The second in a three-part series discusses the current state of e-learning from the point of view of the business organization. Educators have long been aware that people have different learning styles—that is, that they absorb information in different ways; some via doing, some by seeing, some by hearing. Whatever the academic pros and cons of a short vs long list of learning styles, most educators would agree that to get the best out of their learners, they need to include tasks and activities within their content that address as many of these styles as possible. The anecdotes, shared experiences, or even the sharing of other people's superior experiences, provide an additional dimension to how the brain relates an item of knowledge to other known facts, figures and concepts. A good e-learning solution will allow learners to pull learning content on-demand and independent of the device they are using.

T his article is the second in a series of three that take a look at the current state of e-learning from the point of view of the business organisation.

When you think about e-learning, two pictures typically come to mind: rows of students plugged into PCs in a classroom, manacled by headphones and studiously working away independently. Or else it's the student on their own, working late in the office or after work in their homes, again plugged into their own world, in the attempt to further themselves by learning new skills, or possibly even trying to just keep up-to-date in the rapidly changing environment of their work. Either way, e-learning is typically construed to be a solitary experience. But that is changing. Led by new technology advances that allow people to collaborate at any location without specialised equipment, and the increasing awareness of real-time communications (IM, chat, SMS, etc) as a basis for day-to-day contact between team members, the social aspects of learning are becoming more important to businesses as they realise its ability to share "corporate knowledge" and experience beyond the environs of the training suite.

Getting to Grips

So what is "social learning"? Educators have long been aware that people have different learning styles—that is, that they absorb information in different ways; some via doing, some by seeing, some by hearing. Others claim that actually those three are part of a wider list, which would also include logical-mathematical, linguistical, spacial, social, solitary and physical dimensions to learning (see Seven Ways of Knowing: Teaching for Multiple Intelligences by David Lazear, 1991, IRI/Skylight Publishing Inc.). Whatever the academic pros and cons of a short vs long list of learning styles, most educators would agree that to get the best out of their learners, they need to include tasks and activities within their content that address as many of these styles as possible. Their own experience teaches that doing the same things in different ways helps to "fix" the knowledge into their learners. The social aspect to this is sometimes forgotten in the traditional classroom—when learners sit around and chat or question each other, it's just taken as "what people do"; rather than as an important dimension to the individual's understanding of the content being taught. This ability to explore your understanding by talking directly to others also engaged in the acquisition of that knowledge is a powerful way of learning.

Using Your Brain

The anecdotes, shared experiences, or even the sharing of other people's superior experiences, provide an additional dimension to how the brain relates an item of knowledge to other known facts, figures and concepts. The common activity of "bouncing ideas" off other people actually encapsulates several of these "learning intelligences"—forcing participants to verbalise their understanding; re-evaluate it based upon feedback from others; force the application of that knowledge to the different situations of the other participants, and build new mental connections between facts, concepts and skills as you participate in the discussion. Indeed, the ability to hear from others how they applied that knowledge (or could apply it) to the actual work that each person does day-to-day provides a far better way of capturing, retaining and replicating corporate knowledge than is readily appreciated.

You could easily argue that today, businesses actually lose that body of corporate knowledge rather more readily than they retain it—as more and more people work remotely, or in virtual teams, and as time pressures increase on us all, the actual time we have as employees to share common experiences, best practice, etc., has actually decreased over the last few years. So when people leave jobs, they take that knowledge with them. Given that you could also make an extremely strong argument that it's exactly this on-the-job experience that gives a business its strength of knowledge and competitive advantage, losing it is a crime. Modern trends towards e-learning could exacerbate the issue, since a lot of elearning is conducted in solitary, on-demand bursts, so the opportunity to discuss it is minimised.

There is a silver lining to this cloud. These e-learning trends are increasingly taking advantage of advances in real-time communications technology, which enable a blending of learning, not just between classroom and online activities, but between online-singular and online-connected. A good e-learning solution will allow learners to pull learning content on-demand and independent of the device they are using. It will also allow that content to be used in groups—either tutor-led, or peer-to-peer—so that learners can inter-act with the content, as well as each other, and thereby increase the learning potential of the material. Being able to track an individual's interaction with learning content and to audit their scores, even within group activities, opens a new arena for educators.

Let's take a look at an example of simple techniques to create a training programme which covers multiple learning styles (this topic will be covered in more depth in the next article). Firstly, there's the obligatory pre-reading and materials to ensure that everyone is at the same level before the course begins. This is an ideal candidate for the on-demand e-learning treatment: we can create a package (curriculum) of all the content that is mandatory and/or useful. This distinction between what a learner has to do as opposed to what they could do is extremely important: it follows with the whole ethos of this approach that the content should adapt itself to the needs of the learner. In the most simple case, this could be having a pre-test, the passing of which means that the learner does not have to continue with this content topic (because they already know it). Being forced to do what we already know is not just pointless in today's timesensitive world, but very frustrating for the learner—and a bad learning experience is to be avoided.

Connecting People

Having done the pre-work, we can now begin the main body of learning, with a combination of individual work, collective work and have all of this tracked. Then we can step in with the tutor-led social working, via web-conferencing and re-use the same content so the tutor can facilitate the conversation and apply the knowledge gained, including feeding this back into the learner's scorecard.

The capability to get people together in a virtual environment, where they can still partake in almost all the usual social interactions of a real face-to-face, means that suddenly the distance between people is no longer a factor limiting the spread of good ideas, best practice and the sharing of experiences. This isn't about using email and phone calls to talk; it's about real-time video conferencing that allows all users to share and interact with the same con-tent, allowing people to take control and demonstrate their understanding and ideas, and yet relinquish that control to others (or under the tutor's guid-ance) as and when it makes sense to do so. Perhaps the greatest technological advance in all of this is the simple fact that no special equipment is needed. Any computer and any flavour of webcam will do.

For businesses, this is perhaps a vital point. Since most training depart-ments are feeling the financial pinch, that ability to do more with less—and standard—equipment is a boon. It also represents a marked change in the way e-learning is thought about, controlled and deployed. If it's no longer about the technology, then educators can reclaim ownership of corporate training, providing a better level of applicable training that reaches everyone (see previ-ous article) in a more reusable and intimate manner. Handing educators the tools that they need to create professional, interactive, media-rich content that is easy to create will increase the value, time-to-market and effectiveness of training departments. If we then add to this the ability to cater for all learning styles and to elevate the learning from a singular activity to a corporate/department/team-wide interaction, then the future for education within the business looks rosy, and the resulting increase in staff effectiveness should decisively improve the business competitive edge.

Penny Reynolds

NO

Yearning for E-Learning? The Pros and Cons of the Virtual Classroom for Your Call Center

Abstract (Summary)

This article looks at the wide variety of training options available today and helps define the pros and cons of each training medium. Your first choice is doing training the old-fashioned way: traditional, classroom training with a live instructor. This is referred to as ILT, or instructor-led training. It's worked for years and still is the most common way to deliver training in most call centers. Training can be developed and delivered by in-house staff or can be done through professional training firms, either at a public site, or as in-house training. As you begin to evaluate e-learning options, it's important to beware of "techno-lust." Too many call centers have failed with their e-learning initiatives by trying to force too much content into the online medium. A safer approach involves taking small steps into e-learning conversion and realizing that not all aspects of your current training are appropriate for the virtual classroom.

Call center professionals today face a mind-numbing array of training choices. You can choose from dozens of traditional classroom seminars on a wide variety of topics. Or take a class via the Web with other students from across the country from the comfort of your own office. Or choose your own time and pace and take an e-learning module via CD or the Web. So many choices for you and your staff. . . . So, how do you decide?

This article looks at the wide variety of training options available today and helps define the pros and cons of each training medium.

ILT Classroom Programs

Your first choice is doing training the old-fashioned way: traditional, classroom training with a live instructor. This is referred to as ILT, or instructor-led training. It's worked for years and still is the most common way to deliver training in most call centers. Training can be developed and delivered by in-house staff or can be done through professional training firms, either at a public site, or as in-house training.

Much of its success depends upon development of good courseware, with the most successful programs being built upon adult learning principles. A knowledgeable instructor who's adept at facilitation is also key to successful knowledge transfer and learning. If both courseware and facilitation are good, then ILT programs are very effective. And they have the benefit of immediate question/answer, interaction with an instructor and other students, and die leveraging of class questions for further learning.

Classroom training does have its drawbacks however. It's the most expensive type of training and can be quite costly for one-tofew training. Training often happens too late or too soon, with training happening based upon a calendar or schedule plan, instead of the student's immediate needs.

It's best for organizations that have multiple students at a single location at a similar skill level. Classroom training is the top choice when learning needs to involve highly interactive knowledge sharing, or where new skills need to practiced and observed with feedback.

Self-Paced E-Learning

E-learning focuses on delivery of training via an electronic medium: typically either from CD, from a training program residing on an internal server or intranet, or via the Web. Online learning offers an obvious range of benefits, such as self-paced learning, consistency of delivery, approved content, speed of delivery, and round-the-clock accessibility.

And depending upon how it's developed and delivered, it can be quite cost-effective when compared to traditional ILT programs. IBM, for example, estimates that for every 1,000 classroom days of training replaced by e-learning methodology, the company saves nearly a half-million dollars. And that doesn't even include the savings in travel costs.

But it's not for everyone. E-learning requires some level of self-directed motivation which can be problematic for many employees. And the collaboration and interaction with a teacher and other students in a traditional classroom environment is often difficult to replicate in the online learning experience.

It's perhaps best utilized in a "basic training" mode where it's necessary to "teach" certain knowledge. And it's also an obvious choice when there are many students that need to participate stretched over multiple locations.

Real-Time Web Training

There's one other solution that manages to combine the best of both training worlds into one solution. Synchronous, or real-time, training via the Web (or intranet) is a nice "in between choice" for many training applications. It combines the live instruction from the classroom with the cost benefits of the online training.

In most Web training scenarios, training is scheduled and the student participates via a Web connection for the training visuals, and by telephone or VoIP for the instructor audio portion. . . .

Yearning for E-Learning?

As you begin to evaluate e-learning options, it's important to beware of "techno-lust"—the desire to implement the latest and greatest technology to address your training needs. Too many call centers have failed with their e-learning initiatives by trying to force too much content into the online medium. A safer approach involves taking small steps into e-learning conversion and realizing that not all aspects of your current training are appropriate for the virtual classroom.

Using online learning in a preparatory way to teach fundamental concepts followed by the participatory environment of the Web class or traditional classroom ILT program has the following benefits:

- Optimal use of student time, since early learning can take place anytime, anywhere;
- Solidifies the concepts in students' minds before practicing/discussing in social context;
- Frees up more expensive classroom instruction for the practice and polishing of skills; and
- Saves money by shortening (but not eliminating!) classroom time.

So when developing your training curriculum and deciding upon the medium, let your content, your message, and your students guide you in identifying the best fit for elearning in your call center.

POSTSCRIPT

Does E-Learning Actually Promote Employee Learning and Development?

E-learning has been applauded and at the same time criticized for several reasons as organizations try to embrace this training method. E-learning goes by several other terms such as Web-based training, Internet training, and computer-based training (CBT).

Proponents of e-learning endorse this method because it promotes continuous learning, which is an undeniable asset in a knowledge management environment. Advocates also suggest to successfully adopt e-learning initiatives, employees should be able to navigate their way through an Internet culture. Top management support in these initiatives is also critical to their success. The advantages of low cost, dispersed training, and learning flexibility are indisputable advantages of e-learning.

Employees in IBM are able to track the amount of time invested in e-learning, identify their developmental areas, and also get feedback from peers to really enhance their learning and developmental needs. Social aspects of learning, such as discussing, brainstorming, and sharing ideas with others, are being blended into e-learning through Web 2.0 tools. Booz Allen, a global consulting company in Northern Virginia, uses this method predominantly and has adopted about 600 e-learning modules to enhance employee learning. Both Booz Allen and IBM frequently contend for the top training positions of the American Society for Training and Development (ASTD) awards for the tremendous support they provide employees for furthering their learning and development.

However, opponents of e-learning suggest that this method cannot be used for soft skills (such as interpersonal skills) because these skills definitely require an interactive environment. Studies have also demonstrated that organizations prefer to teach sales techniques via face-to face interaction rather than e-learning. Some flaws recognized with this learning method are that they create an information overload, promote passive learning, and do not provide interactive learning.

Suggested Readings

C. Schooley, "The ROI of E-Learning" *KM World* (vol. 18, no. 7, pp. 12–13, July 2009).

George M. Piskurich, "E-Learning Fast, Cheap, and Good," *Performance Improvement* (vol. 45, no. 1, pp. 18–24, 51, 2006).

C. Musico, "The Evolution of E-Learning," *Customer Relationship Management* (vol. 13, no. 10, pp. 36–41, October 2009).

R. Hubbard, "LEARNING about E-LEARNING," *Training Journal* (October 2009).

"E-Learning: Trends, Predictions and IBM's Leading Edge Approach," *Development and Learning in Organizations* (vol. 21, no. 6, p. 21, 2007).

Rebecca Aronauer, "The Classroom vs. E-Learning," *Sales and Marketing Management,* (vol. 158, no. 8, p. 21, October 2006).

Pros and Cons of E-Learning: http://writingandsnacks.blogspot.com/2006/08/pros-and-cons-of-e-learning.html.

E-Learning: The Pros, Cons, and Making the Right Choice: http://www.managerwise.com/article.phtml?id=306.

e-Learning Market to Hit $52.6B by 2010: http://thejournal.com/articles/2007/07/30/elearning-market-to-hit-526b-by-2010.aspx.

ISSUE 12

Does Increased Dependence on Laptops, Cell Phones, and PDAs Hurt Employee Productivity?

YES: Paul Hemp, from "Death by Information Overload," *Harvard Business Review* (September 2009)

NO: Michelle LaBrosse, from "Working Successfully in a Virtual World," *Employment Relations Today* (2007)

ISSUE SUMMARY

YES: Paul Hemp, a Harvard Law School graduate and editor of the *Harvard Business Review,* argues that our current society is facing loss of productivity due to excessive dependence on technology (such as BlackBerrys, cell phones, etc.), blurring boundaries between home and work.

NO: Michelle Labrosse, one of the 25 Most Influential Women in Project Management, contends that modern technological devices allow employees to be connected to form virtual teams.

Psychologists suggest that the modern workplace promotes a work disorder that has been termed *attention deficit trait syndrome.* Employees commit a lot of mistakes because they are constantly connected to different methods of communication, creating a work environment of information overload. At both work and at home, employees are inundated with messages from e-mails, BlackBerrys, and cell phones, not allowing them to give their complete attention to any task at hand. Hence, employees are more prone to errors and also demonstrate reduced attention spans.

A 2008 AOL study on e-mail users and their personal habits indicated that individuals had a compulsion to check their e-mail constantly, with 60 percent of individuals checking their e-mail even in their bathrooms. Employees today live in an Information Age that robs them of having even a single private moment! Further, a tremendous reliance on such external devices has completely blurred the boundaries between work and home. Studies have shown that children feel neglected with their parents' continuous interaction with their BlackBerrys, which have made them feel, in extreme cases, almost like orphans.

How does information overload create decreased employee productivity? Primarily, employees are not able to process the information they receive as quickly as it arrives. Second, they have to prioritize the information they receive quickly and decide which demands their immediate attention. Is it a co-worker's text, a boss's e-mail, or a spouse's call that will get their immediate attention? Employees are constantly in a state of partial attention as they are communicating with one person (co-worker) and thinking of what to say in their next medium of communication (boss's e-mail). Therefore, employees do not provide undivided attention to the task at hand.

How does information overload impact organizations? Productive work time is lost with employees trying compulsively to stay connected with work and home via different forms of communication. In a study of 2,300 Intel employees, employees said that one-third of the e-mails they receive are not important. Employees also indicated they spend two hours a day reading and responding to their e-mails, wasting enormous corporate time. Microsoft researchers have determined that it takes employees about 25 minutes to reverse back to their work-related tasks after they are interrupted by any external method of communication (such as BlackBerrys, IMs, e-mails, Facebook, Twitter). A Harvard Business study demonstrated that an average employee spends 40 percent of his or her time handling information received via such devices (laptops, cell phones, and PDAs) and spend only 60 percent of their work time on value-creation activities related to work. Are such technology devices a boon or a bane?

Proponents of these technological devices suggest that they help employees balance their work and life agenda better. Employees spend less time commuting and therefore can stay connected with their organizations from their homes. Further, in a globalized workplace, such devices help employees stay connected with their international peers, enhancing knowledge capital significantly. Michelle Labrosse, founder of a successful virtual company, insists that such technology was instrumental for the success of her global organization. However, she suggests employees should develop ground rules in using these external technological devices. LaBrosse suggests that such devices should be used to enhance team building and internal employee communication. Every work project should have clear deadlines with frequent updates on employees' progress as a digital work world comes with many disguised distractions. Because e-mail management is very time-consuming, the author advises employees to learn to write effective e-mails with very meaningful subject headers. These headers should indicate what and who needs to take the action. Usually many e-mail communications involve a "daisy-chain" approach where employees spend hours reading e-mails they do not need to provide any definitive inputs. Further, employees should be given a digital protocol—how quickly are they expected to respond to e-mails, BlackBerry messages, and cell phone calls? This will reduce a lot of anxiety for those employees who feel a need to be constantly wired when working remotely. Organizations can use Wikis, an online collaborative environment, very effectively to enhance the productivity of their work environment. Such an online dialogue allows employees to coordinate and plan their work schedules strategically.

YES ↵   Paul Hemp

Death by Information Overload

The value of information in the knowledge economy is indisputable, but so is its capacity to overwhelm consumers of it. HBR contributing editor Hemp reports on practical ways for individuals and organizations to avoid getting too much of a good thing. Ready access to useful information comes at a cost: As the volume increases, the line between the worthwhile and the distracting starts to blur. And ready access to you—via e-mail, social networking, and so on—exacerbates the situation: On average, Intel executives get 300 e-mails a day, and Microsoft workers need 24 minutes to return to work after each e-mail interruption. Clearly, productivity is taking a hit. Technological aids can help, such as e-mail management software for you, a message-volume regulation system for your organization, or even more-sophisticated solutions being developed by Microsoft, IBM, and others. Yet, battling technological interruptions on their own turf only goes so far. You also need to change your mind-set, perhaps by seeking help from personal-productivity experts or by simply accepting that you can't respond to every distraction that flits across your screen. Similarly, organizations must change their cultures, for instance by establishing clear e-communication protocols. In the end, only a multipronged approach will help you and your organization subdue the multi-headed monster of information overload. The secret is to manage the beast while still respecting it for the beautiful creature it is.

New research and novel techniques offer a lifeline to you and your organization. Can everyone just stop whining about information overload? I mean, in the knowledge economy, information is our most valuable commodity. And these days it's available in almost infinite abundance, delivered automatically to our electronic devices or accessible with a few mouse clicks. So buck up, already!

Wait a second: Can I just stop whining about information overload?

The flood of information that swamps me daily seems to produce more pain than gain. And it's not just the incoming tidal wave of e-mail messages and RSS feeds that causes me grief. It's also the vast ocean of information I feel compelled to go out and explore in order to keep up in my job.

Current research suggests that the surging volume of available information—and its interruption of people's work—can adversely affect not only personal well-being but also decision making, innovation, and productivity. In one study, for example, people took an average of nearly 25 minutes to return to a work task after an e-mail interruption. That's bad news for both individuals and their organizations.

cite this!

There's hope, though. Innovative tools and techniques promise relief for those of us struggling with information inundation. Some are technological solutions—software that automatically sorts and prioritizes incoming e-mail, for instance—designed to regulate or divert the deluge. Others prevent people from drowning by getting them to change the way they behave and think. Who knows: Maybe someday even I will enjoy swimming in the powerful currents of information that now threaten to pull me under.

The Problem for Individuals

Information overload, of course, dates back to Gutenberg. The invention of movable type led to a proliferation of printed matter that quickly exceeded what a single human mind could absorb in a lifetime. Later technologies—from carbon paper to the photocopier—made replicating existing information even easier. And once information was digitized, documents could be copied in limitless numbers at virtually no cost.

Digitizing content also removed barriers to another activity first made possible by the printing press: publishing new information. No longer restricted by centuries-old production and distribution costs, anyone can be a publisher today. (The internet, with its far-reaching and free distribution channels, wasn't the only enabler. Consider how the word processor eliminated the need for a stenopad-equipped secretary, with ready access to typewriter and Wite-Out, who could help an executive bring a memo into the world.) In fact, a lot of new information—personalized purchase recommendations from Amazon, for instance—is "published" and distributed without any active human input.

With the information floodgates open, content rushes at us in countless formats: Text messages and Twitter tweets on our cell phones. Facebook friend alerts and voice mail on our BlackBerrys. Instant messages and direct-marketing sales pitches (no longer limited by the cost of postage) on our desktop computers. Not to mention the ultimate killer app: e-mail. (I, for one, have nearly expired during futile efforts to keep up with it.)

Meanwhile, we're drawn toward information that in the past didn't exist or that we didn't have access to but, now that it's available, we dare not ignore. Online research reports and industry data. Blogs written by colleagues or by executives at rival companies. Wikis and discussion forums on topics we're following. The corporate intranet. The latest banal musings of friends in our social networks.

So it's a lot of stuff—but what precisely is the problem? Well, the chorus of whining (punctuated by my own discordant moans) apparently has some validity. Researchers say that the stress of not being able to process information as fast as it arrives—combined with the personal and social expectation that, say, you will answer every e-mail message—can deplete and demoralize you. Edward Hallowell, a psychiatrist and expert on attention-deficit disorders, argues that the modern workplace induces what he calls "attention deficit trait," with characteristics similar to those of the genetically based disorder. Author Linda Stone, who coined the term "continuous partial attention" to describe the mental state of today's knowledge workers, says she's now noticing—get this—"e-mail apnea": the unconscious suspension of regular and steady breathing when people tackle their e-mail.

There are even claims that the relentless cascade of information lowers people's intelligence. A few years ago, a study commissioned by Hewlett-Packard reported that the IQ scores of knowledge workers distracted by e-mail and phone calls fell from their normal level by an average of 10 points—twice the decline recorded for those smoking marijuana, several commentators wryly noted.

Of course, not everyone feels overwhelmed by the torrent of information. Some are stimulated by it. But that raises the specter of . . . [cue scary music] . . . information addiction. According to a 2008 AOL survey of 4,000 e-mail users in the United States, 46% were "hooked" on e-mail. Nearly 60% of everyone surveyed checked e-mail in the bathroom, 15% checked it in church, and 11% had hidden the fact that they were checking it from a spouse or other family member.

The tendency of always-available information to blur the boundaries between work and home can affect our personal lives in unexpected ways. Consider the recently reported phenomenon of . . . [cue really scary music] . . . BlackBerry orphans: children who desperately fight to regain their parents' attention from the devices—in at least one reported case, by flushing a Black-Berry down the toilet.

The Problem for Companies

Most organizations unknowingly pay a high price as individuals struggle to manage the information glut. For one thing, productive time is lost as employees deal with information of limited value. In the case of e-mail, effective spam filters have reduced this problem. Still, a survey of 2,300 Intel employees revealed that people judge nearly one-third of the messages they receive to be unnecessary.

Given that those same employees spend about two hours a day processing e-mail (employees surveyed received an average of 350 messages a week, executives up to 300 a day), a serious amount of time is clearly being wasted.

"Many companies are still in denial about the problem," says Nathan Zeldes, a former Intel senior engineer, who oversaw the study. "And though people suffer, they don't fight back, because communication is supposed to be good for you." Zeldes is now the president of the Information Overload Research Group, a consortium of academics and executives.

Another set of problems involves the constant interruptions we face, whatever the value of the content. When you respond to an e-mail alert that pops up on your screen or to the vibration of your BlackBerry when you're "poked" by a Facebook friend, you do more than spend time reading the message. You also have to recover from the interruption and refocus your attention. A study by Microsoft researchers tracking the e-mail habits of coworkers found that once their work had been interrupted by an e-mail notification, people took, on average, 24 minutes to return to the suspended task.

The scenario the researchers described was unsettlingly familiar. Dealing with the message that had prompted the alert represented only a portion of the time off task. People often used the interruption as an opportunity to read other unopened e-mail messages—or to engage in such unrelated activities as text-messaging a friend or surfing the web. Surprisingly, more than half the time was spent after people were ready to return to their work: cycling through open applications on their computers to determine what they'd been doing when interrupted; getting distracted by some other work in progress as they moved from one window to another; and reestablishing their state of mind once they finally arrived at the application they'd abandoned nearly a half hour earlier.

Distractions created by incoming e-mail and other types of information also have more-subtle consequences. Research by Teresa M. Amabile of Harvard Business School has identified reduced creative activity on days when work is fragmented by interruptions. And we know from other research that even young workers, who have lots of experience frequently switching from one device or application to another, need uninterrupted periods during which to successfully tackle particularly demanding tasks.

Another eerily familiar, if rarely articulated, consequence of information overload is receiving attention from researchers: the delay in decision making when you don't know whether or when someone will answer an e-mail message. If you don't hear back in a timely fashion, you're left wondering: Was your message willfully ignored by the recipient because it ticked him off? Automatically diverted to his junk mail folder? Left for later response? Or is it simply languishing unnoticed because he's swamped by e-mail? (Some of these questions would be answered if more e-mail recipients—though don't count me among them—would click on those annoying confirmation-of-receipt requests that some senders activate.)

The ambiguity created by this online silence can sometimes be worse than a delayed response, according to Northwestern University researcher Yoram Kalman. Our minds go through a series of semiconscious calculations based on past experience: How long does this person usually take to answer e-mail? Should I bother her with a follow-up? Should I escalate my efforts by leaving a voice mail message, and at which number? Should I walk over to Building D to see whether she's at her desk? Shout out the window at the top of my lungs? Meanwhile, you may have to put a project on hold for an indefinite period while you await a response that the recipient could provide in no more than a minute or two.

What does all this add up to? It's not easy to quantify the costs of these and other consequences of information overload. But one calculation by Nathan Zeldes and two other researchers put Intel's annual cost of reduced efficiency, in the form of time lost to handling unnecessary e-mail and recovering from information interruptions, at nearly $1 billion. He says organizations ignore that kind of number at their peril.

Help for Individuals: TECHNOLOGY

During a recent brainstorming session about cutting-edge management ideas, Jerry Michalski was, well, the birdbrain of the group. As recounted in a recent blog post by my colleague Lew McCreary, who was sitting next to him, Michalski would hear something particularly intriguing—and immediately "tweet" to his Twitter network requesting further information. He'd often get a quick response, sometimes with a link to an article or a blog.

If there seemed to be value in the concept—first generated in the room, then enriched by the external commentary of his Twitter flock—he'd share it with others and then add it and relevant links to a software application, called TheBrain, on his laptop. He uses this tool, which visually associates related pieces of information on a computer screen, to save and categorize newly acquired knowledge.

Wow! Michalski, an independent consultant who advises companies on the use of social media, isn't drowning in a cascade of information. He's not even trying to ride it out in a barrel. He's surfing Niagara Falls. So what's his secret?

"You have to be Zen-like," he patiently explained to me. "You have to let go of the need to know everything completely."

Michalski can afford to let go a bit, because he has at his disposal a set of powerful and personalized filters: social networks that gather, select, and value information for him. One of these consists of his friends on Twitter. Another is Twine, a collaborative bookmarking tool that keeps you up-to-date on selected topics of interest, or twines, by channeling to you online content that fellow idea junkies who subscribe to your twines have found useful. The software tool also scans other twines and automatically recommends items that seem relevant to your interests.

"I hardly read blog posts anymore unless someone tweets me about it or I get the link in my feed," says Michalski, who is an adviser to Twine. "Trust your community to filter and flow the right things to you when you need them."

Somewhat less ambitious technologies exist to help those of us who are more enervated than enlivened by the flood of information, especially e-mail. New software tools offer an array of ways to better manage your inbox. Some prioritize Outlook messages by importance, as determined by your history with particular senders; sort e-mail threads according to the work project they relate to; or filter out e-mail that is no longer relevant because, for example, someone else has provided specific information sought by the sender. Others automatically turn e-mail messages into tasks or appointments; let you know how much time you spend responding to messages; and even fetch information from blogs and internet news feeds about people you e-mail, so that you can, for example, congratulate a customer on a recent success (though this, of course, adds to your inflow of information).

If you're more e-mail addict than victim (a semantic difference, perhaps), a Google engineer has devised something to fight your need for a fix. It's an optional link on your Gmail page that, when you click it, turns your screen gray and displays the message "Break time! Take a walk, get some real work done, or have a snack. We'll be back in 15 minutes"—and then counts down the time until you're able to resume checking messages.

Help for Individuals: A NEW MIND-SET

It may be true that people can't overcome an addiction without help, whether support group or technology. But in the end it's up to you to take control of your information problem. And that means modifying your thinking and behavior.

One approach is to religiously adopt one of the disciplines advocated by personal-productivity gurus—for example, David Allen's "getting things done" method (breezily referred to as GTD by the enlightened). But you had better know yourself well enough to determine whether a particular creed is right for you. For example, the familiar advice to check your inbox no more than several times a day won't help if you are someone who is racked by anxiety as you imagine the growing glut of ignored messages.

Or what about a simple mantra? Maybe "inbox zero," Merlin Mann's imperative to never let e-mail accumulate. Or "five.sentenc.es," the address of a single-page website that challenges people to adopt, as an antidote to procrastination in answering e-mail, "a personal policy that all email responses regardless of recipient or subject will be five sentences or less."

Regaining some productivity may require you to shed feelings of guilt and inadequacy about not promptly answering e-mail. Adopt Jerry Michalski's Zen-like attitude. Or follow author Clay Shirky's advice and abandon any hope of keeping up, accepting that you simply cannot read, never mind respond to, all your messages, even those from people you know. The aforementioned AOL survey reported that 26% of e-mail users have either declared or are considering "e-mail bankruptcy." The rash act of deleting all of your messages will leave your e-mail creditors unsatisfied, but it may be just the fresh start you need. (I haven't resorted to this—yet.)

Help for Companies: TECHNOLOGY

Max Christoff is wary of the eye-popping estimates of information overload's cost—one puts the total negative impact on the U.S. economy at nearly $1 trillion—because they often fail to consider the value of information, including that conveyed by the much-maligned e-mail. But Christoff, executive director of information technology at Morgan Stanley, knows the challenges individuals face in managing masses of information. So he's experimenting with ways to ameliorate the problem for employees at the financial services firm.

For example, his team has developed software designed to mediate e-mail interruptions by distinguishing urgent messages from those that may be important but don't require immediate attention. It takes into account a variety of factors, including whether the sender is a client or someone else the recipient has flagged. The software could be tailored to a particular user's behavior—for example, classifying as urgent messages those from senders whose e-mail the recipient typically turns to first. But that makes the classification criteria less transparent, which tends to make users anxious. "If people don't trust the system, they'll interrupt themselves and go check their non-urgent messages to be sure mistakes weren't made," Christoff says.

Christoff's modest efforts to tackle information overload at Morgan Stanley are unusual. Although nearly everyone acknowledges that individuals, to varying degrees, pay a personal price in their struggles to manage e-mail and other types of information, few businesses have viewed the challenge as a corporate issue.

Organizations are increasingly realizing, though, that they stand to benefit from helping people get a better handle on the problem. Besides enabling individuals to process information more efficiently, companies should also encourage them to be more selective and intelligent about creating and distributing information in the first place.

Several new technologies focus on regulating e-mail volume within an organization. A pilot software tool called Postware requires employees to affix a noncash "stamp" to each internal e-mail they send, drawing from a fixed daily allotment. A market-based system known as Attent, developed by a company called Seriosity, allots users equal amounts of a virtual currency, which they use to attach a value to each message as a signal of importance. Recipients can then prioritize their inboxes on the basis of the value assigned to individual messages. The currency on incoming messages is deposited in the recipient's account for use on later outgoing e-mails. Of course, "wealthy" e-mail users, who receive lots of currency from senders seeking their attention, will have more to spend on outgoing e-mail, possibly skewing the apparent importance of messages from them.

Other, more futuristic tools under development aim to sense our work patterns and determine when we don't want to be bothered. Microsoft researchers are developing a set of applications, dubbed Priorities, that might, for example, delay someone's e-mail alerts by gauging not only a message's urgency but also the recipient's receptiveness to an interruption. The software would automatically assess the message (Does it include a phrase like "as soon as you can"?), the user's activity (Are you in a scheduled meeting with someone from your client contact list?), and the user's mental state (Have you been actively working on a document that has led you to ignore other alerts in the past few days?).

IBM is working on a program called IM Savvy, an instant-messaging "answering machine." It senses when you are busy—by, for example, detecting your typing or mouse patterns—and tells would-be interrupters that you aren't available. But the tool gives senders the option of interrupting you anyway if they must. "The problem with intelligent [software] agents that stand between you and interruptions is that if they get it wrong and don't interrupt you, even just once, there may be a high price to pay," says Jennifer Lai, the leader of the IM Savvy team.

Help for Companies: CULTURE CHANGE

A company's responses to information overload will invariably require not only technology but also a change in collective behavior. That can begin with education. Nathan Zeldes, the former Intel engineer, combined technology and education in a real-time software tool called the Intel Email Effectiveness Coach, designed to help users achieve productive e-mail behavior. When the user clicks on Send, but before the message is transmitted, the program gently warns about potential e-mail blunders and breaches of etiquette—for instance, a "Reply to All" that will send the message to everyone on the distribution list.

Companies also need to establish organizational norms for electronic communication, either explicit or implicit. If a standard is implicit, senior executives should set an example. No employee wants to be the first to abandon a practice that contributes to e-mail overload, such as sending weekly reports to all division heads simply to maintain visibility.

A firm might create a weekly "e-mail–free morning": a ban on in-house, though not external, e-mail (and possibly phone calls, instant messages, and drop-in chats). The aim would be to carve out an extended stretch of relatively uninterrupted time.

Or a manager might identify for her direct reports situations in which an in-person exchange or a phone call should replace an e-mail—not so much to foster face-to-face interactions as to speed decision making. When three or four e-mails have bounced around a group, someone may simply need to pick up the phone and settle the issue at hand.

The IT department could come up with guidelines specifying the preferred communication channels for different types of information. For example, e-mail could be reduced significantly if group newsletters and announcements were posted on a company intranet or wiki, which pulls in people seeking the information instead of pushing it at them. A rule of thumb: If the information in an e-mail you're about to send, even if potentially important in the future, is not urgent, post rather than push.

The IT folks could also replace those irksome confirmation-of-receipt requests from senders with auto-responses from recipients. Such responses would alert senders to your personal schedule for answering e-mail and urge them to phone if something needs attention sooner than you are likely to respond. That could reduce confusion stemming from differences in people's unspoken expectations. If I think of an e-mail as something to be answered within the business day and you think of it as something to be answered upon receipt, ill will and bungled decisions may ensue. If you escalate the contacts —instant message, voice mail, a huffy visit to my cubicle—you'll end up increasing the total volume of information related to a single request.

When suggested norms, such as not sending e-mails to colleagues after 10 PM, fail to stick, encouragement can become enforcement—shutting down e-mail servers at 10:01. (In what some saw as a draconian move, an exasperated CIO at ratings firm Nielsen Media Research recently ordered the e-mail system's "Reply to All" function to be disabled.)

Strict measures may ultimately be necessary because information overload has an ethical dimension. One person's urgent e-mail request for information, of unquestioned value to the sender, usually comes at a significant price for the interrupted recipient, for whom the request may be neither urgent nor important. (The down arrow in Outlook, indicating to the recipient that the message is of low importance, has always intrigued me: Even when it is used, which is rarely, many people open the message immediately, curious to see what content warranted the designation.)

In looking for ways to reduce the burden of information overload, an organization must strive to balance sender benefits against recipient costs. And leaders need to ensure that a solution doesn't simply shift the burden from one group to another, whose shouldering of it will come at a net cost to the organization.

The transfer of burdens: Now there's an appealing notion. Let me seize upon it as an opportunity to shift, once and for all, my burden of recipient's guilt—for failing to promptly answer e-mail—onto the shoulders of those selfish senders of the messages in my inbox.

Ahhh, that's better. Maybe information overload isn't so bad after all.

10 Ways to Reduce E-mail Overload

AN OVERWHELMING VOLUME OF ADVICE is available on how to manage e-mail more effectively. Here are some favorite tips I've gleaned from websites such as Lifehacker, 43folders, and Davidco—plus a few that grew out of personal mishaps.

As a Recipient

1. To avoid constant distractions, turn off automatic notifications of incoming e-mail. Then establish specific times during the day when you check and take action on messages.
2. Don't waste time sorting messages into folders; inbox search engines make that unnecessary. (One possible exception: Create an "urgent action" folder—but don't forget to check it.)
3. Don't highlight messages you intend to deal with later by marking them as "unread." In Microsoft Outlook, accidentally typing in the wrong keyboard shortcut will irrevocably designate every item in your inbox as "read." ("Undo" isn't an option, it turns out.)
4. If you won't be able to respond to an e-mail for several days, acknowledge receipt and tell the sender when you're likely to get to it.

As a Sender

5. Make messages easy to digest by writing a clear subject line and starting the body with the key point. Use boldface headings, bullet points, or numbering to highlight action items—and to note who's responsible for each one.
6. To eliminate the need for recipients to open very short messages, put the entire contents in the subject line, followed by "eom" (end of message).

7. Whenever possible, paste the contents of an attachment into the body of the message.
8. Minimize e-mail ping pong by making suggestions ("Should we meet at 10?") rather than asking open-ended questions ("When should we meet?").
9. Before you choose "reply to all," stop and consider the e-mail burden that your choice places on each recipient. If you wouldn't be able to justify that burden, remove the recipient from the send list.
10. For your own sake, send less e-mail: An outgoing message generates, on average, roughly two responses.

Michelle LaBrosse   ➡ **NO**

Working Successfully in a Virtual World

Remember when the word *virtual* sounded futuristic? At a time in the not-too-distant past, corporations and managers tried to imagine a world where they couldn't physically see their employees every day. Today, working virtually is a normal part of our workplace. According to a 2005 report by iGillottResearch Inc., the U.S. mobile workforce stood at 56.6 million in 2004, and that figure will rise to more than 61 million by 2009. (The firm defines a mobile employee as anyone who is out of the office more than 20 percent of the week but is still working.)

Although working virtually is part of the norm, often teams and companies still struggle with how to manage virtual teams and virtual projects. I'm passionate about the virtual workplace because it has been the backbone of the growth of my business. My company has over 20 full-time employees and over 50 contractors who work virtually. It is common for them to go several months without face-to-face meetings—and in some cases they may never meet. A virtual model has allowed us to grow globally, with licensee programs in Europe, Australia, Canada, the Far East, South Africa, and South America. This kind of global growth is possible for companies of all sizes because of virtual teams and the technology that fuels the possibilities of the virtual workplace.

Virtual team members can be working in a variety of environments. They can be working from home offices, or telecommuting centers that their employer operates; they can be sharing offices or desks based on travel and work schedules; or they can be road warriors who spend most of their workday traveling.

Regardless of where employees are working from, building a virtual model provides benefits for the employer and employees, including:

- **A larger talent pool.** Working virtually means you have access to the best employees, because you can recruit from anywhere in the world.
- **Flexibility.** Flexibility is not only attractive to prospective employees, but also a competitive advantage that allows you to respond quickly to changes in your market.
- **Increased productivity.** Employees spend less time commuting, creating less stress and wear and tear from traveling, and affording more time to balance work and family life. The time employees gain to

spend on business tasks can be more focused; often, working outside a traditional office can be more fluid, with fewer interruptions.

- **Opportunities for globalization.** Globalization is no longer for the big guys. It's really about having access. With a global team, the work-day can be 24 hours instead of eight.
- **Fewer expenses.** Both travel and real estate expenses are decreased substantially in a virtual model.
- **Less environmental impact.** Virtual workplaces have an eco-friendly benefit—as they decrease commuting, they also decrease both traffic congestion and air pollution.
- **More inclusive workforce.** Virtual work environments also give work-ers with physical challenges more opportunities.

Who Works Well in a Virtual Environment?

In his book *Good to Great*,[1] Jim Collins told us to put the "right people on the bus." That's even more important in a virtual environment. You not only have to hire the right people for the job, but also hire people who can succeed virtually.

Who are the best candidates for working in a virtual workplace? People who are self-starters and who don't need to be micromanaged or heavily monitored are more likely to succeed in a virtual workplace. They need to be comfortable running projects and responsible for completing the deliverables of their projects.

People who love what they're doing work well virtually. It's difficult to keep people engaged when they don't have a passion for what they're doing. So, when I hire, I look for passion.

If the individuals don't like to carry a BlackBerry and a cell phone or work across multiple time zones and aren't very technically literate to start with, it makes it incredibly difficult to thrive in a virtual environment. We conduct a capability assessment as part of the hiring process to ensure that candidates will fit in this environment. This assessment looks at their current skill level, analyzes their strengths and weaknesses, and maps this information to their job descriptions. Time and again, we see that being highly technically literate is a primary prerequisite for success.

The New Water Cooler

Leaders used to worry about the loss of the water cooler, but I think the virtual world has become the new water cooler—even in physical locations. When you go into companies these days, they are often very quiet—because everyone is communicating via e-mail and instant messaging (IM). E-mail, IM, conference calls, and Webinars can connect teams and create community.

The Tools and the Rules

Once you have the right team members, you need to give them the right tools and some ground rules for success.

The right tools are easy enough to find. Most of us already have them or have access to them: e-mail, instant messaging, conferencing (both video- and tele-), cell phones, BlackBerries, Webinars, and collaborative work tools like the Wiki.

Ground Rules

Once the tools are in place for your organization, the biggest barriers are often around communications and work culture. Ground rules that focus on them can increase your team's productivity and let you reap the rewards of the virtual workforce.

- **Build trust.** In order for people to work effectively virtually, there has to be trust. Trust doesn't happen magically. It is built when you bring your team together for training or team building, and it continues to grow with clear expectations consistently set by leaders and met by the team. Launching the project with a face-to-face meeting is a great way to kick off a virtual project. If you can't meet in person, you can do virtual team-building activities. For example, you can have everyone on the team create a profile on Facebook or MySpace—with the objective of having team members give more of a sense of who they are as people.

    A team builder that we've had great success with when we bring our people together is building kayaks. Our project-management techniques are embedded into the activity, and it's very revealing from a team-building perspective. I often learn a lot as the leader watching the activity, and it gives me insight about people's leadership skills and their ability to follow a process.
- **Set expectations with a project agreement.** Project agreements help to eliminate unnecessary conflict because objectives, expectations, time lines, and roles and responsibilities are clearly defined. In a virtual environment, it's important to regularly update the project agreement and post it to the collaborative work environment or e-mail it out to the team.
- **Manage results, not activity.** In the physical office environment, "busy work" often gets mistaken for real work. In the virtual environment, when you can't see what people are doing, the key is to manage results. Monitor and measure the results, and be clear about the goals.
- **Schedule regular communication.** It's important that there is a regular time for reporting both progress and potential pitfalls to the team. This keeps people on track and gives everyone the discipline of a team check-in. It's ideal if there is a standing time every week or every month—depending on your project milestones. Remember to build in time for feedback, coaching, and support.
- **Create communication that saves time.** Have you created an e-mail culture that wastes time with endless "daisy-chain" conversations that take several hours to read? Does your team spend hours trying to solve an issue with an e-mail conversation that could have been solved with a 30-minute conference call? Because e-mail is such a critical tool in our work environments, it's important to create a new

culture of effectiveness around it. Train employees to write meaningful subject lines that communicate what the e-mail is about. Also, make sure they lead with what is important and who needs to take action on what. Many deadlines can be missed when the action is buried in paragraph 12.

- **Create standards that build a cohesive culture.** What are your standards of quality? How do you define excellence? What does your brand mean to each employee? Making sure everyone knows the answers to those three questions is even more important when people are scattered geographically. Virtually, you need to create cohesion with excellence and a sense of pride in what your company stands for.
- **Define rules of responsiveness.** When people are working remotely, it's important that you define what the rules of responsiveness are for your culture. How quickly are people expected to return an e-mail, an instant message, or a phone call? What is your protocol when people are out of the office or on vacation? If you're in a customer service environment, it's important to have clear expectations regarding how to respond to all customer inquiries.
- **Use collaborative tools like the Wiki:** Working virtually is *not* about platitudes. It is about systems—creating the systems that enable people to do their work from anywhere and everywhere. There has to be a very strong commitment to giving people the tools they need to help run the business and serve the customers. If they have to go somewhere to answer the phone to serve the customers, they cannot work virtually.

We use a Wiki—an online work environment—as a central hub for our work. This allows us to coordinate our projects and processes in one place and easily see the progress we're making. It's a living memory for our organization, capturing our intellectual capital. We started this for the marketing group to reduce the e-mail and to better capture the various marketing initiatives and decisions. Within one week, it was adopted by all the other people in the company: IT projects, facilities to coordinate facility work, accounting to coordinate budgeting with the different parts of the business, and course development to keep track of course upgrades. It has increased our productivity and also created a central "memory" for all of our work.

- **Pay attention to cultural cues and time zones.** When you're working on a global team, you need to be sensitive to the time zones that in which you are working. For example, in which time zone are the deadlines relevant? Are you scheduling calls at a time that works best for all time zones? Also, remember that cross-cultural communication becomes even more of an issue in e-mail. Pay attention to how your colleagues communicate in e-mail. How formal are they? How are they addressing each other? Don't automatically assume an informal tone until you have gained the trust and respect of your team.
- **Create an attitude of gratitude.** Reward people when they do well. Especially when people are working virtually, they need to know when they've made a difference. We created a program called "The Attitude of Gratitude" where people have 2,000 points every month to distribute to their coworkers to thank them for whatever they did during the

month. The top three people with the most points at the end of the month win. First place is something worth $500, second place is worth $300, and third place is worth $200. It's a companywide employee-recognition program that everyone participates in, and it creates both buzz and community.

Working virtually is not a trend. It's a way of life today. So, focus on what you can do to be a better manager or team member. These tips are a good starting point as you build your own best practices for effective project management in the virtual world. Enjoy the journey and invite your team to help you create a powerful work culture.

Notes

1. Collins, J. (2001). *Good to great: Why some companies make the leap . . . and others don't*. London: Random House.

POSTSCRIPT

Does Increased Dependence on Laptops, Cell Phones, and PDAs Hurt Employee Productivity?

Organizations are now truly concerned that increased dependence on external devices that are supposed to make employee more productive is having negative consequences. This phenomenon of wanting to frequently check the communication status on technological devices is being referred to as infomania, infoglut, and click syndrome, among several others. Are employees justified in claiming 40 percent of their payroll for information overload activities that may or may not be related to work?

Studies demonstrate that once employees are distracted from their work, they use that interruption as an excuse to check the communication status from their other technological devices (such as cell phones and BlackBerrys) losing more valuable work time. IBM's global staff of 400,000 employees sends 12 million instant messages to each other daily. Intel has demonstrated that employees lose almost $1 billion in terms of reduced work efficiency and employee work distractions due to such external devices. Further, employees often are either tweeting or texting during corporate meetings and not providing their undivided attention. Will our society overcome this digital addiction?

Morgan Stanley, the financial service giant, has proactively taken efforts to reduce its employees' technology addiction. Employees are encouraged to use software filters to distinguish important and non-important e-mail messages so that they can give priority to the important tasks. Microsoft and IBM are working on futuristic software applications such as Priorities and IM Savvy that allow employees to be interrupted less so that they can have a more productive work environment.

Proponents suggest, however, that technology is a boon for employees. Employees can work from the comforts of their homes to balance work and life. Employees from geographically dispersed locations can integrate information, contributing to a culture of knowledge management. Labrosse suggests that technology (such as the Internet, cell phones, and BlackBerrys) was instrumental in building her international company that allows employees to communicate effortlessly with one another from different continents. Online dialogues on work status and projects can help employees stay ahead of work deadlines. However, proponents do agree that employees need to follow a disciplined digital environment. Identifying specific times during the day to check on their various technologies is a very important first step. Interoffice communication requires a proactive effort to reduce a ping-pong e-mail culture that might consume a lot of employees' time. Ground rules should be established to endorse a philosophy of receiving less e-mail on a daily basis. Employees should be advised to send e-mail with relevant subject headers that will immediately identify actionable items without wasting time to open and read the e-mail. Further, employees should be encouraged not to crowd co-workers' inboxes if they do not have any specific input to the e-mail content.

Suggested Readings

S. Rubel, "Too Much Infotechnology Can Lead to Brain Overload," *Advertising Age* (vol. 79, no. 7, p. 18, February 2008).

Michael Totty, "Office Technology; Operation Overload: Software Tools Allow People to Manage the Clutter That Threatens to Overwhelm Their Daily Lives," *Wall Street Journal* (Eastern Edition), December 11, 2007.

Jonathan Spira, "From Knowledge to Distraction," *KM World* (vol. 16, no. 3, pp. 1, 32, March 2007).

Sherry Sweetnam, "E-mail Tactics," *T + D* (vol. 60, no. 1, p. 13, January 2006).

Information Overload:
http://www.refresher.com/mindfulnetwork/articlelive/articles/35/1/Information-Overload/Page1.html

Information Overload? Relax:
http://online.wsj.com/article/SB124683648696297965.html

Are We Overwhelmed Yet?:
http://www.marketwatch.com/story/information-overload-deal-with-it

ISSUE 13

Do Unions Help Organizational Productivity?

YES: AFL-CIO, from "Unions Are Good for Business, Productivity, and the Economy," (http://www.aflcio.org/joinaunion/why/uniondifference/uniondiff8.cfm)

NO: Dennis K. Berman, from "The Game—Dr. Z's Chrysler Predicament: Selling Unions on Sacrifice," *Wall Street Journal* (Eastern Edition) (April 24, 2007)

ISSUE SUMMARY

YES: The American Federation of Labor and Congress of Industrial Organizations (AFL-CIO) Web site identifies the work of Professor Harley Shaiken, from the University of California-Berkeley, who states the positive impact of unions on HRM outcomes.

NO: Dennis Berman, *Wall Street Journal* journalist and 2003 Pulitzer Prize winner, argues that the current state of the auto industry is mainly due to excessive demands of the unions. The high cost of maintaining labor is passed on to the consumers and reduces organizational profit margins.

Unions are labor organizations that allow employees to negotiate with their employers over several areas of employment such as pay and benefits, employee grievances, hours of employment, labor disputes, and conditions of work. Employees work together as an entity to collectively bargain for their interests with management. The mutual agreement between employers and employees is called the collective bargaining agreement, which covers all the work-related interests of any union.

While 27 percent of the workforce was unionized in the 1970s, approximately 12 percent of the workforce is unionized today. Federal employees are five times more likely to be unionized than private employees. The membership in unions slowly declined over the years as unionized workforces were considered very contentious. The economy also has been slowly moving from a manufacturing environment to a service environment, which tends to be less unionized.

Professor Harley Shaiken, suggests that unionized workforces are associated with several positive organizational outcomes. They include higher productivity, lower employee turnover, improved workplace communication, and a better-trained workforce. Studies also suggest that because of such positive HRM outcomes, unionized workforces are 22 percent more productive than nonunionized workforces. Unions also are known to be associated with an increased quality of products or services. The classic example is that of the Saturn Corporation, the automobile company, and its highly unionized workforce that produced high-quality cars. As unionized workforces are more likely to demand for training, such workforces tend to produce higher quality products and services. Unionized workforces also have demonstrated reduced employee turnover because of opportunities available through collective bargaining to improve work conditions. Unionized workforces also demonstrate a very collaborative and cooperative approach because they are unified to their broader cause.

On the other hand, *Wall Street Journal* journalist, Dennis Berman, strongly suggests that unions have tremendous negative effects on organizations. A contemporary example is that of the auto industry that has filed for bankruptcy due to excessive labor union demands. As unions excessively increase their demands in benefits and wages, the trickle-down effects cause substantial increase in price for the final products and services, which squeezes profit margins for organizations. The bankruptcy filing of the auto companies has demonstrated to the business world the negative effect of labor unions and their selfish obsession with their demands. The United Auto Workers (UAW) has a very tight hold over the operation of the auto industry.

The ability to strike is the union's other biggest weapon that can potentially hamper organizational productivity. The power of a union is demonstrated through strikes as an entire group of employees does not come to work. The word "strike" first appeared in the 1700s when workers in Philadelphia print factories stopped coming to work because they wanted an increase in their wages. The trend to use strikes to meet their work demands continued over the decades. A classic example of the power of strikes was that of air traffic controllers in 1981 when 13,000 out of almost 18,000 employees walked out in strike and demanded better wages, working conditions, and benefits. As the air industry came to an absolute standstill, an intervention from then President Reagan was required. Professor Peter Morici, an authority on unions, indicates that their power to bring work to an absolute standstill is what makes labor unions completely flawed.

An international perspective suggests that European workforces are much more unionized, with countries such as the Netherlands, Denmark, and Sweden having almost 80 percent of their workforces unionized. In countries such as Germany, institutional practices including codetermination and work councils are very powerful expressions of labor unions. These labor practices allow board representation of labor members, making employers and employees negotiate for work-related benefits at the same board level. In several Latin American countries, labor unions are considered more as political platforms, and unions and political parties work very closely toward mutual causes.

Unions Are Good for Business, Productivity and the Economy

According to Professor Harley Shaiken of the University of California-Berkeley, unions are associated with higher productivity, lower employee turnover, improved workplace communication, and a better-trained workforce. Prof. Shaiken is not alone. There is a substantial amount of academic literature on the following benefits of unions and unionization to employers and the economy:

- Economic Growth
- Productivity
- Competitiveness
- Product or service delivery and quality
- Training
- Turnover
- Solvency of the firm
- Workplace health and safety
- Economic development

Economic Growth

During the period 1945–1973, when a high percentage of workers had unions, wages kept pace with rising productivity, prosperity was widely shared, and economic growth was strong. Since 1973, union density and collective bargaining have declined, causing real wages to stagnate despite rising productivity. This decline in union density and bargaining contributed to the current financial crisis and severe recession, as unsustainable asset appreciation and easy credit took the place of wage increases most workers were not getting.

Productivity

According to a recent survey of 73 independent studies on unions and productivity: "The available evidence points to a positive and statistically significant association between unions and productivity in the U.S. manufacturing and education sectors, of around 10 and 7 percent, respectively."

Some scholars have found an even larger positive relationship between unions and productivity. According to Brown and Medoff, "unionized establishments are about 22 percent more productive than those that are not."

Product/Service Delivery and Quality

According to Professors Michael Ash and Jean Ann Seago heart attack recovery rates are higher in hospitals where nurses are unionized than in non-union hospitals. According to Professor Paul Clark, nurse unions improve patient care by raising staff-to-patient ratios, limiting excessive overtime, and improving nurse training.

Another study looked at the relationship between unionization and product quality in the auto industry. According to a summary of this study prepared by American Rights at Work:

> The author examines the system of co-management created through the General Motors-United Auto Workers partnership at the Saturn Corporation. . . . The author credits the union with building a dense communications network throughout Saturn's management system. Compared to non-represented advisors, union advisors showed greater levels of lateral communication and coordination, which had a significant positive impact on quality performance.

Training

Several studies have found a positive association between unionization and the amount and quality of workforce training. Unionized establishments are more likely to offer formal training. This is especially true for small firms. There are a number of reasons for this: less turnover among union workers, making the employer more likely to offer training; collective bargaining agreements that require employers to provide training; and finally, unions often conduct their own training.

Turnover

Professor Shaiken also finds that unions reduce turnover. He cites Freeman and Medoff's finding that "about one fifth of the union productivity effect stemmed from lower worker turnover. Unions improve communication channels giving workers the ability to improve their conditions short of 'exiting.'"

Solvency

Labor's enemies assert that unions drive employers out of business, but academic research refutes this claim. According to Professors Richard Freeman and Morris Kleiner, unionism has a statistically insignificant effect (meaning no effect) on firm solvency. Freeman and Kleiner conclude "unions do not, on average, drive firms or business lines out of business or produce high displacement rates for unionized workers."

Workplace Health and Safety

Employers should be concerned about workplace health and safety as a matter of enlightened self-interest. According to an American Rights at Work summary of a study by John E. Baugher and J. Timmons Roberts:

> Only one factor effectively moves workers who are in subordinate positions to actively cope with hazards: membership in an independent labor union. These findings suggest that union growth could indirectly reduce job stress by giving workers the voice to cope effectively with job hazards.

The benefits of unions in terms of safer workplaces are hardly new. According to one most recent study, unions reduced fatalities in coal mining by an estimated 40 percent between 1897 and 1929.

Economic Development

Unions also play a positive role in economic development. One good example is the Wisconsin Regional Training Partnership, "an association of 125 employers and unions dedicated to family-supporting jobs in a competitive business environment. WRTP members have stabilized manufacturing employment in the Milwaukee metro area, and contributed about 6,000 additional industrial jobs to it over the past five years. Among member firms, productivity is way up—exceeding productivity growth in nonmember firms."

Dennis K. Berman

NO

The Game—Dr. Z's Chrysler Predicament: Selling Unions on Sacrifice

Abstract (Summary)

"They clearly have to do something different than what they're doing now," says Paul Walser, owner of the Walser Chrysler Jeep dealership in Hopkins, Minn. "It's not working."

Piled on when the U.S auto industry was far more dominant, these costs erode what little profit the company can turn. In the past five years, Chrysler's $2.7 billion in operating profit actually morphed into a $1.75 billion loss when factoring in these payments. It is why many bankers say the company's value is a fraction of the $39 billion price Daimler originally paid. In fact, they say this bundle of liabilities is worth zero. Things could well turn around, but Daimler has made it clear it doesn't have the patience. It wants a sale. Fast.

"We're not interested in equity," Mr. [Buzz Hargrove] said. "We've met the test in terms of quality productivity and are not about to give. It ain't going to happen with our union."

Forget about making better cars. Or even about the rise of private equity. The best way to understand the sale of Chrysler Group is as blood sport between parent DaimlerChrysler and its North American unions.

Is DaimlerChrysler willing to get fully ruthless with its employees, in spite of its well-hewn image as loveable corporate citizen? The answer will make for some gripping theater in the months ahead. That is because this deal really is about persuading the company's unions to roll back their own health and pension benefits.

The stock market already is acting like an agreement is nigh, having added $20 billion in value to Daimler since the auto maker said it was considering a sale. But the market underestimates just what rough business this separation is going to be.

"If people buying it think they're going to get concessions out of us, it's not going to happen," said Buzz Hargrove, head of the Canadian Auto Workers union, in an interview.

To first approach the problem, it is best to consider the 82-year-old Chrysler Group less like a car company and more like a hard-luck case. The company carries an estimated $18 billion in unfunded health-care and other benefit costs, all of which weigh heavily on the business.

"They clearly have to do something different than what they're doing now," says Paul Walser, owner of the Walser Chrysler Jeep dealership in Hopkins, Minn. "It's not working."

Piled on when the U.S auto industry was far more dominant, these costs erode what little profit the company can turn. In the past five years, Chrysler's $2.7 billion in operating profit actually morphed into a $1.75 billion loss when factoring in these payments. It is why many bankers say the company's value is a fraction of the $39 billion price Daimler originally paid. In fact, they say this bundle of liabilities is worth zero. Things could well turn around, but Daimler has made it clear it doesn't have the patience. It wants a sale. Fast.

"Unless the [United Auto Workers] is willing to modernize the workplace and abandon its class-warfare labor negotiations, it's impossible to run the company," argues Peter Morici, a University of Maryland business professor and longtime critic of the auto unions.

Daimler suffers from a rich man's conundrum. The profits at its other divisions continue to subsidize Chrysler. The UAW did grant some historic concessions to General Motors and Ford Motor last year. But those were for companies that were truly on the brink. DaimlerChrysler simply isn't. So why should the unions sacrifice?

Daimler's answer is clear: To scare the heck out of the union, by separating it from Daimler. The very idea of separation—any separation—already has proved a windfall for Daimler's stock. There is no turning back now.

But for this gambit to work, DaimlerChrysler's chief executive, Dieter Zetsche, will have to prove exactly the opposite of the affable, avuncular character he played in his company's own television commercials.

Consider his predicament. A buyer isn't going to take on Chrysler without some guarantees of reduced worker costs. Either Daimler can hang on to those costs, invalidating the purpose of the whole exercise, or the new buyers have to coax the workers into giving something up.

Prospective private-equity bidders Blackstone Group, Centerbridge Capital Partners and Ceberus Capital Management are considering trading workers' hard benefit checks for much murkier stock of a newly split Chrysler. That has yet to inspire much joy, and who can blame them. The unions typically value such equity at zero, according to a person who has worked with their bargaining committees in the past. The best bet might come from Canadian car-parts concern Magna International Inc., which at least has a tradeable stock that is easy to value and is said to be the preferred option for the unions.

"We're not interested in equity," Mr. Hargrove said. "We've met the test in terms of quality productivity and are not about to give. It ain't going to happen with our union."

Expect the unions to be especially resistant once the personal wealth of Blackstone founder Stephen A. Schwarzman is revealed when that firm files more detailed initial public offering documents. That number could top a flabbergasting $20 billion—not exactly an owner who compels one to accept a smaller paycheck.

This is where Dr. Zetsche's ruthlessness will be put to the test. If the unions won't budge, he might have to ratchet up the threats to get them to the bargaining table. These threats could be everything from a piecemeal break-up to closing large parts of the company or even a bankruptcy filing.

Whether reasonable or not, such threats ring hollow coming from a company with the both the profits and imprimatur of Mercedes-Benz. No one feels sorry for the guy in the S600 sedan.

This will make it very hard for Dr. Zetsche to really pressure the company's U.S. unions—and run the risk of alienating the company's German workers, too.

Daimler probably will find a willing buyer for Chrysler. But doing so will likely mean it taking on the bulk of the liabilities it thought it was shedding in the first place. C'est la guerre, Dr. Z.

POSTSCRIPT

Do Unions Help Organizational Productivity?

Labor unions were formed initially to ensure that employees have a powerful voice at the workplace and also to maintain a balance of power between employers and employees. In 1935, the National Labor Relations Act was established to provide a mechanism to settle any problems between management and labor. However, over the years, the question of whether unions are friends or foes of the management has become a constant debate.

On the constructive side, unionized organizations have demonstrated several positive results such as increased productivity, reduced turnover, and increased internal communication. The fact that employees have a voice is a strong communication tool to make management aware of their work-related needs. Studies have shown that unionized environments demonstrate higher levels of training and development. This has led to a more efficient workforce and contributed to increased productivity. Unionized organizations also do not have such high turnover because employees feel their work-related needs are frequently met. The increased communication between management and labor makes management more accountable. The question is, if unionization has increased productivity, why has their membership declined?

On the other side, critics of labor unions suggest they are only an expense and do not have any positive effects. In 2008, unionized workforces received 21 percent higher wages than nonunion labor forces and also 40 percent more than nonunionized in terms of benefits. These additional labor expenses cause profit margins in unionized sectors to be very minimal. Unions also have the power to slow down work or stop work through limited workloads, strikes, or slowdowns (slowing down work).

The current debacle of the auto industry seems to make scholars and practitioners very distrustful of their existence. The United Auto Workers (UAW) union has also been ridiculed for its unreasonable demands—a case in point is that of a labor perk called the JOBS bank. This benefit, as an agreement between the auto industry and the UAW, allowed employees to receive 85 percent of their wages even if they are laid off or absent from work. This benefit was referred to as the corporate jet perk of the auto industry labor unions as it seemed ridiculous and unreasonable. The whole nation witnessed the financial debacle when the auto industries sought a bailout from the government because they were not able to stay afloat. UAW workers are more expensive to maintain than Japanese or European autoworkers. For instance, UAW employees receive on average $18 more per hour than Toyota employees. How can the U.S. auto industry stay globally competitive with such high labor wages?

Suggested Readings

"Reasons to Oppose a Union," *Management Report* (vol. 27, no. 11, pp. 7–8, November 2004).

Martin Vaughan, "High State Taxes Hit Union Workers Harder," *Wall Street Journal* (Eastern Edition) (p. A.5, August 25, 2009).

The Pros and Cons of Labor Unions: http://www.ehow.com/about_5097523_pros-cons-labor-unions.html

Pros and Cons of Labor Unions: http://www.edubook.com/pros-and-cons-of-labor-unions/9111/

Unions Are Good for Business, Productivity, and the Economy: http://www.aflcio.org/joinaunion/why/uniondifference/uniondiff8.cfm

Strong Unions Strong Productivity: http://www.epi.org/economic_snapshots/entry/webfeatures_snapshots_20070620/

Labor Day Reverence Is Lost, Say Historians: http://www3.signonsandiego.com/stories/2009/sep/07/labor-day-reverence-lost-say-historians/

How Strikes Work: http://money.howstuffworks.com/strike1.htm

1981 Strike Leaves Legacy for American Workers: http://www.npr.org/templates/story/story.php?storyId=5604656

Dutch Labour Participation Rate One of the Highest in the EU: http://crossroadsmag.eu/2009/07/dutch-labour-participation-rate-one-of-the-highest-in-the-eu/

Internet References . . .

The Good and Bad of Teacher Merit Pay

This site is filled with relevant educator's information about San Benito and their schools, faculty, and the students. It also provides a link for additional research on teacher merit pay.

http://www.sanbenito.k12.tx.us/Hot%20News/042604hotnews.html

How Should Pay Be Linked to Performance?

Harvard Business School Working Knowledge is a forum for innovation in business practices, such as pay for performance. The information here offers readers a first look at cutting-edge thinking and the opportunity to both influence and use these concepts before they enter mainstream management practice.

http://hbswk.hbs.edu/item/5703.html

What Motivates Your Employees? Intrinsic vs. Extrinsic Rewards

Tmcnet.com is one of the largest community and technology Web sites that provides relevant business information from experts. Here you will find a featured article on performance management and employee motivation.

http://www.tmcnet.com/channels/performance-management/articles/
39417-what-motivates-employees-intrinsic-vs-extrinsic-rewards.htm

Intrinsic vs. Extrinsic Motivation

This peer-to-peer based technology Web site provides an open discussion forum on important management concepts, like those discussed here on intrinsic and extrinsic motivation from subject matter experts.

http://p2pfoundation.net/Intrinsic_vs._Extrinsic_Motivation

Forced Ranking: Pros and Cons

AllBusiness.com is an online media and e-commerce company that operates one of the premier business sites on the Web. This site addresses real-world business questions and presents practical solutions. Here you will find discussions on, and see both the positive and negative aspects of, forced ranking.

http://www.allbusiness.com/services/educational-services/4283450-1.html

Compensation and Performance Appraisal

*S*hould organizations promote mediocre work performances? Do employees have preferences in the type of rewards they get? Organizations are striving to compensate employees in a way that will help to retain them. Most organizations reward employees a merit pay regardless of their work performance. Firms are debating best methods to attract, acquire, and retain employees. Employers also want to ensure that performance appraisals actually evaluate employee performance. Can organizations compensate and reward employees truly based on their performance?

- Has Merit Pay Lost Its Meaning in the Workplace?
- Do Intrinsic Rewards Provide for Better Employee Retention?
- Is Forced Ranking an Effective Performance Management Approach?
- Given the Current State of the National Economy, Is Executive Pay Unreasonable?

ISSUE 14

Has Merit Pay Lost Its Meaning in the Workplace?

YES: Fay Hansen, from "Merit-Pay Payoff?" *Workforce Management* (November 2008)

NO: Laura Meckler, from "U.S. News: Obama Seeks to Expand Merit Pay for Teachers," *Wall Street Journal* (Eastern Edition) (March 11, 2009)

ISSUE SUMMARY

YES: Fay Hansen, contributing editor for *Workforce Management*, provides studies of leading professors from Stanford and MIT who suggest that merit pay has lost its meaning because employees are not being actually rewarded for performance. They assert that this compensation system is not distinguishing between success and failure and hence has lost its meaning in the workplace.

NO: Laura Meckler of the *Wall Street Journal* contends that workforces that are traditionally underpaid will benefit from such a pay system. Such workforces will feel motivated to perform better because they have been constantly paid poorly.

Merit pay is by definition providing increases in an employee's pay based on his or her job performance. A lot of money is devoted to providing merit increases and U.S. human resource leaders decided how to distribute $200 billion in merit increases for 2009. The most contentious piece of merit pay is that employees are rewarded their merit increase regardless of their job performance. On average, organizations usually provide employees a merit raise between 3.6–3.8 percent. Why should employees receive an increase in pay when their performance does not justify such an increase?

Professor Jeffrey Pfeffer of Stanford University suggests that organizations have battled with the pay dilemma for several decades. Some organizations such as Hewlett-Packard and Verizon struggle to identify the best methods to reward high performers. Organizations vacillate on whether they should provide higher bonuses or merit increases for their employees. The main question of course is which will lead to higher organizational productivity? However, some organizations conclude that when they try to adopt pay initiatives that will identify star performers, it has resulted in dysfunctional practices. Employees do not like to be differentiated because it destroys a collaborative spirit and also breeds negativity. Hence, organizations continue to use the traditional merit-pay systems. Therefore, employees, regardless of their performance level—superior, average, or low—unanimously get the same merit increase. This practice contributes to a work culture of mediocrity and consequently reduces organizational performance. Therefore, what is the meaning or value of a merit increase?

Emilio Castilla, assistant professor of MIT, in a study of 8,898 employees in a high-tech company, identifies the main problem of this pay system as establishing a consistent formula between performance evaluation and merit increases. It is very important to make employees understand that their annual performance will predict their merit pay. Therefore, organizations should adopt standardized merit increase practices based on performance ratings. This should be a transparent system so as not to create any pay mysteries traditionally associated with compensation. Further, he adds that the profits of any business unit should also predict the range of merit increases employees in that business unit receive. For instance, if a business unit makes significant profits, employees in that unit should therefore get higher merit increases. A significant negative HR outcome of the traditional merit pay is that superior performers feel demoralized and hence leave the organization. Would organizations like to lose their star performers due to a lack of a fair pay system?

Laura Meckler, *Wall Street Journal* journalist, suggests that the merit-pay system has not lost its meaning and would greatly benefit a workforce that is chronically underpaid or unionized. U.S. schoolteachers, as a workforce, are greatly underpaid and are not motivated to perform better. The president supports a merit-pay system for teachers acknowledging that a motivated teacher workforce will churn out quality students. The U.S. educational system has been criticized for producing students that are lacking fundamentally in reading and writing skills. Making teachers accountable for their classes and student performance and linking it to merit pay could be the first step in revamping the national education system, which is falling behind in global standards. A merit-pay system will make teachers feel rewarded and accountable to perform better. Schools generally report a high teacher turnover rate as teachers seek better jobs to get a better standard of living.

Unionized workforces also usually eschew merit pay, choosing uniform pay raises across the board. Introducing merit pay for such groups, though very controversial, might greatly contribute to increased productivity of such workforces. A merit-pay system is a very sensitive topic for public service jobs that traditionally shun a pay-for-performance system. Introducing a merit-pay system with performance criteria might shake off some of the persistent workplace complacency associated with federal jobs.

An international perspective suggests that merit-pay practices are followed by organizations in other countries also. In the United Kingdom, merit pay is called performance-related pay (PRP) and follows a model similar to that of U.S. corporations of providing annual increases of around 3 percent. In Japan, merit pay was introduced in the early 1990s to diminish the practices of seniority pay. It has been received with mixed reactions as the traditional Japanese school of thought perceives it might disturb the concept of group harmony, which is very important to their collective culture. In 2009, China announced that it would implement merit pay in its public sector services, such as teaching and health care, to increase productivity in these sectors.

YES

Fay Hansen

Merit-Pay Payoff?

Abstract (Summary)

Human resources executives help manage the $4.5 trillion that US corporations are spending on wages and salaries in 2008 and determine how to distribute the $200 billion increase in wage and salary spending for 2009. Most of this increase will take the form of merit pay, the nearly universal method for distributing wage and salary raises across the US and, increasingly, around the world. The seemingly self-evident premise underlying merit pay and other individual performance-based pay plans is that they produce higher employee and organizational performance. Most companies, however, do not test the actual impact of performance-based rewards on employee behaviors and financial results. Survey reports show years of flat merit increase budgets that barely meet inflation rates and bear no relationship to productivity growth or profitability trends. Emilio Castilla, assistant professor at MIT's Sloan School of Management and a visiting professor at New York University, advises HR executives to pursue collaboration with academic researchers.

It doesn't exist, several recognized experts say. The issue for companies is not whether they should be paying more for performance compensation programs, but whether they should be paying less.

WHEN VERIZON BUSINESS announced the completion of the first next-generation trans-Pacific undersea optical cable system in September, senior vice president for human resources Robert Toohey was buried in budget decisions. "A big struggle is deciding whether you invest more in merit pay or short-term incentives," he says. "Am I going to get more out of higher bonuses or a 2 percent increase in fixed pay through merit increases? Which will drive employees to perform better?"

Verizon Business, based in Basking Ridge, New Jersey, is one of the three operating units of Verizon Communications. The unit generated $21.2 billion in revenue in 2007 and employs 32,000 workers worldwide. Pay decisions carry huge consequences. "You can't walk into finance and tell them you want to spend another $50 million on merit pay without a business case," Toohey says.

Human resources executives help manage the $4.5 trillion that U.S. corporations are spending on wages and salaries in 2008 and determine how to distribute the $200 billion increase in wage and salary spending for 2009. Most of this increase will take the form of merit pay, the nearly universal method for distributing wage and salary raises across the U.S. and, increasingly, around the world.

A large part of the remainder will go to a complex array of incentive plans. Spending on variable pay plans for salaried exempt employees as a percentage of payroll will reach 10.6 percent in 2009, with 90 percent of all organizations using at least one variable plan, Hewitt Associates says.

The seemingly self-evident premise underlying merit pay and other individual performance-based pay plans is that they produce higher employee and organizational performance. Most companies, however, do not test the actual impact of performance-based rewards on employee behaviors and financial results. The most comprehensive empirical studies flow from the academic world, where evidence is mounting that the assumptions underlying individual performance-based pay programs are wrong.

With the drive for evidence-based management now moving across all corporate functions, the sheer force of intuitive practices and the shortage of obvious alternatives no longer suffice as justifications for rewards programs that tear into corporate resources. The real question posed by the best research is not whether companies should be spending more for individual performance pay programs, but whether they should be spending less.

Meritless Pay

One of the most forceful advocates for evidence-based management is Jeffrey Pfeffer, the Thomas D. Dee II professor of organizational behavior at Stanford University's Graduate School of Business. Drawing from his own work and citing three decades of empirical studies, Pfeffer testified before a 2007 congressional hearing on federal personnel reform that the idea that individual pay for performance will enhance organizational performance rests on a set of assumptions that do not hold in the vast majority of organizations.

Pfeffer, with the full support of other recognized experts, continues to sharpen the challenge that now sits squarely before human resources executives and compensation directors.

"The evidence is overwhelming that individual pay for performance does not improve organizational performance except in very limited cases," he says. "Why do people, when confronted with the facts, turn their backs on them?"

Given the lack of evidence that merit pay boosts employee performance and organizational results, should companies abandon it?

"We've already abandoned merit pay," Pfeffer says. "Merit pay is not based on merit. Performance evaluations are biased; overwhelming studies show this. Even if merit pay was based on merit, the pay increases are not enough to motivate employees, but they are enough to irritate them."

Survey reports show years of flat merit increase budgets that barely meet inflation rates and bear no relationship to productivity growth or profitability trends. The major salary budget surveys point to 2009 merit increases averaging 3.6 to 3.8 percent, with the highest performers receiving 5.6 to 6 percent. In effect, for the vast majority of employees, merit increases are unevenly distributed cost-of-living and market-adjustment increases couched in the language of performance rewards.

Even when companies create seemingly significant pay differentiation between low and high performers, the actual cash increase is insufficient to sustain performance—or it drives the wrong behaviors, Pfeffer says. And, as many studies show, high levels of differentiation destroy engagement, breed distrust and undermine teamwork.

A series of experiments conducted by Hewlett-Packard in the 1990s verified longstanding academic studies demonstrating that high incentives for top performers adversely affect organizational performance. Despite the deluge of consultants calling for companies to boost pay differentiation, Pfeffer cites dozens of studies showing that more dispersed pay distributions generate higher turnover, lower quality and a vast array of unintended results, including serious ethical breaches and business-killing behaviors.

"Individual performance pay plans cost a lot of money and upset everyone," Pfeffer says. Perhaps more important, when companies overestimate the power of financial rewards to affect behaviors, they neglect critical skills development and strong leadership, which Pfeffer and other experts agree play a more central role in raising organizational performance.

"Effective management is a system, not a pay plan," Pfeffer notes. "The mistake is that companies try to solve all their problems with pay."

At Verizon Business, Toohey takes a more holistic view. "I take it beyond pay," he says. "When an employee leaves, does he leave for more money? Managers will say that the employee had a better offer. But why did the employee pick up the phone and call the headhunter in the first place? Was the employee trained and developed? Was there proper management? Are you spending the appropriate amounts on training and do employees know how much you are spending? You must have the right data to determine any of this."

Building the Evidence

At the heart of the performance pay problem sits the assumption that correlation implies causation. That assumption continues to pervade decision making in human resources and pay plan design.

"There is the inferential issue," Pfeffer says. "The CEO drank Wild Turkey; the company performed well; ergo, all CEOs should drink more Wild Turkey. The company uses individual incentives; the company performs well; ergo all companies should use more incentives."

Toohey encounters the difficulty of separating correlation and causation at Verizon Business. "I can look at training dollars for a sales channel and the performance of that sales channel. But does that tell me the training improved performance, or does it mean that the channel had really talented people to begin with?" Without the necessary data collected over time, the actual determinants of performance cannot be verified.

Distinguishing correlation from causation is a substantial part of the evidence-based approach to workforce management and pay plan design. "The first step is to know what the evidence says," Pfeffer says. "Know the research literature that pertains to your business. Diffusion and persistence do not prove effectiveness."

The second step is to run experiments. In companies with multiple sites or divisions, HB executives and compensation directors can take the opportunity to learn by doing. Pfeffer advises executives to run performance pay programs in specific units and test the results. "It's not that hard to do," he says. "Many organizations do not run one consistent pay plan throughout the company, and no law says you have to."

"Treat the organization as a prototype," Pfeffer says. For research models, HR executives can look to marketing, particularly Internet-based marketing, where departments are constantly researching, testing and redesigning. It is critical, he emphasizes, to collect data in a way that does not simply confirm existing biases about pay and behavior.

The objective is to move away from the assumptions that continue to shape pay plan design but are inconsistent with logic and empirical studies. "Evidence-based management is a way of thinking and being open to learning, as opposed to assuming that we already know, which is the ideological view supported by casual benchmarking," Pfeffer says.

"It comes down to how we educate people as executives and HR executives. The goal is to transform human resources into the R&D department for the human system, which is the most important system in almost all organizations," Pfeffer says. "HR executives have to change how they think about their jobs."

"In R&D, you go into the laboratory, you experiment and you keep up with the research that others do. You are not involved in rule enforcement but in value creation for the organization through learning and experimentation. Can you imagine walking into the R&D lab at a pharmaceutical company, asking the chief chemist about an important new study and having him respond that they don't keep up with the literature in chemistry?"

Clearing the Obstacles

"In the whole area of pay for performance, HR has been deficient," says Mark Ubelhart, principal in Hewitt Associates' Human Capital Foresight practice. "When companies look at performance pay design, they look at their business strategy and prevalent practices and best practices, but you have to go beyond benchmarking."

"Improved employee performance may or may not lead to better business performance," Ubelhart says. "Hewitt studies show that when companies pay more, business performance is better. But you have to spend time to determine if this is predictive and causal. And if you have a good company, spending more on performance pay has to make it an even better company for there to be a causal relationship."

The obstacles to building an evidence-based approach are substantial, but not insurmountable. "The first problem is talent," Ubelhart says. "You have to apply rigorous academic techniques to the performance pay issue. A lot of companies have talented professionals in human resources, but to migrate to a decision science, you have to have the in-house talent or tap it from outside. Companies are now trying to bring in analytical expertise."

The second problem is data. "The company has to access its own data on human capital and use it," Ubelhart says. "We are absolutely seeing signs that this is changing. And investors want data on human capital. Not long ago, investors only looked at executive compensation, but now they are looking at human capital."

The third problem is the need for a common language. "You need standardized metrics for reporting, and this is beginning to emerge," Ubelhart says. "Once one or two companies disclose human capital metrics in specific terms, CEOs will demand that their HB departments disclose human capital data as well. In two to three years, we will see HB migrate to analytics for broader disclosure, but for people with a classic HB background, it's quite challenging."

Emilio Castilla, assistant professor at MIT's Sloan School of Management and a visiting professor at New York University, advises HB executives to pursue collaboration with academic researchers. "HB has tended not to be open to collaboration or research or even to understanding the tools involved," he says.

"The very top executives at companies are more open to collaboration," Castilla says. "HB is more resistant at companies where the HB function is viewed as an administrative function and the HB executive is not part of the top executive team. Where they are part of the top executive team, they are more open to collaboration."

Castilla reports that some HB executives are closing the knowledge gap between practitioners and academics through two methods. First, they follow the curricula at the top business schools and participate in university seminars and colloquia. Second, they call in academic experts to collaborate on research work. Both methods can produce a knowledge transfer that builds data for evaluating pay plans.

Pfeffer notes the existing evidence points to group bonuses, profit sharing and gain sharing, which is a form of profit sharing, as more effective forms of performancebased pay than merit pay or individual incentives. "Group plans are more collective and recognize the interdependent nature of work today," he says. "Most employees look at their total compensation and want to see that they share in the success of the organization."

Whether a pay plan is individual or group-based, the point is to put evidence behind the assumption that it improves organizational performance, or if the evidence is not affirmative, to make the appropriate business decision. "We've seen finance and marketing migrate to a decision science on spending issues," Ubelhart says. "Now it's HB's turn."

Laura Meckler

➡ **NO**

U.S. News: Obama Seeks to Expand Merit Pay for Teachers

Abstract (Summary)

Perhaps the most controversial step would increase the number of school districts that benefit from a federal program that supports performance pay for teachers.

WASHINGTON—President Barack Obama laid out a broad education vision Tuesday that includes expanded merit pay for teachers and more charter schools, ideas long troubling to teachers unions.

With his congressional agenda already packed, the president is not proposing a major new piece of legislation. Instead, he spelled out the goal of a "cradle to career" education system aimed at serving Americans better at every level. He said he would use the budget to expand programs that work and encourage voluntary action by states and individuals.

The president's plan, which largely implements promises from his campaign, includes new incentives for states to boost the quality of preschool programs and easier access to financial aid for higher education. Mr. Obama also called on states to raise standards for student achievement.

Perhaps the most controversial step would increase the number of school districts that benefit from a federal program that supports performance pay for teachers.

Mr. Obama also called on states to remove caps on the number of public charter schools. Twenty-six states and the District of Columbia now cap the total, according to the National Alliance for Public Charter Schools.

The president cast his proposals as an effort to move past the debates that have dominated education policy in the past.

"Too many supporters of my party have resisted the idea of rewarding excellence in teaching with extra pay, even though we know it can make a difference in the classroom," he told the U.S. Hispanic Chamber of Commerce. "Too many in the Republican Party have opposed new investments in early education, despite compelling evidence of its importance."

Mr. Obama's support for merit pay breaks with some in his party, who fear it can't be administered fairly. The Teacher Incentive Fund currently supports 34 grant recipients at a cost of $97 million this year, and an additional $200 million was allocated through the economic-stimulus plan. Mr. Obama said he would like to see as many as 150 districts added, but the administration didn't say what its 2010 budget request will be.

"It's time to start rewarding good teachers, stop making excuses for bad ones," Mr. Obama said.

Teachers unions said Tuesday that they welcomed Mr. Obama's overall approach and could support merit-pay plans as long as they are fair to teachers. The presidents of the two largest teachers unions said they were confident Mr. Obama would support only proposals that meet that test.

"This is a president who actually respects teachers for who they are and what they do. We can work many of these things out," said Randi Weingarten, president of the American Federation of Teachers.

Dennis Van Roekel, president of the National Education Association, said merit-pay plans should be negotiated to ensure they are not run in an arbitrary way, and he cautioned: "If you pay one teacher more you have to pay someone else less."

POSTSCRIPT

Has Merit Pay Lost Its Meaning in the Workplace?

Merit pay has been a debatable topic for HRM and line professionals because they feel they are rewarding employees regardless of their job performance. Scholars suggest that organizations need to take a scientific approach to develop compensation practices that will actually award true performance. Managers fear if they isolate star performers, they might lose other disappointed employees. Consequently they follow a merit-pay system, which is, unfortunately, not tied to merit and therefore make many high-performing employees dissatisfied. A Watson/Wyatt 2009/2010 pay survey of 235 companies suggests that U.S. companies continue to pay their employees an average merit pay increase of 3.5 percent. Organizations also indicate that this percentage may be reduced to reflect the state of the current economy. The information technology and financial services were ranked as industries that gave the highest merit increases for their employees. The federal government and education provided the lowest merit increase to their employees.

Advocates of a merit-pay system suggest that some workforces may benefit from pay practices that stress accountability and lead to productivity. Federal jobs and unionized jobs generally prefer uniform raises and do not adopt merit-pay practices. Some employees in these workforces have a sense of entitlement and smugness about their jobs. Making their pay directly related to their performance will greatly contribute to increased productivity. It might also help attract quality talent because superior performers like to see rewards for their hard work. President Obama has taken a very proactive stand on merit pay for the nation's teachers as he feels he should not encourage a pay system that rewards failure. He reiterates that national teachers are the backbone of our economy and not making this talent accountable for their performance could have severe repercussions on the quality of the knowledge, skills, and abilities of our future workforce.

Suggested Readings

H. Risher, "Adding Merit to Pay for Performance," *Compensation and Benefits Review*, (vol. 40, no. 6, p. 22, November 3008).

Anonymous, "Pay Outlook: Raises Are Back, Though They Will Be Small," *HR Focus* (vol. 86, no. 9, pp. 5–7, September 2009).

Pros and Cons of Merit Pay For Teachers: http://k6educators.about.com/od/assessmentandtesting/a/meritypay.htm

Does Merit Pay Make Sense?: http://blogs.edweek.org/edweek/Bridging-Differences/merit_pay/

Unions Call Merit Pay Proposal Unacceptable: http://www.nytimes.com/2000/01/28/nyregion/unions-call-merit-pay-proposal-unacceptable.html

Japanese Starting to Link Pay to Performance, Not Tenure: http://www.nytimes.com/1993/10/02/world/japanese-starting-to-link-pay-to-performance-not-tenure.html

China to promote merit pay system: http://english.people.com.cn/90001/90776/90785/6746707.html

ISSUE 15

Do Intrinsic Rewards Provide for Better Employee Retention?

YES: **Amanda Wilkinson,** from "Total Reward Is Helping to Define a New Era of Benefits," *Employee Benefits* (July 2007)

NO: **Frank Hayes,** from "Reasons to Go," *Computerworld* (June 2008)

ISSUE SUMMARY

YES: Michael Armstrong, who writes extensively on rewards and pay, identifies the benefits of intrinsic rewards and indicates that financial rewards or external motivators are often short-lived and do not contribute to employee retention. However, intrinsic rewards contribute immensely to job satisfaction and employee retention.

NO: Frank Hayes contends that pay or external factors contribute to employee satisfaction and job retention. High compensation has a unique way of attracting and retaining talent.

Intrinsic rewards are defined as the nonfinancial factors in a total pay package. These nonfinancial factors could be challenging assignments, job recognition, career growth, or training and developmental opportunities. In the 1960s, Frederick Herzberg developed the two-factor motivation and hygiene theory suggesting that employees are motivated both by extrinsic (financial) and intrinsic (nonfinancial) rewards. He identified motivation as intrinsic factors (such as the nature of the job, professional growth, development) or internal factors that motivate employees. He identified hygiene factors as extrinsic (such as salary, status, company, working conditions), which are external factors that motivate employees.

Michael Armstrong suggests that the benefits of financial rewards are very transient. While employees do strive for better pay to have a better standard of living and keep ahead in this materialistic world, such job satisfaction does not last long. It is an engaging environment in terms of challenging work, leadership positions, interpersonal relationships, and learning new skills that will sustain employee retention. Armstrong suggests that providing intrinsic rewards have very positive HR outcomes such as reduced employee turnover, increased productivity, and employee engagement.

Towers Perrin, a successful financial global firm, uses a total reward package that adopts a four-quadrant approach to capture both extrinsic and intrinsic rewards. They are pay and rewards, learning and development, benefits, and work environment. Employees therefore are cognizant of what their entire value is worth. There is more than just money. Distinguishing intrinsic with extrinsic rewards helps greatly in the recruiting process as applicants are made aware of their total employee value.

Armstrong also suggests that instead of providing standard intrinsic packages, companies should provide choices for employees by adopting an open communication with employees either through focus groups or interviews to better understand what exactly motivates them. Organizations can then customize their intrinsic rewards to cater exclusively to their organizational workforce. Some employees might want the power and recognition, others might strive on team tasks, and others might want an environment of learning and development. Proponents of intrinsic rewards suggest that external factors (such as pay and benefits) might be very short lived in comparison to intrinsic rewards.

On the other hand, Frank Hayes suggests that providing intrinsic rewards could create opposite HR outcomes. Practitioners suggest that after employees are well trained, developed, or certified, they generally seek greener pastures taking with them their priceless knowledge capital. This is especially relevant in knowledge industries, such as information technology, where current knowledge is very valued.

Professionals and psychologists also suggest that extrinsic factors promote retention more than intrinsic factors do. Extrinsic factors are rooted in the reinforcement theory, which suggests that an employee's behavior (job performance) can be shaped by providing positive rewards (pay and benefits). B.F. Skinner, who proposed this theory, suggests that superior performance, if rewarded, will be reinforced and repeated. Further, extrinsic factors, such as high pay, are very attractive recruiting tools for HR professionals. Organizations that usually use a lead-the-market-pay approach attract the cream of talent because pay and benefits speak their own language. Other advantages of extrinsic rewards are that employees perceive an increased sense of self-worth in receiving higher pay, and it helps them set higher goals to get increased rewards.

An international perspective suggests that different cultural factors contribute to the emphasis of extrinsic or intrinsic rewards. In Asian countries, such as China and India, intrinsic factors are very valued by employees because the culture has such a strong focus on education and learning. Therefore, multinationals establishing in these countries should emphasize this cultural preference in their recruiting strategies and accentuate professional development and growth. In contrast, Latin American countries have a preference for extrinsic rewards (such as club memberships, cars, high pay) because their societies favors status and power displayed by a materialistic world. Similarly, multinationals establishing in Latin American should highlight the monetary rewards of their pay packages.

YES

Amanda Wilkinson

Total Reward Is Helping to Define a New Era of Benefits

Abstract (Summary)

HR consultant and co-author of such tomes as *Reward Management* and *Strategic Reward,* Michael Armstrong, says total reward is about all the ways in which people are rewarded when they come to work—pay, benefits and the other non-financial rewards—put together to make a coherent and integrated whole. Non-financial or intrinsic rewards include factors such as scope for achievement, recognition and opportunities for growth. Armstrong believes the concept of total reward is simple. If people are rewarded both extrinsically and intrinsically then that helps foster engagement with a job, commitment to an organisation and positive discretionary behaviour, for example, by staff undertaking more work than is expected of them or tasks outside of their job description. If employers want to adopt total reward they should start by reviewing the existing package against one of the various total reward models. Armstrong believes the most well-known is that used by Towers Perrin which has quadrants on pay and reward, benefits, learning and development and the work environment.

"**T**otal reward" may be a mis-used term but HR commentator Michael Armstrong believes the less obvious non-financial or intrinsic rewards, such as opportunities for growth, are of vital consideration, says Amanda Wilkinson.

Total reward may be flavour of the month, but although the term first emerged in the US around ten years ago, many employers are still confused as to its true meaning.

HR consultant and co-author of such tomes as Reward management and Strategic reward, Michael Armstrong, however, is adamant that there is only one true meaning. For him, total reward is best encapsulated in a definition used by consumer goods company Unilever which states that it "encompasses all the elements of what it means to come to work".

This extends beyond total remuneration, which is confined to pay and benefits. "There are lots of models about, but essentially total reward is about all the ways in which people are rewarded when they come to work—pay, benefits and the other non-financial rewards—put together to make a coherent and integrated whole," says Armstrong.

Non-financial or intrinsic rewards include factors such as scope for achievement, recognition and opportunities for growth.

Armstrong believes the concept of total reward is simple. If people are rewarded both extrinsically and intrinsically then that helps foster engagement with a job, commitment to an organisation and positive discretionary behaviour, for example, by staff undertaking more work than is expected of them or tasks outside of their job description.

"There is nothing new in total reward. It's a name that has been coined to cover what many people have been saying for years, back to Frederick Herzberg who was writing 40 years ago, that the intrinsic rewards are just as important [as pay and benefits] and probably longer lasting in terms of motivating people," says Armstrong.

Management Green Light

While he accepts that pay and benefits motivate people, the effect, he says, is short-lived. "[The positive effect of] having a pay increase or a bigger car, will pass, always. What really counts in terms of long-term engagement and commitment to the organisation are the other things which are about the environment and the intrinsic rewards that derive from the work itself."

Total reward may sound simple enough, but difficulties can arise in first convincing management to give such a strategy the green light and then actually implementing the concept. "The problem is you can't demonstrate [to management] that you will get a return on investment. This is what you want to cost, but it's difficult because you will have to make all sorts of assumptions," says Armstrong.

While the cost of pay and some benefits can be determined, accurate figures are difficult to calculate for the more intrinsic aspects of reward. Furthermore, there is no way of estimating the return on that expenditure, and the time and effort spent in implementing total reward, although improvements in staff productivity, commitment and recruitment, would be expected along with reduced turnover. The HR team will need to be persuasive if it is to convince management that total reward is worth implementing. The task though is helped by the increasing acceptance and use of the term total reward.

"Many organisations now say they have total reward because it's the thing to have, if you like flavour of the month, but there is a lot of rhetoric about it. I think it's quite a difficult thing to do in reality," says Armstrong.

The Quadrant Definition

If employers want to adopt total reward they should start by reviewing the existing package against one of the various total reward models. Armstrong believes the most well-known is that used by Towers Perrin which has quadrants on pay and reward, benefits, learning and development and the work environment. "That's the first thing, to get total remuneration right. In one sense, that is the easiest because it's clear cut," says Armstrong. However, it is not necessarily quick as it can take years for example to get the pension scheme right or to introduce a flexible benefits plan.

According to Armstrong, the learning and development quadrant includes factors such as workplace learning, career development, training and performance management, while the work environment, includes core values, leadership, job design and employee voice.

"You are really looking much more broadly at your HR policies and saying 'what are we doing to create an effective brand new proposition here—the employment proposition' and you say 'we want to make this organisation a place to which people want to come to work and want to stay to work'," explains Armstrong.

This process can take a long time. "It's really a question of carrying out a review of what is happening now and establishing the gaps, and then progressively doing something about it. You may have to tackle some things one at a time and do it incrementally. What you are trying to do is reinforce the total reward package and trying to reinforce the total value proposition.

"If one can do that, then one is beginning to be in a position to be able to tell people, which is what you want to be able to do when you are recruiting them and while they are with you, 'look, this is what you are getting, not just pay and benefits, you are getting this tremendous learning and development, career planning opportunity programme, we are dealing with flexibility and looking at your work-life balance, we are making sure managers are developed as leaders and so on'. It then becomes a package that can be presented to people."

Involving existing staff in the process of developing the total reward proposition so that they can understand it and help communicate it to a wider audience will pay dividends. This should include discussions with trade union representatives at a local, regional and national level. "The unions could well be suspicious. This is why you start off by saying 'let's get the pay and benefits right', if you can. It's a question of trying to get them on board."

Other ways of involving employees include staff associations, focus groups, workshops and discussions with line managers who, at the end of the day, play a key role in implementing and communicating total reward effectively.

Communication can be executed in a number of other ways including through total reward statements, which Armstrong distinguishes from total remuneration statements that just include pay and benefits. "It's really telling people the value they get from working for this type of organisation. It's not just a handbook-type approach—it's a continuous programme using every media you have got, the Internet, briefing groups, training sessions, workshops, induction programmes, staff handbook, all those things," he says.

Ultimately, the message that needs to be conveyed is that "there is more to working here than just drawing a pay cheque at the end of the month", says Armstrong.

However, there are many organisations that claim to offer total reward when they don't in fact do so, while some even confuse it with offering flexible benefits.

"Some people in organisations I have been involved with say they have introduced flex, and therefore have introduced total reward, well they haven't. Total reward is, in fact, much broader and a much more difficult concept to apply," says Armstrong.

He does, however, believe that flexible benefits are an important part of total reward as they help improve the employee experience by giving more choice when it comes to perks.

If organisations are to do more than merely pay lip service to total reward and to implement a strategy effectively then, as Armstrong says, they must accept "it's a hard road to follow, but one worth following."

Career History

A prolific author of reward and HR books, Michael Armstrong began his career in HR at the coalface as a practitioner.

After 25 years working in this role, including a 12-year stint as the HR director of a large publishing firm, Armstrong is now an independent consultant and managing partner of e-reward.

His publications include a handbook of employee reward management and practice, Reward management, co-authored with Helen Murlis, Strategic reward, co-authored with Duncan Brown, a handbook of human resources management practice and Performance management.

"If people are thinking about their HR strategy, part of this must be total reward. It is becoming an accepted term. There's a better understanding of it now than say five years ago in spite of a lot of people paying lip service to it," says Armstrong.

Q&A

What Is Total Reward?

Various approaches have been taken to total reward, but many experts take a broad view of the total reward package extending it beyond pay and benefits to include intrinsic aspects of work such as the work environment and learning and development. The aim is to use total reward to foster employee engagement with their work, commitment to the organisation and positive discretionary behaviour.

What Are the Benefits of Adopting a Total Reward Strategy?

While it is hard to calculate the return on investment from a total reward strategy, it arguably improves productivity, reduces staff turnover, helps in recruiting key talent and enhances the reputation of the employer both internally and externally.

Frank Hayes

➡ **NO**

Reasons to Go

Abstract (Summary)

Look, turnover is expensive. The real cost of replacing an employee can run as high as 150% of a year's salary once you add up the costs of recruitment, training and waiting for the new hire to get up to speed, plus the lost knowledge, damaged morale and extra work that comes when any employee bails out. That's on top of payroll—it's like paying for 1.5 phantom employees for every one that leaves. Being a great place to work turns out to be like money in the bank. The reasons your IT people would want to leave are: 1. low pay, 2. boredom, 3. no training, 4. career dead end, and 5. no life.

WHY WOULD ANYONE ever want to leave? As you read about the "100 Best Places to Work in IT" in this issue of *Computerworld*, that's a question worth keeping in mind.

No, not about those best places—they're stuffed full of reasons why employees stay. But what about your shop? Why would your employees want to jump ship?

Look, turnover is expensive. The real cost of replacing an employee can run as high as 150% of a year's salary once you add up the costs of recruitment, training and waiting for the new hire to get up to speed, plus the lost knowledge, damaged morale and extra work that comes when any employee bails out. That's on top of payroll—it's like paying for 1.5 phantom employees for every one that leaves.

Average annual turnover for those 100 Best Places to Work? It's a mere 7%—half the industry average. Being a great place to work turns out to be like money in the bank.

OK: What are the reasons your IT people would want to leave? And what can you do about them?

Low pay. There may not be a lot you can do about salaries and raises; they're probably watched like a hawk by your chief financial officer. But you have options. Example: Stop using your bonus pool as a way of supplementing salaries across the board. Instead, pay much bigger bonuses to fewer people for specific, publicly recognized accomplishments. Suddenly, a bonus means something. Everybody on your staff won't hit the jackpot, but everyone will have a chance—based on what he accomplishes.

Boredom. Sure, our job isn't to entertain our IT employees. But if someone is actually bored, something's wrong. Maybe it's the wrong job for him. Maybe it's the wrong company. Or maybe he could be doing a lot more, but the current job won't let him. Hey, if he can polish off his week's regular work in 30 hours, reward that with opportunities for new projects, training, coaching fellow workers—whatever will motivate and challenge him.

No training. Yeah, we all know the excuse: If we pay for training, employees will just take that new knowledge and leave for better jobs. But with no training, they'll get fed up and leave anyway—or rot away with outdated skills. So get creative. Pay for training with loans you forgive only after a certain number of months or years. If an employee is willing to pay out of his own pocket but needs time off for training, be as flexible as you possibly can. And compare the cost of retraining a current employee with the real cost of a new hire. Suddenly, training sounds a lot more cost-effective.

Career dead end. You know all those people you can't promote out of their current jobs because you'll never be able to replace their skills—and can't pay what they're worth because they've topped out the salary range for their jobs?

Put them in charge of finding and training their own replacements.

No life. Insane hours, death-march projects and exhausting demands are just the way IT is, right? Baloney. They're just signs of badly managed IT operations and projects, and they're costing you dearly. So stop the madness. There are better ways to do almost everything in your IT shop—and the people to look to first for ideas are your employees.

Would flextime make them more effective? Telecommuting? Better technology? Improved training? Things you'd never think of? Ask. Learn. Figure out what's possible, then ask some more.

Get rid of the reasons your staff wants to leave and you won't just have a better place to work in IT.

You'll have a better IT shop.

POSTSCRIPT

Do Intrinsic Rewards Provide for Better Employee Retention?

The question of providing intrinsic or extrinsic rewards seems to be a constant concern for compensation specialists. Scholars, practitioners, and psychologists argue that internal motivation of employees is more valuable than external motivation because external motivation or extrinsic factors can be substituted (for higher pay) or short-lived (employees are no longer motivated by their pay levels). On the other hand, intrinsic factors have demonstrated excellent HR outcomes. Container Store, well known for its very strong intrinsic focus, provides its employees annual training and development of approximately 235 hours, while the industry average is about 7 hours. The company's turnover rate is 10 percent compared to the industry norm of 90 percent. Employees value the investment the company provides them in terms of their professional development and growth and return this favor by staying with the company. Container Store has been an Employer of Choice on the Top 100 companies list for almost seven years.

Organizations that focus on intrinsic rewards should also ensure that they frequently provide recognition such as employee of the month (EOM). This could be identified for several purposes such as high performers, best teams, or for organizational tenure. Such professional and public recognition is a very powerful motivator for employees' self-worth and self-esteem. A recent 2008 study at WorldatWork with HR compensation experts suggested that the number of organizations providing EOMs has substantially increased due to its reputation of being a powerful retention tool. Specifically recognizing superior performance, organizational tenure, and also peer rewards demonstrated positive HRM outcomes.

On the other hand, opponents of intrinsic rewards suggest that pay is the most important motivator for an employee's work behavior and subsequent retention. They argue that high pay makes employees feel valuable, is an easy recruitment tool, and provides employees with a better standard of living. Further, if organizations focus on intrinsic rewards, they could lose their employees to poaching as other firms seek their enhanced knowledge. The United States pays the highest salary for its CEOs, almost more than 364 times the average full-time worker. This suggests we live in a society that cherishes and applauds such extrinsic rewards. Otherwise, why would the U.S. CEOs receive such ridiculous pay?

Suggested Readings

"MOTIVATION: Create a Strategy That Earns Respect," *Employee Benefits* (p. S.3, September 2008).

Hao Zhao, "Expectations of Recruiters and Applicants in Large Cities of China," *Journal of Managerial Psychology* (vol. 21, no. 5, pp. 459–475, 2006).

Jonathan Birchall, "Training Improves Shelf Life," *Financial Times* (p. 15, March 8, 2006).

A. Palmer, "Survey: Workplace Recognition Widespread," *Incentive* (vol. 182, no. 6, p. 10,13, June 2008).

Extrinsic Motivation—What Are the Pros and Cons? http://www.artipot.com/articles/400787/extrinsic-motivation-what-are-the-pros-and-cons.htm

The Science of Intrinsic and Extrinsic Motivation, and the Implications for Society: http://beyondgrowth.net/social-criticism/the-science-of-intrinsic-and-extrinsic-motivation-and-the-implications-for-society

CEO Pay: 364 Times More Than Workers: http://money.cnn.com/2007/08/28/news/economy/ceo_pay_workers/index.htm

ISSUE 16

Is Forced Ranking an Effective Performance Management Approach?

YES: Alex Blyth, from "Cull or Cure?" *Personnel Today* (May 2007)

NO: Gail Johnson, from "Forced Ranking: The Good, The Bad, And The ALTERNATIVE," *Training* (May 2004)

ISSUE SUMMARY

YES: Alex Blyth reiterates the thoughts of Microsoft leaders on forced ranking. This performance approach is very good at identifying the underperformers and rewarding the stars.

NO: Gail Johnson, former editor of *Training* magazine, suggests this method is flawed because it encourages a very competitive and dysfunctional work environment.

Forced ranking is a performance management approach that ranks employees in predetermined performance groups. This performance approach was championed in the 1980s by former CEO of GE, Jack Welch, who thought that it was the best way to rank high performers and yank poor performers. This method also came to be referred as the "rank and yank" method. The advantages of this approach are that it rewards top performers, identifies employees with developmental needs, and dismisses employees who are not performing. The traditional forced ranking rated employees in three groups: the top 10 percent, the middle 70 percent, and the bottom 20 percent.

GE was one of the first companies to adopt this performance approach and was very successful in tremendously enhancing its business profits. Today about 20 percent of the Fortune 500 companies adopt this performance method with very positive results. Organizations such as Microsoft also applaud this method because it is very performance driven, which is critical for the knowledge- and customer-focused industries. Microsoft executives believe that 15 percent of the company's employees should be dismissed annually. This kind of system would definitely make sure that the system awards success and penalizes failure. Frequently, even when a business unit is performing well, the stars or high performers carry the load of the mediocre and underperformers. Why should organizations promote a system that rewards failure?

Richard Grote, another champion of forced ranking, suggests a distinction between forced ranking and forced distribution. Forced ranking is a method of ranking leadership and upper-level talent numerically. However, forced distribution is grouping of employees in different performance groups. He also suggests that forced ranking produces best results when adopted for short-term periods (three years). This helps dismiss the underperformers and contributes to bottom-line profits. Eventually the organization will realize that it has no employees who are underperformers.

The other point of view suggests that this method is completely flawed and promotes a lot of dysfunctional organizational behavior. First, when employees are made to compete with another, it results in a very competitive work environment and negativity. Employees might think twice about helping their peers in work-related issues as it might result in a lower rank for them. On the other hand, star employees might feel disillusioned working in a negative work culture. Moreover, who likes a performance appraisal system that ranks and yanks in full public view?

Further, in today's team-oriented work environment, such an appraisal system does not contribute to any collaborative corporate spirit. Also, employees ranked in the lowest rung could file for lawsuits as they may perceive the system to be unfair and discriminary. The classic example of this is that of Ford Motor Company that classified its employees into three performance categories (A, B, C). The organization mandated 10 percent of the employees to be placed in the lowest category. This created many discontented employees filing legal complaints for which Ford Motor Company had to modify this method of appraisal.

Performance experts also suggest that there are several other appraising methods that could identify performance effectively and minimize the use of forced ranking. Several organizations have adopted effective performance management systems without using a ranking method. Lockheed Martin, a major player in the aerospace industry, has implemented a very successful appraisal system that has made both employers and employees very satisfied. Employees are differentiated on five categories of exceptional, high contributor, successful contributor, basic contributor, and unsatisfactory. The definitions of these categories are provided by the concerned managers after detailed and thorough communication of what performance level each category defines. Most employees fall under the successful contributor category, and the extreme categories are used with great caution.

An international perspective suggests that performance appraisal management is a very sensitive topic in many cultures. The paternalistic management approach adopted in many Asian and Latin American cultures make an objective appraisal method quite difficult. Superiors and subordinates form a very close relationship that goes beyond the definitions of the job. Further, dismissal of employees due to poor performance is considered a social stigma and used with great caution. Therefore, practices such as forced ranking and forced distribution is frowned upon in such collectivist cultures.

YES ↵

Alex Blyth

Cull or Cure?

Abstract (Summary)

Microsoft chief executive Steve Ballmer caused a stir last year when he announced to the Institute of Directors conference that he culls one in every 15 employees every year. He suggested that all business, large and small, would benefit from such an approach. His views received support from a recent survey by global talent management consultancy Hudson, which found that 77% of 562 executives and senior managers in the UK believe that a fixed quota for annual staff dismissal would boost financial performance and productivity. Yet despite these many alleged benefits, only 4% of companies surveyed dismiss a proportion of their staff. Many critics of the culling approach believe that companies should instead focus on re-engaging underperforming employees. Tom Barry, BlessingWhite Europe managing director, says it is not good practice to search out the disengaged simply to cull them. However, Ballmer does have some supporters. If a company is to conduct a cull, it needs to ensure it is done properly.

Should HR advise managers to cull less-effective staff, or work with them to improve performance? Alex Blyth considers the arguments.

Microsoft chief executive Steve Ballmer caused a stir last year when he announced to the Institute of Directors conference that he culls one in every 15 employees every year. He suggested that all businesses, large and small, would benefit from such an approach.

His views received support from a recent survey by global talent management consultancy Hudson, which found that 77% [of] 562 executives and senior managers in the UK believe that a fixed quota for annual staff dismissal would boost financial performance and productivity.

The advantages of pursuing this policy were described in Hudson's research as ensuring strong team members are not carrying weaker ones, allowing underperforming staff to pursue a fresh challenge more suited to their abilities, and increasing productivity overall.

Yet, despite these many alleged benefits, only 4% of companies surveyed dismiss a proportion of their staff. The remaining 96% might well be looking at these results and wondering if they should follow suit.

From *Personnel Today*, May 29, 2007, pp. 20–21. Copyright © 2007 by Reed Business Information, Ltd. Reprinted by permission.

Opposition to Culling

Most companies are quick to dismiss the idea. Cathy Monaghan, head of HR at reward consultancy PES, says: "This is a great idea if you want to manage through fear, retribution and paranoia, and create a general air of unease.

"This sort of culling makes people focus on appearing productive, leads to short-termism, and attracts the wrong sort employees. It's also expensive, as you incur recruitment costs to replace the staff you have culled."

Others raise issues with the practical implementation of the idea. "What is the right percentage?" asks Chris Howe, director of ChangeMaker, an HR and change management consultancy. "If you pick an arbitrary number such as 15%, how do you know that is right? What if you have only 7% of underachievers, and you are therefore throwing out 8% of good people?"

Nearly one-quarter (24%) of respondents to the Hudson survey believe that deliberately dismissing underperforming staff increases morale among the rest of the team. But for Hamish Cameron Blackie, partner at accountancy firm and UK200Group member Barlow Robbins, this is a poor way of motivating staff.

"Culling the bottom performers will only ever motivate those on the cusp of success or failure. Those who are at the bottom of the performance table will be demotivated and will not care about their performance any longer. Those in the middle ground, but comfortably distant from the danger of being dismissed, won't care about the policy either," he says.

Finally, there are concerns about the legality of culls. "How would this be explained to an employment tribunal?" points out Nadia Motraghi, a barrister specialising in employment law at Old Square Chambers. "It doesn't appear to be a genuine redundancy situation, because the workforce cull appears unrelated to the level of work that needs to be carried out and the number of employees needed to do that work. From a legal perspective, regular staff culls are likely to require employers to get their chequebooks out."

Alternative Approaches

Many of these critics of the culling approach believe that companies should instead focus on re-engaging underperforming employees. Tom Barry, managing director of leadership consultancy BlessingWhite Europe, says: "It's not good practice to search out the disengaged simply to cull them. It may not be their fault. Companies should try to ensure that the activity of all employees is aligned to strategic goals."

For others, it is more important to focus on the high performers in an organisation. Mike Penny, director of executive search consultancy Warren Partners, says: "Companies often spend so much time on underperformers that they forget to stretch the top performers intellectually and support their development needs. Instead, they can inadvertently punish great performance by overloading them with extra work."

These critics of the culling strategy all agree that it is far better to hire the right people in the first place. Dave Millner, consultancy director of recruitment consultancy Kenexa Europe, says: "If companies have to cull one in 15 staff every year to maintain performance standards, then they are failing to hire the right staff in the first place."

And 72% of respondents to the Hudson survey agreed, admitting there would be less need to release staff deliberately if recruitment processes were more rigorous.

The Case for Culling

However, Ballmer does have some supporters. Stuart Duff, head of development at occupational psychologists Pearn Kandola, believes that the culling approach is simply the logical conclusion of performance management. "Why bother to have a performance management system if you don't act at both ends? Most companies, however, just reward the top performers and ignore the poor performers," he says.

"The reason for this is that it is difficult to manage performance to the extent that you can be confident enough to fire someone. Few managers have the time to do this. Paradoxically, they're too busy to manage their staff properly. However, those organisations that do set their staff clear goals, and manage their progress towards the achievement of those goals over a long period of time, can then act on the results and reap the rewards."

He points to a major IT consultancy that does this. "The HR department sits down once a year with line managers and asks them who are the high performers they want to promote, and who are the poor performers dragging them down, who they want to fire," says Duff.

"Because the company vigorously executes its performance management system, line managers can answer these questions confidently and the organisation can make the right decisions."

This may sound heartless, and Duff says this approach is likely to promote a culture of internal competition and destroy employee loyalty. However, Chris Welford, director of talent and assessment at HR consultancy Penna, believes that culling can even be good for those who get fired.

"The initial reaction to this idea is horror. However, if you think it through, it's more sensible than it sounds. Most people have skills, but they're not always used in the right way," he says.

"In any organisation, there are about 10% of people who are in the wrong job. It makes sense to have adult conversations with them about their future and then to help them find work that will use their skills. It's much better to do that than to hide behind procedures and rules-based management."

All in the implementation

If a company is to conduct a cull, it needs to ensure it is done properly.

Andy Cook, managing director of HR consultancy Marshall James, advises: "Any systems in place to measure staff performance must be objective and non-discriminatory. Communication of company policy must be robust, so that employees are not surprised if they find themselves in the bottom percentile and action is taken to dismiss them. Policies and procedures must always be transparent and, most importantly, legal."

Gail Johnson

$\rightarrow$ **NO**

Forced Ranking: The Good, The Bad, and The ALTERNATIVE

Abstract (Summary)

Whether they call it rank or yank, the vitality curve or top grading, as many as one-third of employers use forced ranking on at least some members of their workforce. Although there is no one specific way to conduct forced ranking, the most common model is to rank employees on a bell curve, designating 20% of employees as superstars, the middle 70% as the average but vital backbone of the company, and the remaining 10% as weakest links. Despite all of the exposure forced ranking has received, corporate America remains fuzzy about the issues surrounding this workforce performance tool. Executives often mandate a forced ranking system because it's the easiest and fairest way to make necessary cuts in a down economy. But Bob Rogers says forced ranking is a poor way to manage poor performers. Rogers, who is the president of Development Dimensions International, a human resource consulting company based in Pittsburgh, has managed and worked under forced ranking systems throughout his career. He claims that forced ranking sends a negative signal to employees and has a tremendous downside in terms of teamwork, culture, competitiveness and legal problems.

One out of five Fortune 500 companies use forced ranking as a workforce management tool to determine whether employees will receive rewards or hit the trail. But is forced ranking the best way to weed out the low-potentials in your organization?

Whether you call it rank or yank, the vitality curve or top grading, as many as one-third of employers use forced ranking on at least some members of their workforce. Forced ranking became all the rage during the tenure of former General Electric CEO Jack Welch. Each year, 10 percent of GE managers are assigned the bottom grade, and if they don't improve they are asked to leave the company. When GE launched forced ranking and the company's profits started to soar, a number of high-profile companies adopted the GE model of forced ranking, among them Pepsico, Conoco, and notoriously, Enron. Today, as many as 20 percent of Fortune 500 companies now apply forced ranking.

Forced ranking is based on the idea that in order to grow, a company must identify its best and worst performers, then reward top performers with bonuses and development opportunities—while showing the bottom-feeders the door, or at least encouraging them to leave.

Although there is no one specific way to conduct forced ranking, the most common model is to rank employees on a bell curve, designating 20 percent of employees as superstars, the middle 70 percent as the average but vital backbone of the company, and the remaining 10 percent as weakest links. Some companies use quintiling, where managers rank the employees they supervise into five groups, from the top 20 percent to the bottom 20 percent. Others take the totem pole approach, ranking employees one on top of the other.

Despite all of the exposure forced ranking has received, corporate America remains fuzzy about the issues surrounding this workforce performance tool. Dick Grote, a former GE executive, is president of Grote Consulting, Addison, Texas, and helps companies launch forced ranking systems. He says people often confuse forced ranking with forced distribution. By definition, forced distribution is part of the performance appraisal process and requires that at least 5 percent of employees be placed in the bottom category, 15 percent in the next category, and no more than 10 percent in the top category.

Forced ranking, on the other hand, is conducted independently of the performance appraisal process and usually only senior executives and managers are ranked to groom and identify potential leaders. "Most people think everyone is ranked from top to bottom," Grote says. "That's a common misconception."

Grote believes that forced ranking works best when used as a short-term fix, not an ongoing process, and he recommends using the approach for a maximum of three years. "The first year you are getting a huge payoff because you identify the 10 percent who are not strong contributors," he says. "By the second year you have narrowed it down. By the third year, you have cut the organizational fat and are getting down to bone and muscle. The job is done and it's time to move on to other processes to manage people."

Executives often mandate a forced ranking system because it's the easiest and fairest way to make necessary cuts in a down economy. "The alternative to forced ranking is promoting people who aren't the stars and retaining poor performers," Grote says.

Robert Rogers says forced ranking is a poor way to manage poor performers. Rogers, who is the president of Development Dimensions International (DDI), a human resource consulting company based in Pittsburgh, has managed and worked under forced ranking systems throughout his career. He claims that forced ranking sends a negative signal to employees and has a tremendous downside in terms of teamwork, culture, competitiveness and legal problems. "Forced ranking is all the rage, but it's also seriously flawed," he says.

When Rogers worked under a forced ranking system in the U.S. Air Force he saw an immediate change in the attitude of his peers. "Our entire division requested to work for the highest ranking commander because we knew that a general wasn't going to let his direct reports get a low rating, as compared to a colonel," he says. "We found ways to work around the system real fast."

Throughout his career, Rogers has come across horror stories of how employees abuse the forced ranking system. "Some managers hire low potential employees from the start," he says. "I met a manager who hired someone he knew was not a top performer, but he needed to fill his quota of C-performers so he offered that employee up."

Eventually, says Rogers, employees under a forced ranking system begin to doubt their abilities to do a good job. "They believe that their continued employment rests not on what they do but on who supports them and how well they can articulate that," he says.

Differentiation or Discrimination?

There is, perhaps, no subject that managers are more reluctant to talk about than forced ranking. "Companies see forced ranking as a competitive advantage," Grote says. "They don't want to share. What's to be gained by going public? Absolutely nothing."

And "nothing" was what we heard after requesting interviews with several corporate giants to discuss their forced ranking systems, including Intel ("we would like to pass on this opportunity"), Capital One ("not able to participate in the story at this time"), EDS ("no comment"), and Microsoft ("not available for interview at this time").

GE declined an interview, but a company spokesperson provided the following comment: "GE believes in rating people, and we have used a ranking system for decades. It's very much part of GE's performance-based culture as well as being part of a holistic process of being continuously assessed. As a result, employees always know where they stand and how they can perform better."

Grote admits to being a vocal, but lonely advocate of forced ranking. "It's very easy to point out flaws and problems with forced ranking because it makes people uncomfortable and there has been so much negative publicity."

Most of the negative publicity stems from a flurry of class action lawsuits by workers who were given low ranks. Take Ford Motor Co.'s experience as an example. Ford's system graded employees A, B, or C, and required 10 percent of employees to get a C. "Their intent was to remove poor performers, but instead the automaker landed in court," says Rogers. "Eventually, after six lawsuits were filed against Ford by disgruntled workers, former CEO Jacques Nasser announced that this unpopular grading system was being modified."

But what many call discrimination is simply a company's way of differentiating their employees, according to Grote. He says that although lower ranked employees might believe that the ranking procedure produces illegally discriminatory results, these lawsuits stem from the fact that managers have not done a good job of telling the truth about how people are doing, "if an employee has always been told he is doing well, and then all of the sudden a forced ranking process comes along and he is told he is in the bottom 10 percent, the employee says, 'This can't be right. I wonder if the reason is because I am elderly, black, female, homosexual . . . take your pick.' That's where the lawsuits stem from."

Grote says it's difficult for managers who have always been told not to discriminate to change their way of thinking, because they have to get used to the idea of discriminating on the basis of talent and ability. "Now they are being forced into a process that does exactly the opposite," Grote says. "It forces them to say Mary is better than George but not as good as Sally—and that's tough. That's why there is so much bad press and unhappiness because forced ranking is necessarily discriminatory."

Alternatives to Forced Ranking

Discriminatory or not, DDI's Rogers says there is a better way to get managers to manage all employees—high and low performers alike—than to resort to forced distribution or forced ranking. He says if a company wants to retain the best employees, it must use a performance management system that holds employees accountable for results, encourages open and honest feedback between employees at all levels, provides a convenient way to develop talent, and features a compensation process that is based on performance and pays the higher performers more than it pays substandard performers.

An example of this type of performance management system is used at McKesson Information Solutions, a healthcare software and services company in Alpharetta, Ga., and a division of McKesson Corp. "We don't believe in forced ranking, we don't think it's right or useful," says Terry Geraghty, senior vice president of human resources for the company's Information Solutions division. Instead, the company uses a traditional performance management system to track and manage the performance of its 6,000 employees. But the solution took years to develop.

When Geraghty was hired four years ago, he walked into a company with an employee turnover rate of 23 percent, dreadful employee satisfaction surveys, low morale and customer service problems "From an HR perspective, we were in crisis mode," he says.

The company had just completed nearly 20 acquisitions to become the largest healthcare IT company in the industry. As a result, there were at least seven formal performance management systems and another 10 hybrid versions floating around. "Our first attack strategy was to use performance management to address morale and bring the different business units together," he says. "We knew that building a single performance management system was the glue that was going to hold the company together."

Geraghty and his team consolidated the company's performance management systems into one common system from San Mateo, Calif.-based SuccessFactors, then sent 600 managers to a full-day training program offered by DDI in just three months.

The company's performance-based system requires employees to have six to 10 objectives that relate to their individual job and the requirements of their department. The employee and manager agree on the top three or four that will have the greatest impact on the employee's success during the year. Managers measure and track those objectives and provide coaching throughout the year.

Geraghty admits that the performance management system is nothing radical, it's just executed very well. The Web-based system tracks the development of 5,000 employees. In addition to 24/7 access, managers can also access Web-based development guides and competency behavior guides used to help set objectives.

An Employee-Driven Solution

While some companies launch performance management systems in response to CEO demand, Lockheed Martin Corp., a Bethesda, Md., advanced technology company, developed its performance recognition system in response to employee demand. That demand came in the form of survey responses in which employees revealed their desire for more feedback from their managers and that the company needed to improve how it recognized and measured performance.

Lockheed had a cultural challenge on its hands. As the result of numerous mergers and acquisitions in the 1990s, Lockheed grew to become the major player of the aerospace industry, bringing together more than 17 companies. But the mergers also brought 17 different company heritages—including dozens of approaches to performance management.

The company needed a single way to differentiate employees and pay for performance. Michael Hopp, director of leadership and employee development, and his team walked a tightrope of trying to balance Lockheed's need with the needs of its employees and managers—and they didn't take this challenge lightly. They formed a best practices team that took two years to research and learn the best ways companies were managing employee performance.

Then Lockheed formed a team of managers to develop its performance recognition system. "We didn't want this process to be developed in a vacuum," Hopp says. "We needed our managers to give us their recommendations and solutions that worked for them as well as supported Lockheed's needs."

Once the managers' recommendations were approved, the HR implementation team rolled out the paper-based performance recognition system in 2002 while simultaneously building a Web-enabled system.

The result was a three-phase process for managers that included setting employee expectations in the first quarter of the year; ensuring that employees were performing to expectations throughout the year with interim reviews, ongoing feedback and coaching; and finally completing an assessment during the first quarter of the second year.

After a three-year planning and implementation process, Lockheed rolled out the Web-based performance recognition system in each of its business units last year and built training around a one-day course. Lockheed trained 15,000 managers to use the system to track and manage the performance of 100,000 employees. The Web-enabled system provides a common process to recognize employee contributions, features a common rating scale, aligns with Lockheed's core values, links to compensation and provides management and employee training.

Distribution Guidelines

Now that the performance recognition system was launched, Hopp and his team faced the challenge of training managers on how to assess employees. Lockheed had a high skew, with 80 percent of employees rated in the top categories of performance. "That information was not very useful because we were telling everyone that they were superior," he says.

Hopp again turned to Lockheed's managers, but this time they developed a distribution scale with definitions and guidelines for the categories of exceptional, high contributor, successful contributor, basic contributor and unsatisfactory.

The rating system uses words rather than numbers or letters. "At first glance it looks like a five-category scale, but it's really three because there is a large, highly successful middle category," Hopp says. "These are the people who are doing everything we want them to do and are doing it well. We want them to do this forever."

Employee differentiation is expected based on their performance relative to the definitions that are written by the managers. The system is unique because managers increment from the middle, not from the top or bottom. Rather than starting with a blank slate for each employee, managers read the definition for "successful contributor" first because most employees fall into this category. The manager reviews the definitions for the "exceptional" and "unsatisfactory" categories, but must have clear evidence to place employees into these categories.

"Part of the philosophy of this system is to make employees feel good because they are successful contributors," he says. "The challenge is that every employee thinks they are above average. So in response, we have defined this category as above average and tell them 'You're doing everything right.'"

Less than 1 percent of employees fall into the unsatisfactory category, and they receive a performance improvement plan instead of a pink slip. Managers are trained not to be rigid when it comes to percentage guidelines. "Many employees look at this as a forced distribution, but we are skittish about calling it that," Hopp says. "These are simply guidelines."

Similar to Lockheed Martin, the first year McKesson Information Solutions rolled out its new system Geraghty noticed a very skewed distribution with more than 70 percent of employees receiving a rating of 1 or 2 on a 5-point scale. Receiving a 1 meant that most employees were significantly exceeding expectations. "Roughly two-thirds of our employees were exceeding expectations in terms of performance," Geraghty says. "That looks great on paper, but our business results didn't line up with the individual performance results."

Geraghty and his team determined they would have to hold managers accountable to accurately rate performance as well as set up challenging objectives. As a result, the company published the following distribution guidelines and holds its managers accountable to them:

1 = Significantly exceeds expectations (7 percent)
2 = Exceeds expectations (23 percent)
3 = Expectations fully met (55 percent)
4 = Met some, but not all expectations (10 percent)
5 = Did not meet expectations (5 percent)

Geraghty is passionate about measuring performance. "McKesson Corp. is a Fortune 20 company in a highly competitive growth business, so it's a good thing when an employee fully meets expectations."

The distribution guidelines are used as a discussion point between managers. "If a manager has business results and can demonstrate that his team has exceeded these guidelines, we allow that," he says. "But if a business unit is struggling and has inflated ratings, managers have to justify why the business results do not coincide with the high percentage of employees ranked superior."

Training's Critical Role

Whether a company chooses to launch forced ranking or a performance management system, experts agree that training plays a critical role in whether the system sinks or swims. Forced ranking advocate Grote refuses to work with any company that will not invest in the training of its managers as part of the forced ranking process. "People's careers are so affected by this, managers better know what they are doing," he says.

Although McKesson Information Solutions' performance management system is successful, Geraghty admits the first year was rocky. "We're into our third year, and it is a much different place," he says. "The process goes smoother, and people understand they have to be trained."

McKesson requires that its managers attend an annual training program where they role play, practice, and learn about the new features and functions of the Web-based system. Managers also go through scenarios on how to rate performance accurately. This increased role of training has been part of a big culture change at the company. "It's now part of our culture that employees must do very well at the company to exceed expectations, and the training emphasizes that message," Geraghty says.

Training also ensures that managers know how to rate people accurately. "Because managers don't like to deliver bad news, most have not been effective raters of performance," says Geraghty. "Our managers must have the guts to sit down with someone and tell them that they did not meet all of their expectations and here's what they need to do. We train them how to do that."

Lockheed's Hopp agrees that teaching managers how to assess employees is vital to the success of any performance management system. "The idea of performance recognition was new for many employees," he says. "Some parts of the company didn't even use the concept of individual employee objectives."

Hopp and his team created a one-day training program to teach managers the Web-based system as well as how to assess performance and communicate the results to employees. Lockheed also provides additional training using modules from Harvard ManageMentor, an online performance support tool from Boston-based Harvard Business School Publishings e-learning division.

The results of the additional training speak volumes. After a five-year planning and implementation deadline, Lockheed has achieved most of its goals for the system. "We have successfully linked performance ratings to salary increases for all of our exempt employees and most of our non-exempt employees," Hopp says. In addition, Lockheed's individual business units have achieved their performance differentiation guidelines.

Results of a recent employee survey found improvements in the perceived link between individual and organizational objectives. Employees said their performance had improved due to ongoing feedback and differentiation. High performers felt they were getting the appropriate amounts of recognition and reward. "I think we are about 60 percent there," Hopp says. "I want to continue to enhance the ability of managers to really use this and to really make those connections."

Three years into McKesson's performance management system the company has gone from crisis to celebration, experiencing 31 consecutive months of declining turnover. This transformation has resulted in the company being ranked #52 in *Computerworld's* top 100 places to work in information technology, as well as being ranked the second best place to work in Atlanta by the *Atlanta Chronicle*.

Recent employee survey results also verify the system's success. The company used Chicago-based global survey firm ISR to survey its employees, and 79 percent of employees said that they understood how their performance is evaluated, compared to an industry norm of 67 percent. Seventy-seven percent of McKesson's employees say that performance reviews are conducted regularly, compared to an industry norm of 60 percent.

Geraghty feels good about these results. "It's been a long road, but McKesson is a different place to work," he says. "Thanks to our performance management system we have a very motivated and engaged workforce."

POSTSCRIPT

Is Forced Ranking an Effective Performance Management Approach?

Performance management should identify high, mediocre, and also under-performers. Scholars and practitioners insist that a clear performance identification process should be the main goal of this system. Any management approach that tolerates mediocrity and poor performance should not be tolerated because it is detrimental to business profits.

Organizations such as Microsoft, GE, and Pepsico are among several Fortune 500 companies that are successful adopters of this performance management approach. The main advantages of adopting this method of appraising are its focus on increased business profits and also a productive workforce. Experts maintain the underpinning emphasis of this approach is superior performance, which becomes an undeniable competitive advantage. The increased financial results are demonstrated in better share prices and subsequent business for the organization. Which CEO would not want such a win-win situation?

Opponents of this system suggest that this system is fundamentally flawed. Practitioners also question how to implement the system if employees in their organization do not fall into a traditional performance curve of superior, mediocre, and underperformers. A collective team spirit is lost as employees compete with each other for the winner's cup. Do organizations want such a contentious work environment? Several different appraisal systems have been implemented by organizations that have been successful without the ranking approach. Organizations could also expose themselves to legal suits, especially if underperformers belong to any protected race, ethnicity, or age.

A case in point is that of Mr. Browne, a senior African American employee at Microsoft, who filed a lawsuit against the company in 2001. He insisted that Microsoft's performance management approach is biased and has a very negative effect on certain ethnic groups. Microsoft adopts a five-level appraisal system with five being the highest grade in employee performance. Employees are allowed to contest their evaluation through an internal procedure. However, Mr. Browne contended that there is a lot of nepotism, and employees who socialized with supervisors frequently received better performance rankings.

In 2001, Conoco received a lawsuit from two senior scientists for their biased performance ranking method. The plaintiffs (employees who have been affected) suggested that they were replaced by foreign-born scientists and sued under national origin discrimination. In another case, Ford Motor Company had eight lawsuits, including two class-actions suits (a group of people seeking to settle similar issues), against their performance method of evaluation. The class-action suits suggested that older workers were being discriminated against intentionally. In 2001, Ford Motor Company mandated that supervisors are not required to put employees in the lowest performance tier. Do organizations want to ruin their reputation with potential lawsuits?

Suggested Readings

B. Hazels, C. Sasse, "Forced Ranking: A Review," *S.A.M. Advanced Management Journal* (vol. 73, no. 2, pp. 35–39, 2, 2008).

S. Boehle, "Keeping Forced Ranking out of Court," *Training* (vol. 45, no. 5, pp. 40, 42, 44, 46, June 2008).

Anonymous, "Forced Rankings of Employees Bad for Business," *Machine Design* (vol. 79, no. 18, p. 30, September 2007).

Forced Ranking Pros and Cons: http://www.allbusiness.com/services/educational-services/4283450-1.html

Forced Ranking: Making Performance Management Work: http://hbswk.hbs.edu/archive/5091.html

The folly of forced rankings: http://news.cnet.com/The-folly-of-forced-rankings/2009-1069_3-950200.html

Forced Rankings: The Latest Target of Plaintiff's Employment Lawyers: http://www.gibbonslaw.com/news_publications/articles.php?action=display_publication&publication_id=790

ISSUE 17

Given the Current State of the National Economy, Is Executive Pay Unreasonable?

YES: Sarah Anderson, John Cavanagh, Chuck Collins, Mike Lapham, Sam Pizzigati, from "Executive Excess 2007," at the Institute for Policy Studies. http://www.ips-dc.org/reports/#84

NO: Robert B. Reich, from "The Economic Argument for CEO Pay," *Wall Street Journal* (Eastern Edition) (September 14, 2007)

ISSUE SUMMARY

YES: Compensation expert and IPS Fellow Sarah Anderson and her colleagues argue that U.S. CEOs are substantially overpaid in a 2008 study conducted for the Institute for Policy Studies.

NO: Professor Reich from Berkeley states that the capitalistic system promotes a principle of supply and demand. There are very few qualified executives, so they are in high demand. Executives have distinguished educational and work records that result in their elaborate pay levels.

U.S. executive salaries usually include salary, bonus, stock option gains, stock grants, executive benefits, and perquisites (perks). In the 1960s, CEO salary was 41 times more than that of the average employee. In the 1980s, CEO salary was 40 times that of the average worker. But in 2009, the average CEO made 400 times more than that of the average employee. The average pay of these executives has become 10 times larger over the decades while the other employee levels have not seen such magnificent increases in their pay levels.

There have been several points of concern about U.S. executives pay levels. Primarily, average employees (nonexecutives) do not experience similar percentage increases in compensation levels as their executives do. Economists observe that the American economy has abundant salaries to offer their top executives but fail to pay their average employees in the same lavish manner. During any decade, the minimum wages and average wage for employees rise barely 7%, while CEOs salaries rise almost 45%. Further, frequent media reporting that the average *daily* pay of U.S. CEOs is approximately equivalent to the *annual* salary of an average worker makes executive pay a very sensitive issue.

Second, the U.S. culture likes to accord a celebrity status to its executives in that they seem to be making much more than their overseas counterparts. CEOs from other countries make only 10 to 12 times more than that of their average employees. In 2006, European CEOs made one-third of what U.S. CEOs made annually. In 2008, CEOs in Japan and Europe made $1.5 and $6.6 million, respectively, in comparison to U.S. executives' average pay of $13.3 million. Further, in the European and Asian economies, executives have taken a financial cut in their salaries if their companies are not performing well.

In addition, often the high executive pay is not related to firm performance. Many executives quit failing companies negotiating a very high golden parachute package (severance package, which is usually four to five times the annual salary, plus stock options and pension). Research suggests that the average departing executive in the United States receives a golden parachute package of almost $16.5 million. Thus these executives actually leave the companies well compensated for their entire lives despite their underperformance. Which average employee can negotiate such a package with a record of poor performance?

Executive employees also negotiate substantial money for their retirement plans. On average, CEOs bargain for almost 10 million in their retirement benefits. In contrast, in 2004, only 36.3% of individuals 65 and older had any retirement benefits. Such glaring differences get even more magnified when considering executive perks like corporate jets, luxurious apartments, exclusive memberships, and elaborate shopping trips.

Advocates of high executive pay suggest that executives rightly deserve their high pay. Primarily, directing and managing an organization is extremely stressful and ruthlessly demanding. It requires long hours with completely disproportionate work-life balance schedules. Therefore, executives need to be compensated more than adequately. Second, executives are fully responsible for the goals and mission of their organizations. They analyze, direct, and coordinate employees and are responsible to their customers. Top executives are ultimately held accountable to customers even if employees from their organization make corporate blunders.

Third, the market economy works on the principle of pure supply and demand. Recruiting and hiring such top talent is very difficult, so when such talent is identified, it comes with a very high price. Many of these executives have distinguished college degrees and boast of solid industry experiences. Why would organizations not pay high salaries for such unique KSAs (knowledge, skills, and abilities)? Customers are willing to pay a very high price for exclusive brands based on the same economic principle.

An international perspective suggests that in other countries, top executives do not get such lavish compensation packages that U.S. executives do. In 2008 in China, the Chairman and President of the top Chinese banks were paid approximately $230,000 annually in comparison to that of $19.6 million awarded to J.P. Morgan's CEO. In many of these emerging economies, governments mandate a cap on executive compensation calculated as a percentage of the net profits.

YES ↩   Sarah Anderson et al.

Executive Excess 2007: The Staggering Social Cost of U.S. Business Leadership

I. Introduction

What's the "going rate" for leadership in the United States today?

This question would once have made little sense. Years ago, we didn't treat "leadership" as a marketable skills set. Today we do. We have academic centers that teach leadership, headhunters who search for it.

Our grand enterprises and institutions still sometimes hire their top leaders from within. But they feel no pressure to hire someone already deeply steeped in the specific work they do. They seek, or at least claim to seek, proven leadership ability, from individuals who have demonstrated a capacity to innovate and inspire, analyze and imagine.

A good leader, we have come to believe, can perform successfully almost anywhere. The CEO of Home Depot can become the head of Chrysler. A military general can become a school superintendent. You need not know how a particular industry operates to play a leadership role within it. You need only know how to lead. Leadership skills, and leadership skills alone, can make you eminently marketable.

Every market, of course, sports a "going rate." Try to collect significantly above that "going rate," if your skill be computer programming or selling real estate, and you'll likely get nowhere quick.

But the market for leadership doesn't seem to work that way. Some individuals with leadership skills in our contemporary United States—those individuals who sit atop America's business enterprises—are capturing far more compensation for their labors than individual leaders in other fields who appear to hold the same exact leadership skill set.

Indeed, our current pay gap between American business leaders and their leadership counterparts in other walks of American life today runs wider, often far wider, than the pay gap a generation ago between business leaders and average American workers.

Back around 1980, big-time corporate CEOs in the United States took home just over 40 times the pay of average American workers. Today's average

From *Executive Excess,* 2007, pp. 7–16, 17, 19–22. Copyright © 2007 by The Institute for Policy Studies and United for a Fair Economy (UFE). Reprinted by permission. www.ips.org

American CEO from a *Fortune* 500 company makes 364 times an average worker's pay and over 70 times the pay of a four-star Army general.

Another example of this growing leadership pay gap: Last year, the top 20 earners in the most lucrative corner of America's business sector, the private equity and hedge fund world, pocketed 680 times more in rewards for their labors than the nation's 20 highest-paid leaders of nonprofit institutions pocketed for theirs.

Most Americans, over recent years, have become aware that business leaders make enormously more than the workers they employ. The gap between business leaders and other leaders in our society has received considerably less attention. This report, our 14th annual examination of executive excess, seeks to remedy that situation.

But we will begin this year's report on more familiar ground, with a review of the current status of the gap between business leaders and their workers. That gap remains at unconscionably wide levels.

The CEOs of major American corporations, the data show, once again last year made as much in a day as average workers took in over the entire year. The 20 top kingpins of the private equity and hedge fund industry last year made more than average worker annual pay *every ten minutes*.

These numbers shock but do not surprise. We have come, as a society, to expect—and even accept—such phenomenally wide pay differentials between workers and business leaders. These differentials have come to appear as a given of modern economic life.

But modern economies, in reality, do not require excessive business executive pay to function. If they did, then the business executives that American executives compete against in the global marketplace would be just as excessively compensated as American executives. They aren't. Top executives of major European corporations, we show in this latest edition of *Executive Excess*, last year earned three times *less* than their American counterparts.

The vast rewards that go to business leaders in the United States represent, in short, not an inevitable unfolding of marketplace dynamics, but a marketplace failure.

Markets that fail need to be corrected, and, in generations past, Americans organized politically to make sure needed corrective action took place. These Americans broke up monopolies. They established a minimum wage. They regulated business behavior. *Executive Excess 2007* spotlights, in this historic spirit, a series of corrective initiatives we here today can take to restore a modicum of balance to modern American economic life.

We ignore initiatives like these at our peril. The outrageously massive rewards now attainable at the top of our economic ladder do our society no good. They ravage the enterprise teamwork that true leaders strive to nurture. They discourage individuals with leadership talent from entering less lucrative fields where their skills could make an important contribution to our common well-being.

In a democracy, we don't depend on leaders to fix problems like these. We citizens take leadership responsibilities onto ourselves. This year's *Executive Excess* aims to help this process along.

II. CEOs v. Workers

The CEO-Worker Pay Gap

Last year, CEOs of major U.S. companies collected as much money from one day on the job as average workers made over the entire year. These CEOs averaged $10.8 million in total compensation, according to an Associated Press survey of 386 *Fortune* 500 companies, the equivalent of over 364 times the pay of an average American worker.

Meanwhile, the private equity boom has pushed the pay ceiling for American business leaders further into the economic stratosphere. Pay data for the chiefs of these privately held firms remain difficult to obtain, but *Forbes* magazine estimates that the top 20 private equity and hedge fund managers, on average, took in $657.5 million last year, or 22,255 times the pay of the average U.S. worker.

These massive private equity take-homes have an enormous impact on inequality in the United States, at both ends of the economic ladder. Private equity managers, to extract such massive personal rewards out of the companies that sit in their portfolios, typically make decisions—on matters ranging from job cuts to pensions—that place steady downward pressure on U.S. working standards.

Astronomical pay packages for managing partners at privately held investment companies also serve to bump up the already overly ample pay of CEOs at publicly traded corporations. CEOs are now routinely leaving their corporate perches to take on far more remunerative leadership slots in the private equity world. Those who remain within publicly traded corporations, meanwhile, use the threat of exit to bargain even higher pay for their executive services.

To retain leadership talent, the argument goes, publicly traded companies must simply pay more. This past March, at a House Financial Services Committee hearing, one business professor cited massive private equity payoffs as evidence that CEOs "may even be underpaid at public companies."

Minimum Wage

This Labor Day, American workers can celebrate the first raise in the federal minimum wage in ten years. But the minimum wage increase that went into effect July 24 makes barely a dent in the gap between pay rates at the American economy's top and bottom. In the decade that ended in 2006, CEO pay rose roughly 45 percent, adjusted for inflation. The real value of the minimum wage, with this year's increase from $5.15 to $5.85, now stands 7 percent below the minimum wage's value in 1996.

Average worker pay has, over the past decade, also lagged far behind CEO compensation. In 2006, average American workers earned $29,544 per year, up 7 percent from 1996.

The Pension Gap

New federal corporate disclosure rules are shining a brighter light on the stark disparity between CEO and worker pensions. According to data available in proxy statements for the first time this year, large company CEOs last year enjoyed a $1.3 million average increase in the value of their pensions. The biggest CEO increase in pension account value—$10.7 million—went to Textron's Lewis B. Campbell. By contrast, the share of ordinary U.S. workers with any type of retirement account has declined in recent years.

According to the most recent Federal Reserve Board survey, only 58.5 percent of households headed by 45-to-54-year-olds had any type of retirement account in 2004, down from 64.3 percent in 2001. Of those in that age bracket who did have such funds, the average account value grew by only $11,325 over those same three years, or roughly $3,775 per year.

According to the Corporate Library, CEOs of S&P 500 companies retire with an average of $10.1 million in their Supplemental Executive Retirement Plan, just one type of special account large American companies regularly set up for their top executives. To place that number in perspective: In 2004, only 36.3 percent of American households headed by an individual 65 years or older held any type of retirement account at all.

Those over-65 households *with* pension protection in 2004, according to the Congressional Research Service, held an average of $173,552 in their retirement accounts, a miniscule 1.7 percent of the dollars in the supplemental accounts set aside for America's top CEOs. Looking at all American households, regardless of age, slightly more than half had retirement accounts in 2004. The average value of these accounts: $129,310.

Among the king-sized supplemental CEO pension stashes accumulated by the end of 2006: $91.3 million for William McGuire of the UnitedHealth Group. Edward Whitacre of AT&T followed closely behind with $84.7 million. Pfizer CEO Hank McKinnell accumulated $77.1 million in his supplemental retirement account before his ouster last year.

With even financially healthy U.S. companies, including IBM, Verizon, Motorola, Hewlett-Packard and Sears, slashing their worker pension benefits, the CEO-worker pension gap is likely to grow even wider.

III. U.S. Business Leaders vs. Other U.S. Leaders

Healthy democracies and dynamic economies require strong leadership, in every sector of society. But current pay practices in the United States send a quite different message: that only for-profit business leadership really matters.

Business leaders, our compensation patterns proclaim, add tens, hundreds, and even thousands of times more value to our society than the leaders we hold responsible for educating our youth, protecting our national security, providing essential public services, or crafting the laws that govern us.

Such extreme pay gaps undermine our future. These gaps siphon off talent from public service and create a nonstop revolving door between government and the business world that breeds conflict of interest and corruption and distorts our democracy.

Top leaders in non-business sectors of our society already earn comfortable incomes. These incomes do not need to be raised. To limit leadership pay gaps, we need to address the problem of excessive pay in the for-profit sector.

Private Equity and Hedge Funds

The top 20 highest-earning leaders of private equity and hedge funds collected an average of $657.5 million in 2006. The top four each pocketed over $1 billion. These men—and they are all white men—are leading a revival of the 1980s leveraged buyout phenomenon that hollowed out a variety of oncevenerable companies, while enriching a precious few. Last year saw more than 1,000 corporate buyouts worldwide, with a total value estimated between $500 and $700 billion. Hedge funds now account for 30 to 60 percent of daily global turnover in financial markets.

Unlike companies that are publicly traded on Wall Street, private equity and hedge funds are not required to report executive compensation to the federal Securities and Exchange Commission. These funds also rely on different forms of compensation. Investment managers reap their rewards primarily from management fees and a share of the profits from fund investments, rather than from stock options, salary, and bonuses.

Private equity and hedge fund managing partners typically receive 20 percent of the profits their funds generate and an annual fee that equals 2 percent of the assets they manage. Some managers demand even higher rewards. For example, James Simons commands 44 percent of profits and 5 percent of assets from investors in his two hedge funds, Medallion and Renaissance Institutional. Last year, he raked in $1.1 billion from Medallion and $395 million from Renaissance. His total earnings: nearly $1.5 billion.

After Simons, Steven Cohen of SAC Capital scored the second-highest Wall Street investment fund windfall, with $1.2 billion. Cohen's wealth has proved a boon to art dealers. He recently acquired an Andy Warhol image of Marilyn Monroe, "Turquoise Marilyn," for an estimated $80 million, nearly three times the price garnered for a similar painting by the pop artist.

Cohen shared second place on the investment fund payday list with Kenneth Griffin, head of Citadel Investment Group. The 38-year-old Griffin has also made a name for himself as an art collector and will soon have his name etched on a section of the Art Institute of Chicago. For the site of his second wedding in 2003, Griffin chose Versailles, where the ill-fated King Louis XVI and Marie Antoinette also tied the knot.

Two of last year's 20 highest-paid hedge fund managers first became public figures as 1980s-era corporate raiders. T. Boone Pickens, for example, made a fortune two decades ago bidding for Gulf Oil and other big oil companies. His current hedge fund, BP Capital, invests almost exclusively in the energy industry and last year generated $1.1 billion in earnings for Pickens.

Another icon of the "greed is good" 1980s, Carl Icahn, cleared $350 million in 2006. Most notorious for his 1986 takeover of TWA, a company he left in bankruptcy, Icahn today heads the Icahn Partners fund, a two-year-old venture that manages about $2.5 billion in assets.

Publicly Traded Companies

The top 20 highest-paid executives of U.S. publicly traded companies raked in an average $36.4 million in 2006. The top earner: Yahoo's Terry Semel, whose $71.7 million in annual earnings consisted almost entirely of options grants estimated to be worth $71.4 million. The Internet services chief also cashed in $19 million in options last year. Semel stepped down as CEO in June, amid widespread shareholder concern over the company's sluggish performance.

The second- and third-highest-paid U.S. CEOs last year both hailed from the oil industry, a sector that continues to benefit from record-high world crude oil prices. Bob Simpson of Texas-based XTO Energy took in $59.5 million, including a $31 million cash bonus and $27 million worth of new options grants. He cleared another $39.8 million exercising previously awarded options.

XTO Energy last year also donated $6.8 million to Baylor University, Simpson's alma mater, for the construction of a sports complex. In exchange, the XTO proxy explains, the university will name the new athletic complex after Simpson—and provide him "access to certain sporting events."

The sixth-highest-paid CEO in 2006 was Angelo Mozilo of Countrywide Financial, with $42.9 million. In July 2007, the company's sub-prime mortgage woes drove its foreclosure rates to the highest level in more than five years and contributed to a global liquidity crisis.

Non-Profits

In 2005, the most current year with data available, the 20 highest-paid nonprofit leaders in the United States averaged $965,698 in compensation. The highest-paid—Harold Varmus, the chief executive of the Memorial Sloan-Kettering Cancer Center in New York—earned $2,491,450. Varmus won the 1989 Nobel Prize for his research on the genetic basis of cancer.

The lowest-paid of the 20 top nonprofit leaders, University of Pennsylvania President Amy Gutmann, collected $675,000 for her labors overseeing a school with nearly 24,000 students and 5,000 faculty members. UPenn's budget last year totaled $4.87 billion, more than the revenues of XTO Energy, whose CEO gathered up nearly $60 million in 2006. Five university presidents, besides Gutmann, appear on the top 20 nonprofit pay list.

Over the last several years, several scandals have taken down nonprofit leaders who seem to have yearned to live the same imperial lifestyles as their corporate counterparts. Lawrence Small, a former banker, stepped down as head of the Smithsonian Institution in early 2007 after reports that his lavish leadership style required $2 million worth of spending on chauffeured cars, private jets, and exclusive hotels. Benjamin Ladner lost his job as American University president in 2005 after news reports revealed he had spent university money on personal chefs, limousines, and extravagant family parties.

Federal Executive Branch

By law, the President of the United States earns the highest salary in the federal government, $400,000 last year. Vice President Richard Cheney, who accumulated enormous wealth in the private sector before entering the Bush White House, made a government salary of $208,575 in 2006. Rounding out the 20 highest-paid federal executive branch officials: 15 cabinet secretaries and other cabinet-level government executives who earn the top executive pay grade of $186,600.

Military Service

In 2006, 15 top brass earned $187,390, the highest military pay rate. These included the chair and vice chair of the Joint Chiefs of Staff, the heads of each branch of the military, as well as the chiefs of various specialized commands, such as John Abizaid, who retired this year as head of the Central Command. Abizaid oversaw some 250,000 U.S. troops in 27 countries, including Iraq and Afghanistan. High-ranking generals round out last year's military top 20. Their base pay: $152,000.

All these generals are operating in an increasingly privatized war-time environment where many basic operations that used to be direct Pentagon responsibilities have been contracted out to powerhouse defense industry corporations. The CEOs of the top six defense contractors last year each pulled in between $12 million and $24 million. These included the chief executives of Lockheed Martin ($24.4 million), Boeing ($13.8 million), Northrop Grumman ($18.6 million), General Dynamics ($15.7 million), Raytheon ($11.9 million), and Halliburton ($16.5 million). Each of these six business leaders last year made more in a week than any of the generals made in a year.

U.S. Congress

The two highest-paid members of the U.S. Congress—the House speaker and Senate majority leader—each earned $212,100 salaries in 2006. The minority leaders in both chambers earned $183,500. All rank-and-file senators and representatives received $165,200 in paychecks last year.

The lowest-paid corporate executive on last year's list of the 20 highest-paid CEOs in America—Viacom's Philippe Dauman—personally pocketed over seven times more compensation for his leadership labors than the 20 top leaders in Congress together.

The huge gaps between congressional and business pay levels keep the revolving door spinning between Capitol Hill and K Street lobby groups. According to Public Citizen, 43 percent of the members of Congress who left office between 1998 and mid-2005 eligible to lobby actually became lobbyists.

This revolving door threatens government integrity in two ways:

- Members of Congress who are hoping to land lucrative private sector jobs have an incentive to shape public policy to please potential future employers or clients.
- Lawmakers-turned-lobbyists have privileged access to their former colleagues that can give them undue influence to advance their clients' interests.

In late July, the House of Representatives passed new ethics legislation that chooses not to extend the ban on lobbying by former House members from one to two years after their congressional service ends.

IV. U.S. Business Leaders vs. European Business Leaders

American executives continue to leave their European counterparts in the compensation dust, even after recent increases in European executive pay levels. In 2006, the 20 highest-paid European managers made an average of $12.5 million, only one third as much as the 20 highest-earning U.S. executives. The Europeans earned less, despite leading larger firms. On average, the 20 European firms with the highest-paid executives on the continent had sales of $65.5 billion, compared to $46.5 billion for the 20 U.S. firms.

The gap between U.S. and European executives is actually running wider than the dollar-equivalence figures below suggest. The drastic fall in the value of the dollar against the euro serves to inflate the compensation European executives received last year.

French executives dominated the list, making up 10 of the 20 highest-paid European executives. The top-earning French executive, Carlos Ghosn of Renault, took in $45.5 million, mostly in stock options. This total does not include Ghosn's compensation from Nissan. Ghosn has been CEO of both Renault and Nissan since 2005. Once considered a hero of the auto industry for resuscitating the Japanese automaker, Ghosn has had to face angry shareholders of late as both firms have performed sluggishly. Ghosn recently gave up his post as head of Nissan's North American operations.

The top-ranked German executive, Josef Ackermann of Deutsche Bank, collected $12.4 million. Ackermann became a lightning rod figure in Germany's ongoing executive pay debate when he faced criminal charges for having helped approve, as a board member, massive bonuses for executives at another German company. Ackermann and five other board members at this company were charged with "breach of fiduciary trust." Ackermann's unapologetic defense of both the bonuses and his own massive paycheck provoked charges that the Swissborn banker was injecting a more ruthless style of American capitalism into a relatively egalitarian German society. The former head of the German Social Democratic Party called Ackermann's behavior "disastrous to the image of democracy."

V. Proposals for Change

This section highlights six practical initiatives that can rein in excessive executive pay. Five involve more equitable taxation, while one would use government contracting dollars to encourage more reasonable pay.

Recent polls suggest that these reforms would enjoy broad public support. The same July 2007 *Financial Times*/Harris poll that found widespread European support for capping executive pay found that 77 percent of Americans feel that corporate executives "earn too much." Only 11 percent admire "those who run" America's "largest companies" either "a great deal" or "quite a bit."

On top of that, Americans—by an overwhelming margin—want to see their nation's top income-earners pay more in taxes. Just 12 percent of Americans feel their country "correctly taxes those who earn the highest incomes." Five times that number, 61 percent, feel wealthy Americans "should be taxed more."

Proposals

Eliminate Tax Subsidies for Excessive CEO Pay

Under current law, corporations can deduct, as a "business expense," whatever excessive pay packages they hand their top executives, simply by defining that excess as a "performance incentive." This tax loophole essentially operates as an incentive for excessive compensation. The more corporations shell out in executive compensation, the less they pay in taxes. And the rest of us taxpayers wind up paying the bill.

Rep. Barbara Lee (D-Calif.) is promoting a reform that would cap the amount of executive compensation corporations are permitted to deduct to 25 times the pay of a company's lowest paid worker. Corporate boards would still be allowed to pay their executives as much as they wanted. They just wouldn't be able to deduct excessive amounts from their taxes.

If such a deductibility cap had been in place last year, the 386 companies included in the Associated Press pay survey would have paid as much as $1.4 billion more in 2006 taxes—just on their CEOs' compensation alone. That additional revenue, if earmarked for reducing class sizes in overcrowded schools, would have been enough to pay the annual salaries of 29,218 elementary school teachers.

And that's just the amount that would have been generated by capping the deductibility of CEO pay at these 386 firms. Rep. Lee's proposal, if enacted, would apply to all top management compensation within a company that exceeds the 25-to-1 ratio.

Down through the years, many noted figures in the business world have argued for reasonable ratios between executive and worker pay. A century ago, financier J. P. Morgan insisted on 20-to-1 ratios, a theme picked up in more recent times by Peter Drucker, the founder of modern management science.

End the Preferential Tax Treatment of Private
Investment Company Executive Income

Rep. Sander Levin (D-Michigan) has introduced legislation that would plug the tax loophole that allows managers of the nation's private equity and hedge funds, individuals who often make hundreds of millions of dollars a year, to pay taxes at lower rates than average Americans.

These managers currently pay taxes on a substantial portion of their personal income at the 15 percent capital gains rate, not the 35 percent rate that would apply if their earnings were treated as ordinary income. Private investment managers earn an annual administrative fee (usually 2 percent) and carried interest on profits (usually 20 percent), often called a "carry." The tax code treats the carry portion of pay as capital gains, even though the investment manager is providing a professional service.

A recent Economic Policy Institute paper estimates that this loophole costs the federal treasury about $12.6 billion a year. This lost revenue, EPI notes, would be enough to fully fund a five-year, $35 billion expansion of SCHIP, the public health insurance program for America's low-income children.

Cap Tax-Free 'Deferred' Executive Pay

Most major corporations in the United States today—85 percent of the companies in the S&P 500—have created special "deferred pay" accounts for their top executives. Dollars in these accounts earn guaranteed interest, compounding on a tax-free basis, until the executives retire. Last year, according to an analysis by Equilar, a compensation analytics firm based in California, the median major company CEO deferred pay account held $3.7 million.

But this median understates the vast sums that some top executives have accumulated. The chief executive at retail giant Target, Robert Ulrich, held $133.5 million in his deferred pay account at year's end, all of this over and beyond the dollars in Ulrich's regular pension and 401 (k).

Standard 401 (k) plans, the only tax-deferral tool available to rank-and-file corporate employees, carry strict deferral limits. Workers under age 50 can this year defer from their taxes no more than $15,500 in 401 (k) contributions. Corporate executive deferred pay plans allow unlimited deferrals.

Senate Finance Committee chairman Max Baucus (D-Montana) and the panel's ranking minority member, Senator Charles Grassley (R-Iowa), earlier this year pushed all the way to a House-Senate conference committee legislation that would have limited annual executive pay deferrals to $1 million. The proposal, attacked fiercely by corporate interests, did not survive the conference committee deliberations. But Senator Baucus has pledged to revisit the initiative.

Eliminate the Tax Reporting Loophole on CEO Stock Options

Corporations are currently allowed to report one set of executive stock option compensation figures to investors on their financial statements and a completely different set of figures to the Internal Revenue Service (IRS) on their tax returns.

Corporations deduct the value of executive stock options, greatly reducing their taxes. At the same time, they often report a significantly lower stock option expense to their shareholders. The IRS examined corporate tax returns filed between December 2004 and June 2005 and identified a $43 billion discrepancy between deductions claimed to the IRS and option expenses reported to shareholders.

The U.S. Senate Permanent Subcommittee on Investigations examined the stock option tax deductions claimed by nine companies over five years. The deductions exceeded their reported stock option expenses by a total of more than $1 billion, or 575 percent. For example, of the 12 million stock options the Occidental Petroleum CEO exercised during the five-year period, the company claimed a $353 million tax deduction—12 times as much as the book expense that, under current accounting rules, would have totaled just $29 million.

This creative bookkeeping is not currently illegal. Senator Carl Levin, chairman of the U.S. Senate Permanent Subcommittee on Investigations, feels these companies "are benefiting from an outdated and overly generous stock option tax rule that produces tax deductions that often far exceed the companies' reported expenses."

Link Government Procurement to Executive Pay

Some of the most excessive executive pay packages over recent years have gone to CEOs whose companies take in much of their revenue from government contracts. Most of these contracts involve the defense industry.

Federal procurement law already limits the amount of pay that a company with a government contract can bill the government for executive compensation. But this "cap" only applies to direct federal dollars. Corporations whose profits or share prices soar after receiving a federal contract remain free to pay their top executives whatever company boards please.

A simple change could end these executive windfalls. The federal government could deny procurement contracts—or economic development subsidies or tax breaks—to all firms that pay their top executives over 25, 50, or even 100 times what their lowest-paid workers receive.

The federal government currently denies contracts to companies that increase, through discriminatory employment practices, racial or gender inequality in the United States. The same principle could be invoked to deny contracts to companies that, through excessive executive compensation, increase the nation's economic inequality.

Increase the Top Marginal Tax Rate on High Incomes

In 2006, not one of the compensation dollars collected by the business leaders discussed in this report faced a federal income tax rate higher than 35 percent.

Back in the 1950s, by contrast, earned income over $400,000—the equivalent of less than $3 million today—faced a top marginal tax rate of 91 percent.

These steeply graduated tax rates, in place for most of the mid-20th century, served to actively discourage excessive compensation. They sent a powerful cultural message that compensation beyond a certain lofty level serves no useful societal purpose.

Our contemporary CEO pay explosion began in the early 1980s, shortly after the Reagan administration sped through Congress legislation that dropped the top marginal tax rate from 70 percent, its level since 1964, down to 50 percent. The top rate has since dropped even lower. These lower rates may not have "caused" the executive pay cascade. But they opened the floodgates.

Any move to restore mid-20th century top marginal tax rates would raise substantial revenue for investments in education and other social programs that could significantly broaden economic opportunity. If the federal income tax rate on all annual income above $10 million were raised to 70 percent—and the tax rate on all income between $5 million and $10 million were raised to 50 percent—federal revenues in 2008 would increase by a stunning $105 billion.

Robert B. Reich ➔ **NO**

The Economic Argument
for CEO Pay

According to research published recently by the Washington-based Institute for Policy Studies, the 20 highest-paid corporate executives earned on average $36 million in total compensation last year. The typical CEO of a Fortune 500 company didn't do quite as well, but at $10.8 million didn't do so badly—that's more than 364 times the pay of an average employee. Forty years ago, top CEOs earned 20 to 30 times what average workers earned.

The trend has ignited a flurry of attention in Washington. Last year the Securities and Exchange Commission ordered companies to reveal more detail about executive pay, but it's still hard for investors to decipher what companies disclose. SEC chairman Christopher Cox recently complained that a typical remuneration report is "as tough to read as a Ph.D. dissertation." In April, the House approved a proposal for a mandatory "say on pay" vote by shareholders. Although the White House opposes it and it has little chance of becoming law, expect Democrats to hammer away at the theme this election year.

Hold on.

There's an economic case for the stratospheric level of CEO pay which suggests shareholders—even if they had full say—would not reduce it. In fact, they're likely to let CEO pay continue to soar. That's because of a fundamental shift in the structure of the economy over the last four decades, from oligopolistic capitalism to super-competitive capitalism. CEO pay has risen astronomically over the interval, but so have investor returns.

The CEO of a big corporation 40 years ago was mostly a bureaucrat in charge of a large, high-volume production system whose rules were standardized and whose competitors were docile. It was the era of stable oligopolies, big unions, predictable markets and lackluster share performance. The CEO of a modern company is in a different situation. Oligopolies are mostly gone and entry barriers are low. Rivals are impinging all the time—threatening to lure away consumers all too willing to be lured away, and threatening to hijack investors eager to jump ship at the slightest hint of an upturn in a rival's share price.

Worse yet, any given company's rivals can plug into similar global supply and distribution chains. They have access to low-cost suppliers from all over the world and can outsource jobs abroad as readily as their competitors. They can streamline their operations with equally efficient software culled from many of the same vendors. They can get capital for new investment on much

From *The Wall Street Journal*, September 14, 2007, p. A13. Copyright © 2007 by Robert B. Reich. Reprinted by permission of the author.

the same terms. And they can gain access to distribution channels that are no less efficient, some of them even identical.

So how does the modern corporation attract and keep consumers and investors (who also have better and better comparative information)? How does it distinguish itself? More and more, that depends on its CEO—who has to be sufficiently clever, ruthless and driven to find and pull the levers that will deliver competitive advantage.

There are no standard textbook moves, no well-established strategies to draw upon. If there were, rivals would already be using them. The pool of proven talent is small because so few executives have been tested and succeeded. And the boards of major companies do not want to risk error. The cost of recruiting the wrong person can be very large—and readily apparent in the deteriorating value of a company's shares. Boards are willing to pay more and more for CEOs and other top executives because their rivals are paying more and more for them. Former Home Depot CEO Robert Nardelli to the contrary notwithstanding, the pay is usually worth it to investors.

The proof is in the numbers. Between 1980 and 2003, the average CEO in America's 500 largest companies rose sixfold, adjusted for inflation. Outrageous? Not to investors. The average value of those 500 companies also rose by a factor of six, adjusted for inflation. In 2005, for example, Exxon Mobil reported $36 billion in profits. Its former chairman, Lee R. Raymond, retired that year with a compensation package totaling almost $400 million, including stock, stock options and long-term compensation. Too much? Not to Exxon's investors, who enjoyed a 223% return over the interval, compared to the average 205% return received by shareholders of other oil companies, a premium of about $16 billion. Raymond took home just 4% of that $16 billion.

As the economy has shifted toward supercapitalism, CEOs have become less like top bureaucrats and more like Hollywood celebrities who get a share of the house. Hollywood's most popular celebrities now pull in around 15% of whatever the studios take in at the box office. Clark Gable earned $100,000 a picture in the 1940s, roughly $800,000 in present dollars. But that was when Hollywood was dominated by big-studio oligopolies. Today, Tom Hanks makes closer to $20 million per film.

Movie studios—now competing intensely not only with one another but with every other form of entertainment—willingly pay these sums because they're still small compared to the money these stars bring in and the profits they generate. Today's big companies are paying their CEOs mammoth sums for much the same reason.

If you assume shareholders would rein in CEO pay, take a look at the United Kingdom. Since 2003, changes in British securities law have given investors more say over what British CEOs are paid. Nonetheless, executive pay there has continued to skyrocket, on the way to matching the pay of American CEOs.

Companies listed on the London stock market have done sufficiently well that British investors don't care what CEOs are paid. Full disclosure with shareholder approval might make it harder for a CEO to claim to be worth it if his company's shares have lost ground during his tenure or risen no more than the average share prices of other companies in the same industry. But given the intensity of competition for star performers, disclosure and approval might cause CEO pay to soar even higher.

This economic explanation for sky-high CEO pay does not justify it socially or morally. It only means that investors think CEOs are worth it. As citizens, though, most of us disapprove. About 80% of Americans polled by the Los Angeles Times and Bloomberg in early 2006 said CEOs are overpaid. The reaction was roughly the same regardless of the respondent's income or political affiliation. But if America wants to rein in executive pay, the answer isn't more shareholder rights. Just as with the compensation of Hollywood celebrities or private-equity and hedge fund managers, the answer—for anyone truly concerned—is a higher marginal tax rate on the super pay of those in super demand.

POSTSCRIPT

Given the Current State of the National Economy, Is Executive Pay Unreasonable?

U.S. executives are frequently criticized for getting very unreasonable total pay packages. Executives in the health care industry led the way in 2009 with an average compensation of $12.45 million. In 2008, the most attractive compensation package of $103.5 million was awarded to Sanjay Jha, new co-CEO of Motorola. While executives seem to be getting the lion's share of a company's profits, their employees struggle for reasonable salary levels. Critics do not fail to comment that these executives seem to be affluent even with a poor and failing economy. The irony of the Detroit automakers flying in their private jets to Washington DC to appeal for their federal bailout did not escape any viewer's attention.

Executive perks, another aspect of their compensation package, are the frequent attention of media journalists. For instance, in 2008, the biggest earner of perks was Johnson & Johnson CEO William Weldon who received about $154,000 for personal travel. It is when the perks become unreasonable, such as when the Tyco's top executive spent an extravagant $6000 for shower curtains, that it leaves the "average employee" simply stunned.

However, proponents of high executive pay levels suggest that making comparisons of executive pay to that of other professional levels seems inappropriate. Do you compare the salary of a software professional to an administrative assistant? The analogy drawn by journalists, politicians, and economists of executive pay to the "average worker" therefore seems meaningless.

Advocates of high executive pay also argue that such talent is required to perform from their very first day of work. Most jobs usually provide probation or a trial period, but executive jobs allow no time for experimentation. Therefore, such talent needs to be compensated at high levels to provide these employees the required motivation to perform at high levels. The market economy works on the simple principle that products high in demand come with a lofty price. That seems to be the storyline of hiring U.S. executives.

Nonprofit, political, military, congressional, and educational leaders are making a meager amount compared to private CEO salaries. Therefore, policymakers suggest that several interventions should be adopted to keep the executive pay in check. First, executive pay should not be treated as an expense that allows firms to claim tax concessions. Second, executives of investment companies are eligible for preferential tax treatment, which should not be encouraged. Third, an executive cap in dollar amount should be imposed on the deferred pay that executives accumulate. Fourth, stock option reporting should be closely monitored so that the dollar amount stated is the same for both company and tax statements. Finally, the federal government should advocate not doing business with organizations whose CEOs are making excessive salaries.

Suggested Readings

J. Marquez "5 Questions: IN DEFENSE OF CEO PAY," *Workforce Management* (vol. 86, no. 16, p. 8, September 2008)

Eric Krell, "Getting a Grip on Executive Compensation," *Workforce* (vol. 82, no. 2, pp. 30–34, February 2003)

Anonymous, "Compensation Paid to CEO/Shareholder Was Reasonable," *Practical Tax Strategies* (vol. 82, no. 5, pp. 298–300)

Jack Welch and Suzy Welch, "CEO Pay: No Easy Answer: The Free Market May at Times Overcompensate. But There's Not a Better System," *Business Week* (vol. 4092, p. 106, July 2008)

Overall CEO Pay Falls, But Top Executives Still Get Lavish Perks Like Tax Prep and Chauffeurs: http://bulletin.aarp.org/states/fl/2009/17/articles/overall_ceo_pay_falls_but_top_executives_still.html

Wall Street Journal report: U.S. Executive Perks "Flourished" in 2008: http://www.wsws.org/articles/2009/apr2009/ceos-a04.shtml

Cutting the Perks: Execs Lose Jets, JETCO's Lose Execs: http://currents.westlawbusiness.com/Articles/2009/08/20090803_0011.aspx?cid=&src=WBSignon

Executive Perks: What's Appropriate Today: http://www.compensationresources.com/press-room/executive-perks—whats-appropriate-today.php

Study shows U.S. bank CEO pay dwarfs rest of world: http://www.reuters.com/article/idUSTRE58M2QU20090923

Indian CEOs Get What They Deserve: http://online.wsj.com/article/SB10001424052748704500604574482560792145116.html

Internet References . . .

Mixing and Matching Four Generations of Employees

FDU Magazine is published by Fairleigh Dickinson University, which is the largest private university in New Jersey. This article discusses generational differences and how these differences effect the dynamics within the workplace.

http://www.fdu.edu/newspubs/magazine/05ws/generations.htm

Different Generations in the Workplace Can Collaborate Successfully

This Web site provides a column by generational expert and internationally known consultant, coach, writer, and speaker Phyllis Weiss Haserot on intergenerational relations and navigating the challenges of the multi-generational workplace for better productivity, retention, succession planning, and business development results.

http://www.accountingweb.com/topic/education-careers/different-generations-workplace-can-collaborate-successfully

High Performance Work Practices and Human Resource Management Effectiveness: Substitutes or Complements?

This site discusses how HPWPs and HRM effectiveness act both as substitutes and as complements. Research results here suggest that effective HRM can offset HP WP's expense and that HPWPs can enhance the flexibility of effective HRM systems.

http://www.allbusiness.com/business_planning/business_structures/3501627-1.html

Best HR Practices for Today's Innovation Management (The Human Side)

This Web site hosts a number of articles and literature on HR management. Here you will find an article that provides the best HR practices and innovation management techniques.

http://www.allbusiness.com/human-resources/108204-1.html

The Effect of HRM Practices

Can different generations work harmoniously together at the workplace? Do elaborate HRM practices provide strategic advantages? The current workforce has employees from different generations working together that HRM professionals are concerned might require different HRM practices. On the other hand, both practitioners and scholars applaud the results of effective HRM practices on firm performance with many blue-chip examples from U.S. corporations. Can HRM practices be different and rewarding at the same time?

- Does Attracting, Developing, and Retaining the Millennial Generation Require Significant Changes to Current HRM Practices?

- Do Human Resource Management Practices Contribute to Increased Firm Performance?

- Is Outsourcing a Good U.S. Business Strategy?

ISSUE 18

Does Attracting, Developing, and Retaining the Millennial Generation Require Significant Changes to Current HRM Practices?

YES: Charles Woodruffe, from "Generation Y," *Training Journal* (July 2009)

NO: Dana Kyles, from "Managing Your Multigenerational Workforce," *Strategic Finance* (2005)

ISSUE SUMMARY

YES: Dr. Charles Woodruffe, author and CEO of a company that focuses on managing winning talent, states that, based on experience, expectations, and personality needs, Gen-Yers might need a new set of management practices.

NO: Dana Kyles, freelance writer for *Business Week* and *Strategic Finance* magazines, believes that multiple generations can work together harmoniously. Several HRM practices appeal to all the generations unanimously, and it is these common practices that organizations should try to identify.

The American corporation is witnessing a new kind of workforce diversity. Four multiple generations born in different time periods are currently working together: the Pre-Boomers or Matures (1900–1945), Baby Boomers (1946–1964), Generation Xers (1965–1979), and Generation Yers or millennials (1980–1999). Researchers suggest that each generation depicts unique personality characteristics shaped by their historical, economical, and cultural times.

Organizations are concerned that the current millennial generation may require a new set of management practices. The positive characteristic of the millennial generation is that its members are very techno-literate due to growing up with the Internet. For a majority of them, their school, college, and projects have been done only on computers. They have a strong need to achieve and will even work on the weekends to get their jobs done. Their boundaries between work and life are quite blurred, so they will not hesitate to take work home and vice-versa. They are very comfortable working in teams because their entire academic career has been shaped in a collaborative spirit.

The negative side is that this generation has predominantly dealt with only positive feedback. Therefore, they do not take criticism very well, whether it is from management or from co-workers. They also do not like to show deference to hierarchy because their generation has always demonstrated a casual approach to both professors and peers. They are fiercely ambitious as they have performed well in both their core and extra-curricular activities. They have generally been successful academically and hence are not able to take failure very well. They feel they should be able to Facebook, text, and surf at work, and in the same way, they are very comfortable texting messages to their supervisors from the privacy of their homes.

Why would the millennial generation need different HRM practices? First, an attractive compensation package is very important for Gen-Yers who have generally lived in such comfort and luxury. Money and materialistic pleasures are important for this generation as they would like to at least maintain similar living standards to that of their parents. Second, they are so used to learning opportunities being provided to them—whether it is for class projects or extra-curricular activities—that training and development are important for them. Third, their high sense of achievement and urgency will see them crave for titles and also of professional visibility. Finally, they have grown up with brand names—whether it is cars or retail merchandise—that they are going to yearn to work for the employers of choice.

The other side of this debate suggests that it is possible to have similar management practices with diverse generations in the workplace. It requires a thorough understanding of each generation's core work-related values and personality traits. Research suggests that the Matures are loyal and motivated by public recognition, the Boomers are competitive and good at networking, Gen-Xers crave for opportunity and autonomy, and Gen-Yers have a great need to stay connected with their peers and technology. Organizations can provide an excellent workplace for multi-generations by creating work projects that appeal to all generations. For instance, a single work project can be adjusted so that different generations enjoy the same work from diverse perspectives. The Boomers for example, might want to lead the project while the Gen-Yers might want to be the technical experts. It is also important to acknowledge each generation's strengths so that it helps design appropriate work projects.

Despite their differences, the four generations would like some form of flexibility in their work schedule whether it is in flexible scheduling, job sharing, or telework. Gen-Xers might want the extra time to spend time with their school-going children while the Boomers might want that time to spend with their aging parents. Similarly for compensation and benefits, organizations can provide cafeteria benefits that would provide flexibility in benefit choices to different generations. The Matures and Baby Boomers would definitely prefer more money in their retirement package, while the Gen-Xers would want more money toward college tuition reimbursement, and Gen-Yers definitely would want more hard cash to build their personal lives. A recent study of WorldatWork said organizations should consider generational differences by providing flexibility in the same core practices.

YES

Charles Woodruffe

Generation Y

Abstract (Summary)

Finally, a survey last year by the CIPD and Penna came out with findings that run counter to the Generation Y stereotype. It found that Generation Y members were less concerned about CSR than Baby Boomers and also "far less likely to rapidly change jobs than was thought." Maybe another Generation Y quality is the ability to pick up on, and adapt rapidly to, changing economic circumstances.

Charles Woodruffe asks why?

In the run-up to the recession, there was a plethora of articles and conferences claiming to unlock the perplexing nature of Generation Y.

They are the pipeline of new talent available for employers but their values, needs—indeed, demands—were seen as different to those of their forebears. Employers were trying hard to understand them in order to attract and retain them. They were presented with a stereotype of very demanding, "want it all now" young people who were difficult to recruit but easy to lose. Generation Whine was rather cruelly applied as an alternative epithet.

The Generation Y stereotype has a logical basis in the way in which members of that generation were parented. In talking about Generation Y, we are talking about people brought up by active parents Although, somewhat irritatingly, every writer seems to date the generation differently, Generation Y is broadly the group of people born in the early 1980s and runs through to those still in secondary school. Their parents are broadly from the group known as the Baby Boomers—those born between the end of World War Two and the mid 1960s.

The key feature of Generation Y's upbringing is that their Baby Boomer parents have been heavily involved in it. We are talking about the huggy parents who ferry their children from event to event, do their homework for them, help them with their applications and, most importantly, have given them a high sense of self-worth.

Nor has the active parenting ended. The Americans have conjured the marvellous term 'helicopter parents' to describe the ongoing vigilance of the parents of Generation Y. This vigilance extends to a willingness to take issue with HR managers who do not recruit their progeny!

From *Training Journal—TJ*, July 2009, pp. 31–35. Copyright © 2009 by TJ—Training Journal. Reprinted by permission of Fenman Ltd.

So where has all this left the children? Supposedly, members of Generation Y are marked out by their self-belief. They have had a history of positive feedback, understanding and parents answering their every need. They have little track record of frustration and having to wait. They have tended to be able to obtain what they want when they want it—be it a lift to a party or the latest Game Boy/Xbox etc. And the members of Generation Y that you are seeking to recruit and train will, almost by definition, have had a history of academic success.

As if having doting parents was not enough, members of Generation Y came to the labour market—until last autumn—at a time of plenty. But autumn 2008 might, of course, be where the story ends. In summer 2009, we need to take stock. Firstly, we were only ever talking about a caricature. Secondly, we need to decide whether the caricature still applies and matters.

The Caricature

If you follow Maslow's Hierarchy of Needs, with basic survival and security needs at the bottom and self-actualisation at the top, the parenting and background economy were said to have resulted in Generation Y being able to move directly to address higher-order needs. By the caricature, they are self-actualisers. In the workplace, they are painted as a high-maintenance generation, marked out by:

- High ambition
- Sense of entitlement
- Outspoken—they show a high willingness to challenge managers and are undeterred by traditional hierarchy, giving off an air of over-confidence
- Inability to take criticism
- Wanting work-life balance and flexibility. One survey suggests that 85 percent want to spend 30–70 percent of their time working from home
- Wanting attentive management from supervisors and regular appreciative feedback.

Generation Y is also said to:

- Struggle with processing failure and criticism
- Unable to internalise lessons
- Have difficulty with unclear guidelines or minimal management—yet not want to be told what to do
- Be ready to resign if their jobs are not fulfilling and fun, with decent holidays and the opportunity for career breaks and time off for charity work.

At the same time, Generation Y offers several positives, including:

- A complete at-oneness with IT—they have been brought up with it
- Team-working skills
- Self-belief to achieve

- A high level of drive. Seemingly in contradiction with the emphasis of Generation Y on work-life balance, people comment on their willingness to work after hours and at weekends to get a job done.

That was the caricature of Generation Y up to the recession—a time when Generation Y did not fear unemployment, having every belief in its ability to secure alternative employment. What is the status of the caricature now?

Firstly, like all caricatures, it would be foolish to apply it without thought or inspection to everyone born in the decade and a half from the early 1980s. Secondly, there is probably a germ of truth in it that it would be equally foolish for managers to deny.

On one hand, the caricature is an exaggeration and shorthand for a particular type of person. On the other hand, it recognises changes that have taken place in people's expectations at work that have spread beyond people born in those specific years.

Dealing first with the characteristics of the Y generation, you should clearly not think that everyone born within their timeslot will embody all their characteristics—good or bad. Their stereotypical behaviour was generally an unrealistic and irritating way for people to approach employers (I recall hearing of a person in their mid twenties throwing a strop because their bonus was merely half a million pounds); nowadays it is just plain ludicrous.

Of course, there will be some who, recession or not, continue to live out the caricature to its extreme. It seems to me that you do not have to adapt to their shortcomings, which—taken to an extreme—might stop them being seen as talent in the first place. Instead, your selection systems need to pick out the ones who will adapt to work life in your organisation.

However, and returning to the germ of truth in the caricature, there has to be some mutual adaptation. You will choose members of Generation Y who seem the most productive people or the best investments. They will choose you if you have recognised that the centre of gravity of what you offer people has changed.

This change has also spread outside the confines of Generation Y, just as Facebook and iPods are not the monopoly of a particular generation. It is a change from which it will be hard to turn away, even in a recession, though, of course, people might well have retraced their steps down Maslow's hierarchy. Everyone might be concerned with job security, but that does not mean they will be positively engaged if their other needs are ignored.

So how do you engage people who have become used to the new generation of employment? Essentially, you have to get alongside their needs and values and make sure you address their priorities. For several years, I have used a needs triangle to try to summarise what people nowadays are looking for in work. This is not perfect science but it does offer a way of ordering people's needs.

1. The package

Generation Y—particularly males—are said to be quite focused on their salary. This has been put down to their student debt burden and the need for a good salary to join the property ladder. However, although the package is a vital component of being an employer of choice, few people flock to an otherwise bad employer purely because it pays well. Generally, the package is the least sure way of retaining people for it is the inducement that is most easily matched by another employer.

2. Employability

We do not go to work just to earn today's money, but tomorrow's also. People are concerned with an income stream rather than just immediate money. There are four major factors that affect employability:

- *Being developed* People nowadays demand development. They recognise that the future is uncertain and that even a committed employer cannot guarantee a job. They want to be ready with a passport to alternative employment. Organisations must give a high priority to people's development in order to attract and retain them. Development must cover professional and managerial/leadersip skills. The most powerful development comes from providing people with new experiences, particularly experiences that challenge them.
- *Involvement with prestige projects* Ambitious people, notably today's Generation Y graduates, like visibility. They relish the opportunity to tackle prestigious projects, particularly those that will give them exposure to people with power within the organisation. Assuming their contribution is a positive one, such exposure enhances employability.
- *Career advancement* Drive and motivation is part of what makes people talented. Advancement feeds their goal of securing and maintaining an income stream. Part of being an employer of choice comes from letting good people get ahead quickly.
- *Being part of a prestigious organisation* There is an advantage to the employee in working for a prestigious organisation that is at the leading edge of its sector. It has a currency on the job market that will generate future income. The importance of this factor is clear from organisations' thirst to be among the list of Top 100 employers (e.g., The Times Top 100 Graduate Employers).

3. Job satisfaction

If people go out to work to generate the income for a style of life, they also want to be happy while doing so. Six components of job satisfaction can be separated:

- Achievement to be an employer of choice, you want your staff to be telling their friends about the tremendous achievements they have notched up, not how they are bored out of their brains and underutilised. Generation Y puts great store by using its strengths.
- Respect and recognition People are less tolerant than in the past of status distinctions and barriers. They want to be trusted with information and to have their hard work noticed. Members of Generation Y are also said to be intolerant of status barriers: they expect to be able to email

senior people and might well extend this to those at the top of their employing organisations. Raising managers' skill levels is vital to being an employer of choice. Indeed, they need to lead rather than manage. Generation Y is also described as in particular need of regular feedback, having grown used to regular testing at school and university.

- Autonomy People enjoy a sense of autonomy and of being trusted to get on and deliver. They can be frustrated if they do not feel a sense of ownership over their projects or if they lack real responsibility. It was partly satisfying this sense of autonomy that made 'dot coms' so attractive.
- Balance between work and private life Generation Y is said to be particularly intolerant of a lack of integration between work and private life. It is not so much a sense of balance as a blurring of the two that matters. Members expect to come to work and be logged into Facebook or MSN at the same time as doing their work. At university, they are used to mixing work (study) and their private life and would see it as restrictive to have boundaries at work. They are the permanently connected generation.
- Congruent values People want to work in an organisation with values that are congruent with their own. By definition, values are something on which we differ. However, at any period of time there is a dominant value system with which employers would be better off being congruent than discordant. For example, nowadays, organisations strive to parade their CSR credentials and this must be for their staff to witness as much as their customers. But it is vital that this is authentic: Generation Y is vigilant to a lack of integrity. Generation Y is also said to be particularly vigilant to identity and intolerant of working towards something that does not reflect its own sense of identity.
- A sense of fun in a good working environment Many people prefer to work in an informal and fun atmosphere. Organisations have sought to meet this in all sorts of ways, such as by having trendy office environments, 'dress-down' days and team-building events of various sorts. A lack of teamwork/cooperation was cited as a turnover driver by 19 percent of leavers in a survey by TalentDrain.

Individual Focus

Perhaps more important than any of the above needs is the requirement to treat people as individuals. In response, organisations are doing their best to customise what is provided to employees, ensuring as far as possible that each person's particular needs are met.

But They'll Leave Anyway

However, the image of Generation Y is that you can meet its members' needs as much as you like but they'll leave anyway to build their CVs. They do not have staying with their first employer as their game plan, so what is the point of bothering with them?

There are two responses to this. Firstly, will they all leave? The answer, surely, is of course not, especially in the current economic circumstances. If you can offer them the chance to build their employability, some will stay, some will go with the possibility of coming back and some will be lost forever.

Secondly, the ability to build employability is, in truth, probably greater for large organisations than others. Certainly, small firms would be naïve to think they can readily take on graduates who will stay to lead their organisation in the future. It is simply not in the Generation Y blueprint. Quite realistically, they will see that they need to move around and build their CVs. On the other hand, large multinationals can offer a series of employments akin to moving between organisations.

This is fortunate because opting out of employing Generation Y is only realistic for smaller organisations. Large volume recruiters like retailers, the civil service, law firms and accountants have to keep topping up their talent pipeline. Other organisations could consider leaving their recruitment of future leaders until people have matured into the ways of work. That is not to say that they should boycott Generation Y: it is just that the relationship is likely to be an affair rather than a marriage.

Conclusions

Generation Y makes up approximately 20 percent of the workforce and is vital to our economic future. Some of them will behave in line with their caricature. In a recession, one hopes for their sake, many will not. However, it is also the case that what people expect from work has evolved and this evolution extends beyond Generation Y.

The task of employers is to separate the employable from the unemployable but also to adapt to the changing demands of each generation in just the same way that they adapt to the changing expectations of their customers.

Finally, a survey last year by the CIPD and Penna came out with findings that run counter to the Generation Y stereotype. It found that Generation Y members were less concerned about CSR than Baby Boomers and also "far less likely to rapidly change jobs than was thought." Maybe another Generation Y quality is the ability to pick up on, and adapt rapidly to, changing economic circumstances.

Dana Kyles

NO

Managing Your Multigenerational Workforce

Abstract (Summary)

For the first time in American history, corporations are challenged with managing four generations of employees at once, each with different values, expectations, and attitudes. The old models of who works and what they work for are steadily changing, but this new workplace diversity does not have to wreak havoc on productivity or retention. If leveraged properly, it can actually increase efficiency and employee satisfaction. The four groups are Matures, Baby Boomers, Generation Xers, and Nexters. Regardless of what group you are in or what group you manage, success can be achieved through understanding. Consider the following strategies: 1. Create both function- and project-oriented assignments. 2. Watch your mouth. 3. Acknowledge strengths and commonalities. 4. Listen. 5. Look beyond appearances. 6. Keep an open mind. The main thing to keep in mind is that each generation has something valuable to add to the workplace, and managers need to make sure that happens.

It takes time, talent, tact, and perseverance—but the end product can be a great place to work with a wonderful talent pool.

What happens when multiple generations work together in a department or on a team but they don't know or understand the generational values of their colleagues? BAMU!!! Sparks fly, and production may implode. For the first time in American history, corporations are challenged with managing four generations of employees at once, each with different values, expectations, and attitudes. The old models of who works and what they work for are steadily changing, but this new workplace diversity doesn't have to wreak havoc on productivity or retention. If leveraged properly, it can actually increase efficiency and employee satisfaction.

The four groups are Matures, Baby Boomers, Generation Xers, and Nexters. After describing them, I'll suggest some effective ways to manage them.

Name: Matures (aka Pre-Boomers, Silents, Traditionalists, Veterans)
Age: Born between 1900 and 1945
Population: 75 million in workforce
Characteristics: Loyal, consistent, conforming

Matures, the oldest group, aren't known to go against the grain or challenge authority. They are structure-loving, abide-by-the-rules-type folks who came of age during the Great Depression and World War II. Influenced by war times and military backgrounds, most are comfortable with conformity and a top-down management style. Their values are based on respect for authority, integrity, and delayed gratification. Often motivated by verbal or written recognition, awards, and public acknowledgment for a job well done, this segment is most loyal to their employer and doesn't believe in job switching. They often prefer being an "expert" in their function, and employers enjoy the consistency that comes with that preference.

Name: Baby Boomers

Age: Born between 1946 and 1964

Population: 80 million in workforce

Characteristics: Competitive, political, hardworking

The influence of their stay-at-home moms, Western heroes, and hopes of post-war prosperity weren't enough to counter influences from "free love" societies, civil rights protests, and Vietnam. This free-spirited generation rebelled against conformity and everything that resembled it. In doing so, they redefined traditional family roles, changed social norms, raised the divorce rate, and accumulated unprecedented amounts of credit card debt. Known for their workaholic ethic, Boomers will do whatever it takes to get the job done and get ahead, and they expect to be rewarded with status symbols such as advanced titles, more money, special parking spaces, and large private offices. They outnumber all other generations and hold a majority of management-level positions in the workforce. Baby Boomers are master networkers who rank relationship building higher than most other work virtues. They are also approaching retirement and are heavily concerned with financial and job security.

Name: Generation Xers

Age: Born between 1965 and 1979

Population: 46 million in workforce

Characteristics: Individualistic, disloyal, techno literate

Generation Xers are considered the most challenging group to manage. Often viewing corporate relationship building as a degree of "bootlicking," they, unlike the former generation, could care less about titles or hierarchies and prefer to stay out of corporate politics. This computer-savvy generation finds security in their own skills. If they can't continue to learn and develop in their work environment, they will leave it. Their values aren't hard to understand considering they entered the job market during a period of massive corporate layoffs and a brutal economic recession. It's quite logical that they are skeptical of authority and don't trust corporate America. Being the first generation reared in single-parent/nontraditional homes where their "caretaking" duties were critical to the family's survival also makes their strong belief in work/life balance understandable. Opportunity and autonomy are the ultimate corporate rewards for this generation. Not only is it a reward—it's a requirement for them to be happy and productive in the workplace.

Name: Nexters (aka Generation Y, Millennial)

Age: Born between 1980 and 1999

Population: 75 million just entering the workforce

Characteristics: Techno literate, purposed, multitasking

Generation Next is coming of age during a time of technological sophistication, extreme economic swings, individual/entrepreneurial prosperity, terrorism, and HIV/AIDS. Also products of nontraditional families, they are developing the self-resiliency of the previous generation. Nexters are looking for purpose and fulfillment in their careers. Not so much concerned with the American Dream as defined by the Baby Boomers or the individuality of the Xers, Nexters want meaningful jobs that allow them to cater to the greater good of society. They want their managers to relate to them and value their contributions. If they aren't valued or feel they aren't contributing, they will leave. Their greatest reward is internal, not external.

Getting Along

Regardless of what group you are in or what group you manage, success can be achieved through understanding. Consider the following strategies:

- Create both function- and project-oriented assignments. Creating a mixture of function- and project-oriented assignments appeals to all generations. The Matures get to be experts within their function, Boomers can lead a project or function and satisfy their need for status, Xers can continue to develop/acquire new skills by jumping from project to project to project, and Nexters can fit in the slot they deem most valuable to them.
- Watch your mouth. Generational clashes typically stem from miscommunication. Choose a communication style suitable for the audience and that is considerate of their work drivers. For example, using the work-hard/play-hard motto and bragging about working evenings and/or weekends during a job interview as a description of a work culture is more likely to repel the younger generations and attract the Boomers. Also, knowing that Matures may feel a little anxious about computer technology, other generations should seek understanding of Matures' competency levels when implementing new technology instead of assuming they know as much as everyone else, and they should offer the appropriate technology training.
- Acknowledge strengths and commonalities. Acknowledging the strengths of each generation provides a strategic edge in workforce planning or team formulation. For example, if a department wants to establish a new activity-based management (ABM) system, a Mature can provide functional knowledge and expertise about drivers and metrics, a Boomer can act as coordinator using his/her network to gather necessary support and cooperation, and the Xers and Nexters can determine or develop the technology for tracking and rolling out a training and implementation plan.
- Listen. When a Mature tells a Nexter she is shooting herself in the foot, she should take heed and learn from the wisdom. If an Xer requests a month to create a new decision model that proposes to do in one mouse click what it takes two clerks eight hours a week to do, let him. It probably works.
- Look beyond appearances. Diversity is difficult to manage if the mere sight of someone automatically puts them into a category. Get to

know employees and their backgrounds before making judgments. For example, if Mr. Boomer's idea of business casual is a blazer, starched blue shirt, and creased slacks but the Xers dress in Polos, khakis, nose rings, and boots, he shouldn't assume they aren't serious about their careers.

- Keep on open mind. It's a must!

Obviously, I've just touched on a few main points here so you can get a quick overview of the groups. Remember, though, that not every person fits all of the characteristics of his/her generation's description. For example, the older Baby Boomers may reflect more characteristics of the Matures, and the younger Baby Boomers may be more like GenXers. And the Nexters may reflect a number of the values of the Matures.

The main thing to keep in mind is that each generation has something valuable to add to the workplace, and we, as managers, need to make sure that happens.

POSTSCRIPT

Does Attracting, Developing, and Retaining the Millennial Generation Require Significant Changes to Current HRM Practices?

Scholars have defined each generation with special work-related characteristics. Pre-Boomers are considered loyal and conforming, the Baby Boomers are known to be competitive and hardworking, the Gen-Xers are individualistic and tech-savvy, and Gen-Yers are considered to be multitasking and demanding. Organizations are currently concerned as the workforce is beginning to hire Gen-Yers that their HRM practices might seem a little old-fashioned for this generation.

The millennials have led a life of comfort in comparison to that of the other generations. Their times have also seen some of the best technological revolutions. The Internet was introduced to the world in the 1990s, which the Gen-Yers grew up with and so are very confident about. This generation is also the champion of multitasking, shaped again by technological innovations such as cell phones, BlackBerrys, and other technological devices that allow them to do multiple things at the same time. Though they have several characteristics that are laudable, their generation may come with some characteristics that may require organizations to change some of their current HRM practices.

First, most of the research suggests that this generation wants everything in their career rather quickly—whether it is titles, promotions, or money. They prefer to join brand name companies, make lots of money, and move up the career ladder very quickly. Their times have seen the best of everything from fashion to retail to automobiles, and they want extra money to maintain those high standards. They would rather be in a constant learning mode because future employability is very important to them. Their boundaries between home and work are so blurred that they do not think it is wrong to stay connected with their peers from work. They are very unlikely to stay in a job for more than two to three years as building their resumes and also paychecks are important career criteria for them. Recent studies done by Nike Corp. on different generations indicate that Gen-Yers also demonstrate high social responsibility—a deep caring for others. Some scholars suggest that HRM practices may have to be changed to cater to this generation that is focused on high performance.

However, the other side of the coin suggests that there are certain universal practices that might appeal to all the generations. Who would not like a little flexibility in their work schedule? HRM professionals can provide this option as all the generations would like some flexibility in their workplace.

Providing choices in compensation packages also would greatly benefit the different generations. Each generation might like the benefits toward a different cause whether it is retirement or college tuition. Training and development can be provided unanimously to all employees but to serve different purposes. For instance, the Pre-Boomer and Boomers might prefer any technology training, and the Gen-Yers might benefit from any leadership training. Performance appraisals might mean providing more consistent feedback as this generation needs a lot of reassurance that they are doing well on their jobs. Therefore, attracting, developing, and retaining the millennial generation might just require providing the same HRM practices with a little flexibility.

Suggested Readings

Gen X vs. Gen Y: Nike Compares the Two: http://www.primacy.com/primetimes/200804/featured_article.html

To Engage Gen Y Workers, Adopt New Approaches: http://www.andersonperformance.com/News/Articles/ToEngageGenYWorkersAdoptNewApproaches.htm

ISSUE 19

Do Human Resource Management Practices Contribute to Increased Firm Performance?

YES: **Anonymous**, "Google's Lessons for Employers: Put Your Employees First," *HR Focus* (September 2008)

NO: **Tony Pettengell**, from "OOMPH! Heroes or Zeroes?" *Personnel Today* (September 2007)

ISSUE SUMMARY

YES: This article helps to identify how HRM practices have provided phenomenal success and growth to the Google, Inc. organization. HRM leader of Google Lazlo Bock, insists that it is employees that make his organization outstanding.

NO: Tony Pettengell suggests that HRM leaders are never in the forefront in most organizations. Hence, they do not provide any substantial profits or growth in organizations.

HRM includes an entire range of management practices right from an employee's entrance into an organization to his or her final exit. The concept of strategic HRM or the adoption of effective HRM practices to enhance a firm's competitive advantage emerged in the early 1990s. Until then, organizations competed mainly on the basis of their product or service, which could be subsequently imitated by competitors. However, Professor Jay Barney provided scholars and practitioners a revolutionary theory, the resource-based view, suggesting firms can enhance their sustainable competitive advantage with strategic HRM practices. He suggested that organizations look inward to their employees and adopt HRM practices that can provide uniqueness. Therefore, an increased awareness that employees and their HRM practices can provide organizations with sustainable competitive advantage emerged.

Google Inc. is a classic example of a company that has adopted strategic HRM practices effectively to enhance performance. This 10-year-old company, with about 11,000 employees, had an annual revenue of $19 billion in 2009. The company boasts 50.8 percent of the Web service market. How has Google achieved such a phenomenal growth in such a short time? Is it their effective strategic HRM practices?

Google's HRM practices are applauded by both scholars and practitioners to be among the best. The company recruits mainly from elite colleges, headhunters, or employee referrals because these forms of recruitment ensure a qualified applicant pool. Google's hiring practices are elaborate with the goal of hiring the most qualified. It involves multiple behavioral interviews and cognitive ability tests. Behavioral interviews allow employers to ask very specific job-related questions based on applicants' past experience. Cognitive ability tests are considered to be one of the best predictors of job performance. The company provides extensive opportunities for training such as self-directed (e-learning), on-the-job learning (from other team members), and external presentation (subject matter experts) rendering for a well-developed workforce. Google's performance appraisal system, unique and inimitable, follows a format of 70 percent (main work), 20 percent (any Google project that interest employees), and 10 percent (any extra-curricular class or learning) work policy as the company insists that a variety of work-related activities can tremendously enhance creativity and innovation. Some of the benefits the company offers its employees or "Googlers" as they are called include the 15 ethnic restaurants that provide breakfast, lunch, and dinner free for all employees. In addition, employees can claim $8,000 annually for tuition reimbursement, and new parents get $500 for 4 weeks after the birth of a baby.

On the other hand, Tony Pettengell, senior journalist, argues that HRM practices are never in the forefront in most organizations. Most small and mid-sized companies do not have a separate HRM department. They manage very well with functional (line) managers doing both their core jobs and also any additional HRM responsibilities (such as hiring, training, etc.). Successful small and mid-sized organizations manage without exclusive HRM leaders. Why would organizations increase their overheads with an HRM department? Even in large organizations, only a small percentage of HRM directors are directly represented on the board. A board representation allows its members to be involved in the strategic outcomes of the firm. What is the point of an HRM department if it doesn't have any strategic input? The department's role then becomes predominantly administrative, which does not serve any strategic purpose.

In today's drive for lean and mean organizational structures, many have started outsourcing HRM functions. Generally, 401(k) programs (80 percent), health benefits management (70 percent), and pension benefits (69 percent) functions are outsourced. Organizations are trying to save costs and HRM outsourcing seems an excellent option to reduce costs and increase revenues. In a study of Fortune 500 companies, two-thirds of the U.S. companies surveyed indicated that they outsourced at least five HRM functions. Outsourcing HRM functions would be valuable if the HR leaders were involved in strategic decisions of the firm. They could then focus on core strategic and planning activities. However, if the HRM leaders do not provide any strategic input and their organizations frequently outsource, their positions seem superfluous.

YES ↵

Google's Lessons for Employers: Put Your Employees First

Abstract (Summary)

Freedom and curiosity are what popular employer Google is all about, Laszlo Bock told attendees at a session at SHRM's annual conference and exhibition in Chicago.

Freedom and curiosity are what popular employer Google is all about, Laszlo Bock told attendees at a session at SHRM's annual conference and exhibition in Chicago. Bock is VP in charge of people operations, a key role in an organization that focuses on hiring and developing the right people. Being open to ideas from employees is really what's central to Google's success as a workplace, Bock maintained, although people may assume it has more to do with the fact that employees can bring their pets to work or the availability of onsite car washes.

Freedom and curiosity are what popular employer Google is all about, Laszlo Bock told attendees at a session at SHRM's annual conference and exhibition in Chicago. Bock is vice president in charge of people operations, a key role in an organization that focuses on hiring and developing the right people.

Being open to ideas from employees is really what's central to Google's success as a workplace, Bock maintained, although people may assume it has more to do with the fact that employees can bring their pets to work or the availability of onsite car washes.

Google's People Ops group includes hundreds of employees with experience in three key areas: "classical" HR people, people from business consulting with good problem-solving skills, and detail-oriented experts in areas such as statistics and psychology. The group has developed an efficient list of questions to ask job applicants that helps predict success within the organization. And a "self-nomination" system is used for promoting people: When they feel they are ready, the company conducts an extensive evaluation, relying heavily on input from peers.

Google's rules of engagement with employees, according to Bock:

- Hire learners. They are inquisitive, and when they fail, they will ask how they can do better.
- Give people the tools and resources to succeed; then let them.

From *HRfocus*, September 2008, pp. 8–9. Copyright © 2008 by IOMA—Institute of Management and Administration. This text is republished with the express written permission of IOMA. Further use of, electronic distribution or reproduction of this material requires permission of IOMA. For information, go to www.ioma.com

256

- Work on small projects in small teams.
- Keep structures flat. Especially as the company gets big, information needs to flow up.
- Discuss everything you can publicly.
- Give performance-driven raises. This is helpful in controlling turnover and enhancing retention.
- Reward success, don'tpenalize failure. "If you don't fail, you're not doing your job well." Quarterly goals are set and performance evaluations are based on these; the company aims for a 70 percent success rate.

Tony Pettengell   ➡ **NO**

OOMPH! Heroes or Zeroes?

Abstract (Summary)

Many would argue that oomph has no part to play in HR. That HR is there to provide the stability; to be the constant in the business firmament, helping other stars burn more brightly. Yet no matter how great your latest HR initiative is, it will come to nothing if the organization you work for lacks oomph. Two of HR's key skills are its ability to empathize and to influence. Yet given the fact that only half the senior roles in HR are occupied by women, there is a long way to go before women's influence is felt in the workplace. HR will never have oomph until the glass ceiling has been breached and women have an equal say in the boardrooms of the UK. For until women are ensconced in the world of business, business will plod on the same as it ever has.

It's time to make your mind up. Is HR ever going to take the lead in changing the way we work? Tony Pettengell argues that we need more than just oomph and men at the top.

As you settle into your ergonomically designed executive posterior advantage device (chair to you and me), and adjust the levers and pulleys that constitute HR's most vital piece of equipment, spare a thought for the hard-working "worker" of the world or the sad manager who has no need to indulge in such self-indulgent self-inspection.

The fearless, the feckless and the downright foolish who will surely rise to the top without noticing the trail of bodies he leaves in his wake. Those, in short, who have little time for such introspection and self assessment. Those not working in HR.

For navel-gazing and self-doubt seem to have become a national obsession in the HR community. Why am I here? What am I doing? Why am I doing it? Does the company need me? Does the company want me?

To misquote Luigi Pirandello, it's like 125,000 HR professionals (Chartered Institute of Personnel and Development estimate) in search of a role.

When in Greece

So does HR have enough oomph? And if it has got it, is it being used wisely? HR and oomph? Naturally, the ancient Greeks had a word for the relationship between HR and oomph—oxymoron.

From *Personnel Today,* September 18, 2007, pp. 36–38. Copyright © 2007 by Reed Business Information, Ltd. Reprinted by permission.

In addition to creating what we now know as civil society, the Greeks also had a whole heap of gods, including: Ares, the god of war; Aphrodite, the goddess of love; Hades, the god of the underworld; and top god and all-round serial adulterer Zeus, who was so scary his dad ate him and who ended up as god of law and justice and was allowed to get away with it. One of his sons, Apollo, was the god of music, prophecy, poetry, painting, animal welfare and plagues, and Ponos was the god of hard labour, but it was Hard with a capital H—strictly for the eternal kind of endeavour favoured by Sisyphus (he of the rolling rock lifestyle).

There was also a god of doctors and nurses (Achelois), and then there was Atlas, the god of great burdens, who had to hold the cosmos on his back. To prove his similarity with the traditional British worker, Atlas tried to get out of this job by lending the cosmos to eternal chum Hercules. Being the god of the union movement, Hercules thought: "This is not my job, mate" and duped him into taking it back by feigning an itchy back.

Tellingly, there was no god of personnel, despite the fact that our ways of trading, working and our legal system are largely derived from the ancient civilisations of Greece and Rome. We know all this from the writings of Plato and Homer (author of the Iliad and the Odyssey, not author of his own destruction in The Simpsons). Of equal importance, although glossed over for the past 2,000 years, is the fact that all the really top roles went to men. But that was then . . .

Leaping philosophically to a more enlightened age, HR's mantra could be "I doubt, therefore I am," making HR truly the existentialist profession of the modern age. But could things work better without HR? Does HR have a role to play? After all, smaller firms get by without it, don't they?

Well, no. They don't, they just don't call it HR. And does your organisation really, really want you? Of course it does. It has an HR department (or at least role) and it pays your wages—i.e., it passes valuable financial resource to your pocket. It also would presumably like to see some kind of return on that investment, so spending hours pondering the value of your existence is probably not high on its list of priorities.

On a Voyage of Discovery

That said, while HR tends to overdo it somewhat on the voyage of self-discovery—with endless books with unlikely titles.

But are HR continuing to learn? Do they still have the hunger for knowledge that got them to their current position? Hopefully, they do, but you wouldn't know it from their public personas, as ego seems to play a bigger part in their decision-making than business acumen or touchy-feely feelings towards their employees. And in retail in particular, people policies occupy their very own world.

Going for a Killing

Clearly, they've taken lessons from the gods, for if something doesn't go their way, they lash out and cast thunderbolts (or more likely PR-generated spin) in the direction of their detractors/competition.

However, these knights are only doing what knights have done for centuries, steaming in, cutting through the fat and making a killing. But while the crusades of the past were carried out in the name of God—the pantheon of Greek gods having been subjected to a downsizing exercise resulting in the deployment of a single deity (at least in the West)—in the modern world we worship at the high altar of the banknote. These modern-day knights are businessmen with oomph, running businesses with oomph. This approach is called commercial reality and this is often where HR becomes sidelined.

Many would argue that oomph has no part to play in HR. That HR is there to provide the stability; to be the constant in the business firmament, helping other stars burn more brightly. Yet no matter how great your latest HR initiative is, it will come to nothing if the organisation you work for lacks oomph. And the sad reality is that most organisations lack oomph. Oomph is not a common commodity in any walk of life. Where the gods used to use and abuse people, often for nothing more than mild amusement, commercial businesses—especially in high-staff turnover industries such as retail and catering—still like to play God. And while our aforementioned knights in shining armour of the modern era may not be the cowboys of the Western world, some of their peers leave a lot to be desired.

Reality Kicks In

Most organisations would not beat themselves up about this in the same way as the HR community. But HR's latest bout of doubting has its roots in reality, as many of the mundane HR functions that make HR such a safe haven have been outsourced, leaving the HR practitioner even more confused.

Yet where there's muck, there's brass. For while the business of business is no longer about lopping off heads and arms, but about making money, as large companies brazenly cut a swathe through the commercial landscape, there will inevitably be casualties. In any merger or major reorganisation there will be job losses, with all-too-human consequences for the all-too-human workforces being affected. Being higher beings, managers wouldn't want to sully their hands by getting rid of people themselves, and that's where skilled HR practitioners are plying their trade, carrying out what is undeniably a thankless task.

And ask anyone outside HR what they think its main function is and they'll say: "They fire people, don't they?" Which is true. Their other response—"They do the fluffy stuff"—is equally revealing.

It's true that HR deals with the dirt and the fluff. Hardly the stuff of oomph. Yet a dose of the right fluff at your fingertips can make all the difference between a failing company and a survivor, between a mediocre organisation and a world leader—as a glance at some of the other features in this issue of Personnel Today demonstrates.

Women's Influence

Two of HR's key skills are its ability to empathise and to influence. Yet given the fact that only half the senior roles in HR are occupied by women—despite more than 70% of CIPD-registered professionals being women (according to the Women and Work Commission's 2006 report Shaping a Fairer Future)—there's a long way to go before women's influence is felt in the workplace.

The fact that women are paid 17% less than men and that so few women occupy senior roles in all other business sectors, demonstrates that HR's influence is being used only sparingly, if at all. And there's the rub. For unless HR women get their own house in order, how can they hope to influence the male-dominated bastions of business?

HR will never have oomph until the glass ceiling has been breached and women have an equal say in the boardrooms of the nation. For until women are ensconced in the world of business, business will plod on the same as it ever has.

A mischievous god might say: "For every glass ceiling, there's a glass floor. And do you really want people seeing your underwear?" But unless women break through that ceiling, it is unlikely that HR will ever get close to gaining any respect, let alone having oomph.

So the time has come to stop all this navel-gazing. After all, you want your finger to be on the pulse, not buried in a disgusting blend of stomach juice, fluff and goo.

And while overturning more than 2,000 years of a "male, pale, stale" work ethic will be a real Herculean task, there are signs that HR's women are showing the confidence to change the way we work forever.

As one of the HR GRRRLs putting her head above the parapet—Gillian Hibberd, corporate director, Buckinghamshire County Council—told *Personnel Today* last year. "HR serves business's needs, but that doesn't mean being treated like a servant. If you act as a servant you will be treated like one, and then you will lack real credibility."

It's time for the HR GRRRLs to kick off the shackles and strut their stuff. Unless they do, HR oomph will remain a dream.

POSTSCRIPT

Do Human Resource Management Practices Contribute to Increased Firm Performance?

The resource-based view theory suggests that organizations can enhance their competitive advantage and firm performance with strategic HRM practices that are valuable, rare, inimitable, and nonsubstitutable. Strategic HRM practices that are unique and cannot be easily imitated by competitors will provide organizations the sustainable competitive edge. Google Inc., a company founded by doctoral students Larry Page and Sergey Brin from Stanford University in 1998, is a successful multibillion-dollar company today. The company has made an elaborate effort on its people or human resource practices. Their HRM department at Google is called People Operations and is comprised of employees from three different fields: traditional HRM, consulting, and psychology backgrounds. This multidisciplinary approach to understanding HRM practices has produced a model of HRM practices for other companies to emulate.

Google's careful and elaborate selection practices are applauded for the quality of hires they identify. On an average, each applicant has about four interviews before being selected. The company receives on average 250 applications for every vacant position. The employees are enriched in an environment of continuous learning. Google's performance appraisal process embraces the concept that failures are natural stepping stones to success. Therefore, employees are encouraged to fail because it provides a learning curve that is undeniable. The benefits the company provides make both the Googler (current employee) and Noogler (new employee) feel very bonded to their work environment. Nooglers are sent new presents every week from the time they receive the offer letter until they join. Googlers have on-site dry-cleaning and snack rooms (unlimited supply) as some of their unusual benefits. Are these practices valuable, rare, inimitable, and nonsubstitutable?

On the other hand, research and practice also suggest that HRM might not be wearing the strategic cap that it should. Thus they do not provide any benefits of increased performance. This is because organizations still believe the traditional school of thought that their functional departments of finance, marketing, and sales are the profit centers. Therefore, organizational efforts concentrate on upgrading these divisions. HRM departments are still predominantly viewed as the administrative effort behind the hiring and firing of employees. In most organizations, they are considered as the administrative experts and not as change agents as strategic experts would like them to be. Most small- and mid-sized organizations do not have an HRM department. Are they not successful? The line managers are able to carry the load and navigate between their functional and human resource management roles very well. Also, in today's flat world, organizations would not hesitate to outsource specific functions of the HRM department. Outsourcing HRM practices has shown to be very cost-effective, and a majority of companies are already choosing to do so. Organizations have realized they do not need to have a specialized HRM department to manage their employees. Therefore, the ultimate question becomes whether HRM practices are a boon or a bane.

Suggested Readings

Strategic HR Planning at Google Inc: A Descriptive Case Study of Human Resource Strategy at Google Inc: http://www.scribd.com/doc/13286610/Strategic-HR-Planning-at-Google-Inc.

Google Adjusts Hiring Process as Need Grows: http://www.jobbankusa.com/News/Hiring/google_adjusts_hiring_process.html

Building a Googley Workforce: http://www.washingtonpost.com/wp-dyn/content/article/2006/10/20/AR2006102001461.html

Companies Increasingly Outsourcing HR, Study Shows: http://hr.blr.com/news.aspx?id=3863

When Is an HR Department Necessary?: http://www.ewin.com/articles/whnHR.htm

ISSUE 20

Is Outsourcing a Good U.S. Business Strategy?

YES: John E. Gnuschke, Jeff Wallace, Dennis R Wilson, and Stephen C. Smith, from "Outsourcing Production and Jobs: Costs and Benefits," *Business Perspectives* (Spring 2004)

NO: Murray Weidenbaum, from "Outsourcing: Pros and Cons," *Executive Speeches* (August 2004)

ISSUE SUMMARY

YES: Professors from the University of Memphis insist that outsourcing is a good business strategy because it creates higher profits, delivers cheaper products, and enhances customer response time.

NO: Professor Weidenbaum from Washington University suggests that there are several barriers to a smooth outsourcing process such as language barriers, technology glitches, and intellectual rights.

Outsourcing can be defined as using vendors (domestic or overseas) to complete any specific organizational tasks (either in manufacturing or service). Traditionally, manufacturing jobs have moved blue-collar jobs to locations where the labor costs have been more cost-effective (also referred to as offshoring). Currently, outsourcing development has moved professional white-collar jobs to places where it is more cost-effective.

Thomas Friedman, distinguished author of "The World Is Flat" identifies the launching of the World Wide Web as the most important contributing factor for the current overseas outsourcing trends. In 1995, when the Internet was made accessible to all, organizations could then use global vendors to complete domestic organizational tasks.

Professional jobs that are most likely to be outsourced are 1) jobs that do not require much face-to-face contact, 2) jobs that can be performed with technology, and 3) jobs that can be performed at much lower rates overseas. Currently, the largest percentages of jobs that are being outsourced are office administration (32%), information technology (28%), and human resource functions (15%).

Proponents of outsourcing suggest that it allows organizations to take advantage of labor costs. Professional labor costs in emerging economies are

25 percent lower than that in the United States. As a result, using lower labor costs allow organizations to supply their final products or services at a much reduced price to their customers. Reduced product or service costs ultimately enhance profits and business opportunities for organizations. Increased profits and customers, will definitely have a positive effect on the domestic economy. Outsourcing has been identified as providing competitive business advantages because it definitely allows organizations to focus on their core strategic activities.

Practitioners also suggest that overseas outsourcing is driven by the business demands of wanting to provide a 24/7 customer service culture. It could also be guided by the fact that overseas destinations have the qualified talent. Further, today many global communities speak the same business language, which makes outsourcing tasks a very viable option. Finally, this could also be an extension of businesses having been successful in domestic outsourcing to try overseas vendors also.

On the other hand, several disadvantages have been associated with outsourcing. The primary concern is that local people are increasingly losing their jobs. While organizations traditionally have been moving blue-collar work overseas, current outsourcing trends include moving white-collar professional jobs. This issue has been discussed in national debates causing locals to be increasingly insecure in their jobs. Therefore, such public discussion has created a sense of national pride about local jobs and a feeling of prejudice against outsourcing.

Second, many businesses have expressed concerns that overseas employees have not be able to communicate with U.S. customers effectively even though they speak the English language. For instance, Dell moved its overseas customer support back to its domestic base as customers frequently complained of difficult accents and miscommunication. Third, many emerging economies, where most of the outsourcing is done, experience energy shortages with frequent power outages. This definitely would cause interruption of the outsourcing work unless contingent plans are clearly established. Finally, intellectual and privacy rights regarding outsourcing work may not be strictly enforced in emerging economies, whereas U.S. organizations must be very mindful about those rights.

Scholars and practitioners also imply that there may be exaggerated emotions with this national issue as it has reached high political levels. While outsourcing may be causing professional jobs to move overseas, it also helps in creating a robust local economy. Policymakers have suggested federal interventions in terms of placing a cap on outsourcing activities. However, this defeats the very essence of a capitalistic system that dictates business freedom, market competition, and consumer choice.

An international perspective suggests that other countries also outsource professional jobs to countries where labor is most cost-effective. The most popular outsourcing destinations are India, China, and Philippines. The main reasons outsourcing jobs are moving to such emerging economies is because employees in these countries have the adequate educational backgrounds and local infrastructure to be employed in such fields.

YES ← John E. Gnuschke et al.

Outsourcing Production and Jobs: Costs and Benefits

The current economic expansion has generated an atypically anemic quantity of new employment opportunities. Compounding the loss of over two million actual jobs since 2000 is the loss of six to seven million potential jobs that would have been created in a typical economic recovery. In the absence of strong job creation, the weak labor market and the prolonged economic recovery have generated an enormous amount of concern about the outsourcing of production and jobs to other countries. If the economy had expanded rapidly and started creating job opportunities after the recession ended in the fall of 2001, the intensity of concerns about outsourcing would have been swept away by the euphoria of the economic expansion. Since job creation has been non-existent since 2000 for most areas of America, it is understandable that American workers, businesses, and government officials are increasingly concerned about the welfare of the U.S. economy.

What actually is outsourcing? Simply defined, outsourcing occurs when an organization transfers some of its tasks to an outside supplier. Offshore outsourcing occurs when these tasks are transferred to other countries. This outsourcing may take the form of constructing facilities and hiring labor offshore to produce services or products for sale and consumption offshore. Alternatively, offshore outsourcing may involve the utilization of offshore facilities and labor for the importation of goods and services into the U.S. In both scenarios, the purpose of offshore outsourcing is to take advantage of lower production costs, increase profits, and remain competitive in an increasingly global economy.

Economists and managers easily focus on the gains that may be generated from meeting global competition in an unencumbered world economy where all competitors face the same set of constraints. Cheaper and frequently better products are generated for consumers both domestically and in the world economy. New employment and income generating opportunities in foreign markets generate new market opportunities for domestic and international producers of goods and services. Finally, international outsourcing of production and employment causes the domestic economy to undergo a new wave of evolution that sets the stage for the next surge of economic growth. An example might be that the outsourcing of parts of the manufacturing supply chain have shifted

U.S. jobs from manufacturing to services and simultaneously prepared the U.S. economy to shift its attention to activities that have a higher market value.

Financial institutions and service providers subsequently found outsourcing to be a source of competitive advantage for their businesses. The Boston Consulting Group cites the following companies (and the locations where they outsourced) as among the most prominent early movers:

- GE Capital (India, China, and Ireland);
- American Express (India and the Philippines);
- Bank of America (India and the Philippines);
- Citigroup (India, the Philippines, Malaysia, Taiwan, and Singapore);
- HSBC (India and China); and
- Standard Chartered Bank (Malaysia, India, and China).

Based upon this history, outsourcing will likely increase, continuing in the manufacturing sectors and expanding significantly into the service sectors including healthcare.

What factors are driving these sectors to outsource their production and employment? According to Bill Sweeny, Vice President of EDS—Global Government Affairs, the decision to outsource is based upon the following factors:

- The demand of the customer;
- The type of local talent available;
- Cost;
- Productivity;
- Political risk; and
- Infrastructure delivery.

Ashok D. Bardhan and Cynthia Kroll with the Fisher Center for Real Estate and Urban Economics at the University of California, Berkeley, further develop this thought by explaining that the "push" factors for outsourcing services are cost driven much like they are for manufacturing, but the "pull" factors provided by the countries where services are being outsourced are somewhat different. As Bardhan and Kroll clarify, the "pull" factors include the following:

- Widespread acceptance of English as a medium of education, business, and communication;
- A common accounting and legal system, with the latter based on either the U.K. or U.S. common law structure;
- General institutional compatibility and adaptability;
- Time differential determined by geographical location leading to a 24/7 capability and overnight turnaround time;
- Simpler logistics than in manufacturing; and
- A steady and copious supply of technical-savvy graduates.

All of these factors result in the potential for significant cost savings by taking advantage of skilled, quality labor at a fraction of the cost associated with producing domestically.

Understandably, from producers and consumers points of view, moving jobs to minimize production costs means some combination of higher profits, lower prices, and improved economic conditions around the world. From the perspective of the workers displaced and the families forced to downsize their expectations, the losses are much more personal and difficult to justify on the basis of the gains in other countries. In previous periods of economic disruption, critics voiced concern over jobs being moved overseas but understood that domestic economic growth would soon accommodate the workers who were displaced. In addition, the majority of the jobs shipped elsewhere were either high-wage, (frequently unionized) blue-collar jobs in manufacturing that generated abundant envy and little public understanding or sympathy, and low-wage and low-skill jobs that could not be protected in a world market overrun by a glut of low-wage workers. Outsourcing was a necessary evil for the betterment of consumerism and capitalism. As long as white-collar, high-wage professional, managerial, and service jobs were immune, there was no real alarm.

Now, however, white-collar jobs are very much at stake and are a new-found cause for concern. As John C. McCarthy noted, these once sacred jobs are now moving to other locations. In Tables 1 and 2, Bardhan and Kroll provide more detail regarding specific industries and jobs at risk to outsourcing, primarily to India and East Asia. Globalization, faster communications, lower costs, and the Internet have all been contributing factors in this evolution. Daniel W. Drezner adds, "The reduction of communication costs and the standardization of software packages have now made it possible to outsource business functions such as customer service, telemarketing, and document management". As Thomas F. Siems and Adam S. Ratner note:

> Specialized tasks—such as software development, financial research and call centers—can often be accomplished elsewhere in the world at a fraction of U.S. costs. . . . It is often in a firm's best interest to outsource certain tasks and use the abilities of its remaining workers in other, more productive activities.

Service-sector jobs that are subject or most vunerable to the risk of outsourcing share some common attributes. Among these are:

- No face-to-face customer servicing requirement;
- High information content;
- Work progress is telecommutable and Internet enabled;
- High wage differential with similar occupation in destination country;
- Low setup barriers; and
- Low social networking requirements.

Unquestionably, workers who have lost and will lose jobs to offshore outsourcing have suffered and will suffer economically, especially in the short run. Consumers ultimately benefit from the lower market prices as a result of businesses seeking the lowest-cost methods for producing goods and services. But, all of this depends on the assumption that U.S. workers can retain the means to earn a living in an increasingly competitive global economy.

Table 1

Employment Change in Industries at Risk to Outsourcing*

Industry Name	U.S. Employment (000) % Change		
	Q1–2001	Q2–2003	2001–2003
Non-manufacturing Sectors			
Software Publishers (except Internet)	276.1	247.9	−10.2
Internet Publishing and Broadcasting	50.6	33.7	−33.4
Telecommunications	1,323.4	1,138.9	−13.9
ISPs, Search Portals, and Data Processing	516.0	433.2	−16.0
Data Processing and Related Services	320.9	292.2	−8.9
Accounting, Bookkeeping, and Payroll	976.3	875.7	−10.3
Payroll Services	158.9	124.6	−21.6
Computer Systems Design and Related Services	1,341.2	1,148.1	−14.4
Business Support Services	784.4	746.2	−4.9
Telephone Call Centers	406.2	363.2	−10.6
Telephone Answering Services	54.8	50.9	−7.1
Telemarketing Bureaus	351.4	312.3	−11.1
Manufacturing Sectors			
Computer and Electronic Products	1,862.1	1,415.9	−24.0
Semiconductors and electronic components	308.7	237.9	−22.9
Subtotal: At-risk Industries	6,853.9	5,791.8	−15.5
All Non-farm	131,073.0	130,513.3	−0.4
Manufacturing	16,932.3	14,757.7	−12.8
Nonmanufacturing	114,141.3	115,757.7	1.4

*These industries have been most often noted as outsourcing to India and East Asia.
Source: US Bureau of Labor Statistics

How many U.S. service jobs will be outsourced? The most frequently cited figures have been those from Forrester Research that estimates almost 600,000 U.S. service jobs will be outsourced by 2005 and up to 3.3 million jobs will be outsourced by 2015. Although this news seems dismal at best, Drezner tempers the Forrester number with the following observation:

> The Forrester prediction of 3.3 million lost jobs, for example, is spread across 15 years. That would mean 220,000 jobs displaced per year by offshore outsourcing—a number that sounds impressive until one considers that total employment in the United States is roughly

Table 2

U.S. Employment in Occupations at Risk to Outsourcing

Sectors	Average Annual Employment 2001	Salary 2001
All Occupations (Total U.S. Employment)		
Occupations at Risk of Outsourcing	127,980,410	$34,020
Office Support*	8,637,900	$29,791
Computer Operations	177,990	$30,780
Data Entry Keyers	405,000	$22,740
Business and Financial Support**	2,153,480	$52,559
Computer and Math Professionals	2,825,870	$60,350
Paralegals and Legal Assistants	183,550	$39,220
Diagnostic Support Services	168,240	$38,860
Medical Transcriptionists	94,090	$27,020
Total in Outsourcing Risk Occupations	14,063,130	$39,631
Percent of All Occupations	11%	

*Office support aggregates data from 22 detailed Office and Administrative Support categories.
**Business and financial support aggregates data from 10 detailed Business and Financial Occupations.
Source: U.S. Bureau of Labor Statistics

130 million, and that about 22 million new jobs are expected to be added between now and 2010. Annually, outsourcing would affect less than .2 percent of employed Americans.

While it is clear that Drezner's observations about job creation seem wildly optimistic, it is true that the disruptions caused by the flight of jobs overseas is probably equally overstated.

Gartner [Consultants] assumed that more than 60 percent of financial-sector employees directly affected by outsourcing would be let go by their employers. But Boston University Professor Nitin Joglekar has examined the effect of outsourcing on large financial firms and found that less than 20 percent of workers affected by outsourcing lose their jobs; the rest are repositioned within the firm. Even if the most negative projections prove to be correct, then, gross job loss would be relatively small.

Although the U.S. has overcome more challenging obstacles, the nation (especially policymakers and businesses) cannot ignore the responsibilities and needs of the labor force. The key to the success of the U.S. will be how the nation deals with the challenge. Bardhan and Kroll offer some possible scenarios:

1. Services job outsourcing proves more costly to the economy than the earlier round of manufacturing outsourcing. The U.S. will no longer dominate the next wave of innovations since centers of skilled, high-tech professionals build up in other parts of the world. As a result of outsourcing, workers displaced through outsourcing face prolonged periods of unemployment. Such workers would finally be absorbed in lesser-paying service jobs. Alternatively, there could be a downward adjustment of salaries and wages, making the outsourced occupations internationally competitive again.
2. A backlash against globalization could occur within the U.S. and worldwide, slowing down the process of business services outsourcing. Protectionism, although inefficient from an economic point of view, may result in the retention of some outsourceable jobs.
3. Industry shrinkage may come in part from a redistribution of jobs within the U.S. rather than a net loss. This scenario could result from the shifting of jobs from large employers to smaller firms in support sectors, as well as domestic outsourcing from high-cost regions within the U.S. to relatively low-cost regions elsewhere in the U.S.

Some critics of outsourcing suggest that while the gains from free trade are clearly true, the issue of fair trade must be considered. As strong and patriotic as it sounds, protectionism results in increased prices and ultimately long-term jobs losses. But, the long-term benefits of participating in the international exploitation of either people or resources are equally dubious.

Largely ignored in this article, but keenly understood, is India's relation to the U.S. in regard to offshore outsourcing. Indeed, most articles written and comments cited use India as the main comparison. With support from the U.S. and by nurturing a large, educated technical workforce, India became the market it is by being the second-largest English-speaking nation in the world. However, somewhat neglected in discussions and consideration are other Asian nations, particularly China, that are also emerging as serious contenders in the global economy. Simply put, a nation hungry to grow economically will compete at many levels. For the U.S., complacency is not an option, and time is definitely not a luxury.

Globalization means that the U.S. is no longer the only significant economic power and must be innovative in its actions to remain competitive. The first solution must be the creation of new jobs. The next administration, either Bush or Kerry, must not only promise new jobs, but actually deliver them. U.S. Secretary of State Colin Powell recognizes this as a priority:

> Outsourcing invariably does result in the loss of jobs and we have to do a better job in the United States, a good job in the United States, of creating opportunity in the United States to provide more jobs, so that those who have lost jobs will have opportunities in the future.

Retraining of displaced workers must occur. In the past, retraining sometimes meant transferring a displaced worker from one low-skilled job to another. This type of retraining is no longer an option. Retraining must be for high-tech and high-skilled positions and will require increased funding for post-secondary education.

Foresight in dealing with ongoing globalization means the challenge must also be met at the primary and secondary levels of education. The global market has a focus on Math and Sciences; U.S. education must also focus on Math and Sciences. U.S. education has fallen short of its goals. Lael Brainard, Senior Fellow with the Brookings Institution, makes a dire observation: In five years, we're going to be having a debate about one of the worst skill shortages we've ever seen because the demographics are actually going to start moving in the other direction and demographers are forecasting that starting in five years, and certainly 10 and 20 years out we are going to be seeing skill shortages of the sort that we didn't even really begin to see in the late '90s. So this issue about trying to integrate our labor force with international labor forces is going to become absolutely critical to our competitiveness into the longer-term future.

In order for the U.S. to remain competitive, it must meet this new challenge. Proactive, sound, successful measures must be implemented immediately. Realistically, businesses will continue to minimize costs to maximize profits. As Siems and Ratner note:

> Businesses in India and elsewhere are developing an important competitive advantage in outsourcing by providing quality services at low costs. In the Internet Age—where a company's physical location is of little relevance and information travels quickly and cheaply—firms will continue to boost productivity and keep costs low by doing what they do best and outsourcing the rest.

And consumers reap the benefits.

Murray Weidenbaum

➡ **NO**

Outsourcing: Pros and Cons

Overseas outsourcing of jobs has quickly become a controversial national issue. Some see outsourcing as a way of maintaining or increasing a company's competitiveness. Many others view outsourcing in a far more negative light, focusing on the people who lose their jobs.

Clearly, outsourcing is not a subject that can be dealt with on a bumper sticker or even on a 30-second sound bite. Let us start with a little background before we try to come up with any firm conclusions. Outsourcing involves far more complicated advantages and disadvantages than the debaters on either side are willing to admit.

Why Do Companies Outsource?

Many service companies started creating jobs overseas to gain access to foreign markets. They had to audit, consult, and repair where customers are located. To state the matter mildly, they did not tell their overseas customers that they had to come here. Moreover, many foreign markets have been growing quickly while some domestic areas have become relatively saturated or at least mature.

Simultaneously, some domestic businesses hired specialized workers stationed overseas to respond to U.S. limits on immigration. When these American employers could not get those workers to come here, they had to send the work to them. While doing so, the companies learned how to use modern technology to shift the location of work economically. They thus became accustomed to taking advantage of lower costs, domestic and foreign.

Moreover, the shift of some telemarketing and customer service jobs overseas followed an earlier pattern within the United States when such work was outsourced from urban to rural areas where labor costs were lower. Telecommuting from employees' homes also helped pave the way for some enterprises to extend the process to new suppliers, at home and abroad.

Viewing these matters in a broader perspective, the age of economic isolationism has long since passed. In various industries—ranging from banking to consumer products to job placement services-leading firms report that their overseas revenues exceed their domestic sales. Despite the shift to India of some domestic call center work, approximately 60 percent of the revenue of American information technology companies originates overseas.

From *Executive Speeches,* vol. 19, issue 1, August/September 2004, pp. 31–35. Copyright © 2004 by Murray L. Weidenbaum. Reprinted by permission.

Most fundamentally, many companies are focusing their efforts on their core competence. It is the rare enterprise that produces an entire product by itself—or even half of the end value. Most businesses subcontract out most of their activities to other companies, mainly domestic. Viewed from that perspective, overseas sourcing is a minor part of the trend to decentralize business operations.

Nevertheless, over time many American corporations came to appreciate how frequently the higher productivity of U.S. workers offset the wage differentials and other costs of operating overseas. Thus they quickly encountered practical limits to offshore outsourcing. To put the matter bluntly, no company can outsource the management, responsibility, or accountability of its activities.

On the other hand, outsourcing can help a company operate in an increasingly competitive global marketplace. Many U.S. companies learned the benefits of drawing on workers stationed in other countries. Outsourcing can enable a business to provide 24/7 coverage, especially for consumers who need around-the-clock support. It is frequently impractical for a firm to adopt a unilateral policy against outsourcing work especially when its foreign and domestic competitors are doing it.

There is also a growing division of labor. For example, system designers in the United States working closely with the retailer may conceive the inventory-management software that helps use electronic product tags more effectively. But once the system has been mapped out, the actual software code can be written by programmers in India. All sorts of adjustments are being made in this complicated world. For example, in 2003, Delta Airlines outsourced 1,000 jobs to India, but the $25 million in savings allowed the company to add 1,200 reservation and sales positions in the United States. Large software companies Microsoft and Oracle have simultaneously increased both outsourcing and their domestic payrolls.

It is important to gain some perspective by seeing the relative importance of domestically and internationally produced services. Much of the current controversy focuses on information technology (IT). In 2003, approximately $120 billion was spent on IT in the United States. Approximately 1.4 percent was moved offshore. However, the 98.6 percent of the work that stayed here was not deemed newsworthy.

In total, about 400,000 U.S. positions in information technology have gone offshore. Meanwhile, total U.S. employment rose from 129 million in 1993 to 138 million in 2003, mainly in services. It turns out that, contrary to much of the heated public discussion, the international movement of services is very positive to the American economy.

That is so because American corporations are not the only companies that engage in offshoring. In 2003, for example, the United States imported (that is, offshored) $87 billion of business services. Yes, that included a lot of relatively low-skilled call center and data entry work done in lower-cost developing countries.

But, in the same year, we exported (that is, companies in other nations offshored to us) $134 billion of business services. That "insourcing" generated a substantial array of relatively high-skilled jobs in engineering, management consulting, banking, and legal services. On average, "insourced" jobs pay 16 percent above the national average. A net balance of $47 billion flowed to the United States. That is more than a 60 percent increase over 1994, a decade earlier. This good news rarely surface in the often emotional debates on offshoring.

The Limits to and Dangers of Outsourcing

A word of warning, however, is necessary in the face of the current business enthusiasm for overseas workers. Companies who outsource just because "everybody is doing it" may be surprised by unexpected costs and complications. About one-half of the outsourcing arrangements are terminated, for a variety of reasons. Some new overseas vendors encounter financial difficulties or are acquired by other firms with different procedures and priorities.

Businesses that arbitrarily set a fixed percentage of work to be outsourced likely will regret it. Newcomers to overseas contracting may find themselves dealing with unreliable suppliers who put their work aside when they gain a more important client or their overseas vendor may suffer rapid turnover of skilled employees who find jobs with more desirable firms. Typical Indian operations in business processing—including call centers and offices handling payroll, accounting, and human resources functions—often lose 15–20 percent of their work forces each year. While software programming skills are plentiful in some parts of Asia, good managerial experience is very limited.

Other costly complications can arise. Local highways and transportation networks may be inadequate. Some overseas companies wind up busing their employers to and from work. Also, electricity may not be available as assuredly as in the United States, where blackouts are very infrequent.

Some American companies are paying much more for real estate for their offshoring activities than they would in the United States. That negative differential occurs for two reasons. One is the cost of upgrading poor infrastructure overseas. The second reason is the fact that inexpensive overseas labor pools are usually found in very large cities, while facilities such as call centers back home are located in lower-cost suburban and rural areas.

Some U.S. companies limit their outsourcing to routine engineering and maintenance tasks because they worry that their core technology may be swiped by vendors in Asia that do not respect intellectual property rights. U.S. firms also may encounter a variety of unanticipated difficulties, such as dealing with arcane legal systems and meeting the requirements of different tax and regulatory agencies. Moreover, they may more frequently encounter corrupt officials in the public sector.

Furthermore, overseas managers often do not understand the American business environment—our customers, lingo, traditions, and high quality control and expectations for prompt delivery of goods and performance of services. Dell moved its call center support for corporate business from India back to the United States in 2003. Its clients had complained about foreigners speaking English in hard-to-follow accents and giving vague answers to technical questions. Given the continued flow of complaints from individual customers, we may wonder what further pullbacks may occur.

What Happens to the Company's Employees?

The effect of outsourcing on U.S. employment is far more complicated than it appears at first. The visible part (the tip of the iceberg) is widely known. Some U.S. employees lose their jobs or get shifted to less desirable work. In recent years, this iceberg may have a very large tip. However, any serious analysis must extend to the rest of the iceberg.

Looking at the total employment effects of outsourcing, the less visible part of the impact is much larger. Far more U.S. employees keep their jobs because outsourcing helps the company stay competitive. Some get new or better jobs because the firm enhances its financial strength. For example, as companies upgrade their software systems, there may be less domestic demand for basic programmers—but more need for higher paid systems integrators.

Corporate IT departments report that they are changing their mix of in-house skills. They now give more emphasis to managerial experience, business process knowledge, and understanding the domestic customer. These capabilities rarely can be provided effectively from an overseas location.

Outsourcing and the savings it generates are the beginning—not the end—of the adjustment process. Cost reductions from outsourcing can open up new market opportunities for U.S. companies and thus generate additional jobs here at home. The companies also can afford to buy new equipment and expand training programs. Hence, higher domestic labor costs can be offset by higher worker productivity. Over time, there is a positive feedback effect from outsourcing. As poor countries overseas develop their economies, new markets are created for U.S.-made products and services. China already has become a major importer of industrial and consumer goods as well as of agricultural products and raw materials. In time, India is likely to do the same.

Moreover, economic trends rarely move in a straight line for long periods of time. Salaries of IT personnel in India are reported to be rising at 15–20 percent a year. In addition, a lot of hidden costs arise, such as the need for U.S.-based managers to visit the overseas sites from time to time to assure that the work being performed meets the standards of the American firm.

Some historical perspective is also useful. In the early 19th century, the United States was a poor developing country. European capital helped finance our canals, railroads, steel mills, and other factories. American workers began to manufacture goods that competed with European production.

Because markets were relatively open, Europeans as well as Americans benefited in the process. Economic growth and job creation occurred on both sides of the Atlantic Ocean. Currently, service providers overseas require American-made computers, telecommunications equipment, and software. They also obtain legal, financial, and marketing services from United States sources. Their employees and their families increasingly are customers of American products.

What Is the Net Effect on the USA?

On reflection, most service jobs cannot be outsourced. Personal contact is vital in virtually all business activities. It takes domestic companies to tailor new products and services to the needs of local customers. Most of the people we work with regularly remain close by. We normally do not take long domestic trips to see our doctor or dentist or lawyer or accountant. Much less do we go to New Delhi or Manila for those purposes.

One of the great strengths of the American economy is that we have a very open labor market. That characteristic is basic to this nation's economic vitality. Approximately one million workers are laid off or quit each week and an equal number is hired in their place. It is much harder to lay off workers in Europe or Japan than here. However, there is another side to the coin. Employers there are very reluctant to take on new workers. In striking contrast, American companies are much more likely to add personnel—and they do so.

Over the years, far more new jobs are created in the United States than are outsourced. Moreover, many foreign companies have been setting up operations in the United States and they hire American workers to staff these operations. Our more realistic labor policies do work, while their labor policy "straightjackets" do not. By its nature, a strong and flexible labor market has plenty of movement—out of some jobs and into others.

The bottom line is clear: the United States creates far more new jobs (net of layoffs) than Europe and Japan combined. We have the highest proportion (66 percent) of the population employed of all industrialized countries.

The record also shows that groundbreaking technology—rather than international competition—is the major cause of layoffs, and of new hires. Technological progress is the heart of the dynamic American job-creating economy. Our positive technology environment also encourages foreign manufacturers, such as pharmaceutical companies, to set up laboratories here.

Let me add a factual note to the emotional debate on the loss of manufacturing jobs. Despite lower wages abroad, foreign firms have chosen to produce automobiles made by high-wage American workers. Examples include Honda in Ohio, Mercedes Benz in Alabama, BMW in South Carolina, and Toyota in California.

Moreover, while direct manufacturing employment has been declining, total U.S. production of manufactured goods has risen about 40 percent over the past decade. This is a tribute to rapidly advancing productivity. By the way, this combination of trends is an international phenomenon. In recent years, China, Japan, and Brazil each lost more manufacturing jobs than did the United States.

A portion of the reported decline in manufacturing employment is a statistical quirk. So is a part of the rise in service employment. That offsetting change results when a manufacturing company contracts out some of its support activities. After all, converting a business function from an overhead burden center in an industrial corporation to a profit center in a service firm is a prod to achieving greater efficiency. It helps keep American businesses more competitive. As for the corporate profits that may result from outsourcing, we tend to forget that the typical shareholder is a pension fund or a mutual fund representing ordinary Americans.

What Should We Do?

Do those who advocate laws against American business outsourcing overseas really believe that foreign governments would not retaliate? My guess is that they never even thought about the fact that, in a global marketplace, companies all over the world are outsourcing. The United States is both the world's largest exporter as well as the world's largest importer. In other words, we have the greatest stake in maintaining open markets—at home and abroad.

As in many other forms of regulation, proposed government restraints on outsourcing would have all sorts of unanticipated adverse consequences. Recently, the University of Maryland requested an exemption from a proposed prohibition on outsourcing by agencies and departments of the federal government. It turns out that the university maintains a network of training centers at many U.S. overseas installations. The alternative to increasing the skills of Americans stationed overseas via "outsourcing" would be to hire foreigners with the needed skills!

Hysterics aside, the Information Technology Association reports that setting up the "do-not-call" list already has eliminated more call-center jobs than all of the outsourcing to India. Conversely, not every job created overseas means that an American job has been lost. For example, in the past, U.S. airlines traditionally did not pursue small billing discrepancies with travel agencies because it was not worth the cost. Now, using cheaper Indian workers, the airlines can afford to correct small billing errors. For the airlines, it is a welcome saving, while those are new jobs in India.

Ironically, experts on offshoring report that all of the publicity on offshoring unfavorable as well as favorable—has been generating more awareness on the part of U.S. companies of the potential benefits of outsourcing overseas!

Nevertheless, the national debate on offshoring requires a constructive response, especially in a presidential election year. Many of the people who lose their jobs are truly hurting. If old-style protectionism is not a good answer, what should we do?

The positive approach is to enhance the productivity and competitiveness of American workers. IBM recently announced the creation of a new $25 million retraining program for employees who worry about losing their jobs to outsourcing.

More fundamentally, the fact that we have the highest high school dropout rate of all industrialized nations is nothing that can be blamed on foreigners. Nor can we be proud of the fact that, at the other end of the skill spectrum, the United States has fallen from third to seventeenth among nations in terms of the share of 18 to 24 year olds who earn degrees in science and engineering. Also, let us not overlook all the regulatory and tax barriers to innovation and to more efficient domestic production of goods and services that have been erected by the U.S. government.

An agenda of economic reforms is long overdue in order to make the United States a more attractive place to hire—and keep—productive employees. It is fascinating to contemplate that, if we would adopt such a positive approach to the outsourcing debate, the unexpected results would be real and positive for American workers.

POSTSCRIPT

Is Outsourcing a Good U.S. Business Strategy?

Economists suggest that the outsourcing trends have their roots in early trading patterns. Realizing that other countries have unique products and services to offer, Europeans established trade with the United States and the rest of the world. This established the concept of trade, exchange, and multilateral relations among nations. Currently, western nations are using the labor of emerging economies for outsourcing work as these economies have talent that can perform the necessary work at a much reduced cost. The technological revolution introduced by the Internet in the 1990s and subsequent Y2K crisis (computer mediation problem) set the stage for global technical communities to collaborate in an unprecedented way.

Researchers predict that 3.3 million service jobs will be outsourced by 2015. Outsourcing allows organizations to become more strategic and focus on their core business activities. It allows organizations to take advantage of differing labor costs and therefore maximize their profits. The global business culture is increasingly focused on how to provide uninterrupted customer service to their customers which outsourcing allows organizations to achieve. For instance, U.S. software engineers send a design or customer-support problem to their Indian counterparts at the end of their business day. The Indian engineers then complete the job by the end of their business day providing uninterrupted customer support to their global customers. This is possible only because of technology and time zone differences.

Outsourcing is considered controversial because it takes away jobs from the local economy. This has created quite a stir among professional white-collar employees who have never experienced any external threats to their jobs before. Domestic customers also have been complaining of communication problems with overseas vendors. Emerging economies have not been very strict in enforcing intellectual rights and privacy issues, which can potentially become contentions if the outsourcing task is information-sensitive. Some organizations may perceive a loss of control when organizational tasks are performed externally. Policymakers also fear that not providing federal interventions for outsourcing might potentially lower the position of the United States in the global economy.

Organizations most often are dictated by the single premise to maximize their business profits. Therefore, global trends such as outsourcing have to be dealt with by both employers and employees with different consequences. As technology is allowing myriad jobs from health care to accounting to software to be outsourced, the most important question that employees of the future need to ask is "When will my job be outsourced?" Do employees of tomorrow need to focus on developing job-related skills that can ensure that their jobs cannot be outsourced? Will labor costs remain an issue?

Suggested Readings

Andrew B. Blackman, Mitchell Freedman, & John Levy, "Outsourcing by CPAs: Are We a Business or a Profession?" *The CPA Journal* (vol. 74, no. 5, pp. 6–8, 2004).

D. Prentis, "Look Before You Leap," *Public Finance* (pp. 26–27, January 2009).

Charlie Masi, "Pros and Cons of Global Outsourcing," *Control Engineering* (vol. 53, no. 12, pp. 14–16, December 2006).

Gary S. Shamis, M. Cathryn Green, Susan M. Sorensen, & Donald L. Kyle, "Outsourcing, Offshoring, Nearshoring: What to Do?" *Journal of Accountancy* (vol. 199, no. 6, pp. 57–61, 2005).

Outsourcing Statistics: http://www.cyfuture.com/outsourcing-statistics.htm

Outsourcing Pros and Con: http://www.prlog.org/10181084-outsourcing-pros-and-cons.html

The Pros and Con of Outsourcing: http://www.entrepreneur.com/humanresources/hiring/article49616.html

Outsourcing Statistics—what figures will tell you: http://ezinearticles.com/? Outsourcing-Statistics---What-Figures-Will-Tell-You&id=2621948

Contributors to This Volume

EDITOR

PRAMILA RAO has been an assistant professor of Human Resource Management (HRM) at Marymount University in Arlington, Virginia, since August 2005. She graduated from George Washington University, Washington D.C., in May 2005 with a major in human resource management and a minor in international business. Her dissertation titled "Executive Staffing Practices in U.S.-Mexico Joint Ventures" is an international empirical research, which has been published as a book. Some of her subject research has been published in *Employee Relations, Cross-Cultural Management, The Business Journal of Hispanic Research,* and the *International HRM Best Practices Series of Routledge,* among others. She is also interested in debate as a teaching tool for HRM and is testing this type of learning method in her classes. Her research interest focuses on HRM practices in a cross-cultural context with a special focus on Mexico and India.

AUTHORS

STEVE ALLISON is senior technical consultant for Adobe Connect, which provides enterprise Web communication solutions for training, marketing, and so on.

SARAH ANDERSON is a compensation expert and IPS Fellow.

DENNIS K. BERMAN is the *Wall Street Journal's* Global Deals editor, responsible for M&A coverage in the world's leading business paper. He is author of a biweekly column, "The Game," which covers Wall Street. Mr. Berman joined the *Journal* in 2001 as a telecom reporter and technology columnist. He covered the historic financial collapse and subsequent accounting scandals at companies such as Lucent, Global Crossing, and WorldCom. Mr. Berman was one of the *Journal* reporters who shared in the 2003 Pulitzer Prize in explanatory journalism for a series on corporate scandals. His work is honored in the 2005 anthology of "Best Newspaper Writing" published by the American Society of Newspaper Editors. He is a magna cum laude graduate of the University of Pennsylvania, a guest lecturer on journalism at New York University, and a Kentucky Colonel.

DINA BERTA was the senior editor of *Nation Restaurant News* for nine years. She is an award-winning writer who has developed, written, and photographed stories on restaurant industry trends in human resources and culinary arts, as well as best business practices among companies in the Rocky Mountain region.

IRA BLANK is a litigation attorney with Lathrop & Gage with an emphasis in employment law. Blank has extensive experience in the areas of employee coaching, discipline and discharge, managing unionized employees, labor arbitration, workplace harassment risk avoidance, and union avoidance. He was formerly industrial relations manager for a Fortune 100 manufacturing company. He also served as vice president of human resources and human resources counsel for a service company that was one of *Inc.* magazine's 500 Fastest Growing Companies in America. Blank received his undergraduate degree from the University of Alabama School of Business. He received a Master of Industrial and Labor Relations (M.I.L.R.) from the School of Industrial and Labor Relations at Cornell University. He obtained his juris doctorate from the Washington University School of Law.

ALEX BLYTH has been a freelance writer for eight years and works for several magazines such as *Accountancy, B2B Marketing, Financial Director, First Voice, Growing Business, New Business, Personnel Today, PR Week,* and *Revolution,* among others. His first book, *How to Grow Your Business for Entrepreneurs,* was published by Pearson in 2009.

DIANE CADRAIN, a frequent contributor to SHRM online and *HR Magazine,* is a West Hartford, Connecticut, attorney who has been covering workplace legal issues for 20 years.

JOHN CAVANAGH has been director of the Institute for Policy Studies (IPS) since 1998. In this capacity, he oversees programs, outreach, and organizational development.

CHUCK COLLINS is a senior scholar at the Institute for Policy (IPS) and directs IPS's Program on Inequality and the Common Good.

JAMIE ECKLE was the managing editor at *Computerworld* for 9 years. He has more than 25 years of experience in editing reports, articles, and Web site content. He also has expertise in the specialized languages of business, technology, and medicine.

MARTHA J. FRASE is a freelance writer in Martinsburg, West Virginia.

ANNIE GENTILE is a freelance writer in Vernon, Connecticut. She has published several articles related to employment issues.

DR. JOHN E. GNUSCHKE is director of the Bureau of Business and Economic Research and the Center for Manpower Studies and Professor of Economics at The University of Memphis.

LESSING GOLD is an attorney and partner of Mitchell Silberberg Knupp and has legal expertise on shareholder disputes, mergers and acquisitions, representation of nonprofit associations, representation before regulatory agencies, and contractual negotiations. Some of his key professional achievements have been the formation of several major security alarm and integration companies and serving as leading counsel in the acquisition of one of the largest security alarm companies in the United States. He publishes a monthly column in *SDM Magazine,* a national trade publication for the security industry.

ROBERT J. GROSSMAN, a contributing editor of *HR Magazine,* is a lawyer and a professor of management studies at Marist College in Poughkeepsie, New York.

FAY HANSEN is a contributing editor for *Workforce Management* and is very prolific in writing about employment-related issues.

FRANK HAYES, *Computerworld's* senior news columnist, has covered IT for more than 20 years.

PAUL HEMP, a Harvard Law School graduate, is a contributing editor to the *Harvard Business Review* and was the Senior Editor of the same for nine years. He is the author of several *HBR* articles. He also has appeared as a commentator on CNN, CNBC, NPR, and the BBC and as a panelist at the Yale CEO Leadership Summit.

HERMINIA IBARRA is the Cora chaired professor of Leadership and Learning, professor of Organizational Behavior, faculty director of the INSEAD Leadership Initiative and a member of the INSEAD Board. She received her M.A. and Ph.D. from Yale University, where she was a National Science Fellow. Prior to joining INSEAD, she served on the Harvard Business School faculty for 13 years. Her co-author, Otilia Obodaru is a Ph.D. candidate at the INSEAD.

GAIL JOHNSON was the managing editor of *Training* and currently is the president/CEO at Face to Face Communications and Training. Ms. Johnson has designed and delivered thousands of communication-related workshops throughout the United States. Ms. Johnson earned her B.A. degree in journalism and M.A. in communication studies from Northern Illinois University.

JUNE KRONHOLZ, ROBERT TOMSHO, DANIEL GOLDEN, and ROBERT S. GREENBERGER are educational reporters from Wall Street who won the prestigious national award of first prize (Breaking of Hard news) for this article "Race Matters" from the Education Writers Association.

DANA KYLES is a published writer for *Business Week* and *Strategic Finance* magazines. She works as a principal analyst in the utilities industry with a decade of leadership, valuation, financial modeling, strategy, and project management experience. She is a frequent public speaker on multigenerational workforces.

MICHELLE LABROSSE, PMP, is the founder of Cheetah Learning, a virtual company of about 100 employees, contractors, and licensees worldwide. The Project Management Institute recently selected Michelle as one of the 25 Most Influential Women in Project Management in the World, and only one of two women selected from the training and education industry. She is a graduate of the Harvard Business School's Owner President Managers (OPM) program and also holds engineering degrees from Syracuse University and the University of Dayton.

MIKE LAPHAM is an associate fellow at the Institute of Policy Studies.

JESSICA MARQUEZ is the New York bureau chief for *Workforce Management*.

LAURA MECKLER is a staff reporter since 2005 at the *Wall Street Journal* for the Washington D.C. Metro area. She currently covers topics on presidential health and social policies. She also was the national staff reporter at the Associated Press in Washington for nine years.

JOE MESSERLI has maintained and authored the balancedpolitics.org Web site, which has had more than 5 million hits for the past 7 years. He has college degrees in computer science and finance/economics. Currently he works for Zyquest, a technology consulting firm in De Pere, Wisconsin. Most of his consulting work is with National Audit, an auditor of major health insurance companies for the entire country.

RANGARAJAN (RAJ) PARTHASARATHY is a process improvement manager with a leading retail business in Chicago, Illinois. He is a senior member of ASQ and a certified quality manager and quality engineer. Parthasarathy has worked in manufacturing engineering, quality engineering, and process improvement for more than 10 years. He may be contacted by e-mail at rpartha463@aim.com.

TONY PETTENGELL is a journalist with more than 20 years' experience in editorial roles and is the group production editor at *Personnel Today*. He writes on various HR-related topics.

SAM PIZZIGATI is an associate fellow at the Institute for Policy Studies (IPS).

ANN POMEROY is senior writer for *HR Magazine*. She has provided several in-depth analytical articles on various work-related issues. She was the former managing editor of *SHRM Professional Emphasis Group* newsletters.

DR. ROBERT D. RAMSEY is a freelance writer from Minneapolis with extensive frontline experience in supervision and personnel administration. He is the author of several successful trade books and a frequent contributor to *Supervision* and numerous other popular journals and newsletters.

ROBERT REICH, professor of public policy at the University of California at Berkeley and former U.S. Secretary of Labor under President Clinton, is author of the just-published *Supercapitalism: The Transformation of Business, Democracy, and Everyday Life* (Alfred A. Knopf).

PENNY REYNOLDS is a contributing editor to *Customer Inter@ction Solutions*. She is also a founding partner of The Call Center School, a Nashville, Tennessee-based consulting and education company. She is the author of several call center management books, including *Call Center Staffing—The Complete, Practical Guide to Workforce Management.*

STEPHEN C. SMITH is the editor/research associate for the Sparks Bureau of Business and Economic Research/Center for Manpower Studies, Fogelman College of Business and Economics, at the University of Memphis.

DANIEL J. SOLOVE is a professor of law at the George Washington University Law School, Washington D.C. He is the author of *Understanding Privacy* (Harvard University Press, 2008), *The Future of Reputation: Gossip, Rumor, and Privacy on the Internet* (Yale University Press, 2007), *The Digital Person: Technology and Privacy in the Information Age* (NYU Press 2004), and *Information Privacy Law* (Aspen Publishing, 3rd ed. 2009), among other titles. His book, *The Future of Reputation,* won the 2007 McGannon Award. An internationally known expert in privacy law, Solove has been interviewed and quoted by the media in several hundred articles and broadcasts, including the *New York Times, Washington Post, Wall Street Journal, USA Today, Chicago Tribune,* the Associated Press, ABC, CBS, NBC, CNN, and NPR.

CHAD TERHUNE is a senior writer for *BusinessWeek* based in Florida. Terhune previously worked for *The Wall Street Journal* for 11 years. He won a National Press Club award in 2003 for his coverage of abuses in the health insurance industry. Terhune graduated from the University of Florida.

JEFF WALLACE, PH.D., is a senior research associate at the Sparks Bureau of Business and Economic Research/Center for Manpower Studies, Fogelman College of Business and Economics, at the University of Memphis.

MURRAY WEIDENBAUM holds the Mallinckrodt Distinguished University Professorship at Washington University where he is also honorary chairman of the Weidenbaum Center on the Economy, Government, and Public Policy.

ERIN WHITE is a staff reporter covering management and workplace issues for the *Wall Street Journal* in New York. She graduated cum laude from Yale University.

DENNIS R. WILSON, PH.D., is a senior research associate at Sparks Bureau of Business and Economic Research/Center for Manpower Studies, Fogelman College of Business and Economics, at the University of Memphis.

DR. CHARLES WOODRUFFE is the managing director of Human Assets Ltd that he founded in 1987. Human Assets is a team of results-oriented and highly qualified business psychologists who help organizations choose, develop, and engage the winning talent they need. Dr. Woodruffe is a well-respected expert and author of many books such as Assessment Centres: Identifying and Developing Competence and Winning the Talent War as well as countless articles on HR strategy, executive development, coaching, talent management and the talent war, recruitment, and employee engagement.

VICTORIA ZELLERS is a labor and employment attorney in Cozen O'Connor's Philadelphia office. Victoria has significant federal and state court litigation experience representing both private and public employers under Title VII, the Americans with Disabilities Act, and the Age Discrimination in Employment Act, among other employment-related claims. She earned her law degree from Temple University Beasley School of Law, cum laude, where she was a member of the *International and Comparative Law Journal.*